THEORY AND PROGRESS IN SOCIAL SCIENCE

This work attacks questions that have long troubled social science and social scientists – questions of the cumulative nature of social inquiry. Does the knowledge generated by the study of social, political, and economic life grow more comprehensive over time? Do today's social scientists in any meaningful sense know more than their intellectual predecessors did about such perennial concerns as the origins of war and peace, or the causes of economic growth, or the forces shaping social stratification, or the origins of civil upheaval? These questions go to the heart of social scientists' soul-searching as to whether they are indeed engaged in "science" and, if so, what kind of science is involved.

The author pursues these questions through in-depth examination of various theoretical programs currently influential in social science, including feminist socia, and others.

THEORY AND PROGRESS IN SOCIAL SCIENCE

JAMES B. RULE

The State University of New York, Stony Brook

PUBLISHED BY THE PRESS SYNDICATE OF THE UNIVERSITY OF CAMBRIDGE
The Pitt Building, Trumpington Street, Cambridge, CB2 1RP, United Kingdom

CAMBRIDGE UNIVERSITY PRESS
The Edinburgh Building, Cambridge CB2 2RU, United Kingdom
40 West 20th Street, New York, NY 10011-4211, USA
10 Stamford Road, Oakleigh, Melbourne 3166, Australia

© Cambridge University Press 1997

First published 1997

Printed in the United States of America

Typeset in Sabon

Library of Congress Cataloging-in-Publication Data
Rule, James B., 1943–
Theory and progress in social science / James B. Rule.
p.   cm.
Includes bibliographical references and index.
ISBN 0-521-57365-3. – ISBN 0-521-57494-3 (pbk.)
1. Social sciences. 2. Progress. 3. Rational-choice theory.
4. Feminist theory. I. Title.
H61.R76   1997
300 – dc 20   96-28260
                                                  CIP

*A catalog record for this book is available from
the British Library.*

ISBN 0 521 57365-3 hardback
ISBN 0 521 57494-3 paperback

For Alix and Adam

Contents

Preface   *page* xi

Introduction: Progress: Formal and substantive   I

                 PART I   21

1. *Dilemmas of intellectual progress*   23
    Theoretical programs and closure   25
    Three models of closure   28
    The uses of intellectual history   34
    Relativism and progress   38
    The ends of theoretical inquiry   40
    The critique of closure   44

2. *The reckoning of progress*   49
    The sociological study of science   49
    The revolt of the constructivists   52
    The quantification of progress   57
    The rise and fall of interaction process analysis   60
    The rise and decline of ethnomethodology   63
    The sociology of science: Reprise   68
    Conclusion   72

                PART II   75

3. *Rational choice*   79
    The essential doctrine   80
    The expressive appeals   82
    Supporting cases: The "or-else" clause   83
    The claims to generality   86
    The limits of rational-choice analysis   88
    When rational choice goes wrong   92
    Conclusion   95

Contents

4. *From Parsons to Alexander: Closure through theoretical generality* — 98
   Parsons's view of the whole — 99
   Generality à la Alexander — 102
   The attack on empirically informed theory — 107
   The "or-else" clause — 112
   Theories of everything — 116
   Conclusion — 118

5. *Network analysis* — 120
   Early history of the network approach — 123
   American network studies — 125
   The "or-else" clause — 128
   Claims to generality: Network nominalism and network realism — 136
   Conclusion — 139

6. *Feminist analysis in social science* (James Rule and Leslie Irvine) — 144
   Feminism: Theory and social movement — 145
   The intellectual evolution — 147
   The claims to generality — 151
   Relatedness as a feminist principle — 157
   Criteria for analytical success — 161
   The "or-else" clause — 163
   Conclusion — 165

PART III — 171

7. *Theory as expression* — 173
   Model 1: Theory as objective mapping — 174
   Model 2: Theory as expression — 179
   Theory as end: Theory as means — 183
   The origins of expressive rewards — 187
   The shifting appeals of theory — 190
   Struggles for theoretical supremacy — 195
   Safety in numbers — 198
   The limits of theory as expression — 200

8. *Theory for coping* — 203
   Hermeneutic exceptionalism — 205
   "Soft causality" — 208
   Some theoretical successes — 215
   Conclusion: In quest of generality — 222

9. *Summary and conclusions* — 226
   The hope of progress — 227
   Between literature and science — 230

viii

Contents

Between relevance and system   233
Can social science solve social problems?   238

References   243
Index   253

Preface

This book concludes a two-part work that began with *Theories of Civil Violence* (1988). The two works, written over a period of more than ten years, seek judgments on the progressive character of social science. Can our overall understanding of social life reasonably be said to increase over time? Do the analytical successes of earlier thinkers form necessary stepping-stones for the work of those who follow? Do present-day social scientists in any meaningful sense know *more* than our predecessors knew decades or centuries ago?

My concern with such questions has grown out of deeper perplexities about the conduct of social inquiry and its role in the larger social context. On the one hand, working social scientists normally defend their chosen approaches as superior to the alternatives – that is, as providing more accurate, more profound, more veridical insight into the subject matter. Yet even casual acquaintance with our literatures reveals the predictable obsolescence of such perceptions. The appeals of any particular way of studying the social world over others are enormously context-sensitive. In retrospect, prevailing theoretical mind-sets often seem to tell us more about the tensions or obsessions affecting particular ages or intellectual constituencies than about the social world. To the extent that our under-standings have this context-bound character, it would appear that every theoretical school begins the work of social analysis anew. And insofar as this is true, it is hard to argue that the sum total of knowledge grows over time.

The question is: Should we expect anything else of social inquiry? Should we simply expect our theories to capture and focus the perceptions and concerns of a particular age or intellectual constituency? Or should our analyses aim at insights that withstand shifts of social context and, hence, of theoretical fashion? Any answers to such questions, I hold, have the most far-reaching implications for the way we go about our work.

These questions challenge all the disciplines involved in the study of social institutions and behavior – including sociology, political science, anthropology, economics, elements of legal and policy studies, and various other endeavors. In this book, I focus most often on examples and works from my own discipline, sociology. But the arguments put forward here apply to all domains of social science. If discussion were to trace the vicissitudes of such theoretical programs as game theory (most avidly pursued by economists and political scientists), or identity theory (more the province of psychologists), or theories of cultural change (as pursued by anthropologists), I am convinced that similar patterns and conundrums would be evident. Indeed, the four theoretical programs discussed in detail in Part II of this book – rational-choice theory, "general theory" in the tradition of Talcott Parsons, network analysis, and feminist social science – sprawl across disciplinary boundaries. All have had practitioners and detractors from most social science disciplines.

And all our disciplines are evidently subject to the phenomenon of central interest here, the transience of theoretical programs. Concomitant with such transience is endemic uncertainty as to whether achievements registered in any one line of theoretical inquiry will matter to theoretical "outsiders" – or, indeed, will continue to move anyone at all, once the immediate flush of theoretical sex appeal has subsided.

An apparent exception here is economics, often vaunted as more "successful" than its sister social sciences. The usual accounts for this supposedly more authoritative status point to the high levels of quantification and the allegedly more settled state of its theoretical structures. Yet these distinctions are misleading. The familiar, highly quantified modes of analysis are indeed characteristic of the neoclassical school. But this theoretical program predominates mainly in the English-speaking world, where its supremacy dates back no further than the 1940s (Yonay forthcoming). The historically recent advent of this mind-set suggests that it may ultimately prove no more permanent than other theoretical ascendancies considered in this book.

In *Theories of Civil Violence,* I sought to trace the course of theoretical change with regard to a single substantive issue – the history of attempts to understand the origins of such phenomena as riot, rebellion, and other forms of militant collective action. This book pursues the same underlying questions in a yet broader context. Rather than comparing theoretical accounts of a single subject matter, this work weighs the progressive claims of broad theoretical visions of social life – "theories" in the sense of comprehensive programs of social inquiry.

Enthusiasts of such programs typically see them as spearheading intellectual progress, as constituting decisive "steps ahead" in our overall understanding. My question is simply: What should we make of such claims? Does the characteristic promise of new theoretical movements to "move the field forward" withstand close examination? Does the historical record indeed reveal patterns of theoretical change that could be interpreted as progressive?

As I look back on the completed manuscript of this volume, I am struck by what a conspicuously *un-trendy* work it is. As in *Theories of Civil Violence,* many of the ideas targeted for attention here are now utterly out of fashion, if not anachronistic. I have tried to take them no less seriously for that. By the same token, where discussion focuses on works of high intellectual sex appeal at the moment of my writing, I have resisted the temptation to climb on the bandwagon.

There are good reasons for such an approach. I have grown convinced that social scientists' obsession with remaining ahead of the curve of theoretical fashion – by pursuing the latest theoretical "revolutions," "breakthroughs," "reorientations," "new syntheses," and the like – comes at a cost far greater than we usually acknowledge. Perhaps the best that can be said for this obsessive revamping and redefinition of basic directions and concepts is that it generates steady outlets for the talents and energies of those engaged in it. The drawback is that theoretical innovations are developed more for show than for use. Who would deny that the marketplace of theoretical ideas often recapitulates the frenzy of the stock exchange – with no distinction being made between the enduring value of ideas and their current selling price?

Thus I conclude that theory in social science is too important to be left exclusively to professional theorists. If the "selling price" of theoretical ideas indeed fluctuates too rapidly for comfort, perhaps we need to consider more enduring standards of value. The best way to do this, I maintain, is to weigh the potential of different sorts of insight to outlast the special social and intellectual contexts in which they arise.

As in *Theories of Civil Violence,* I have struggled to pursue these goals with the greatest possible clarity of language. I am convinced that the obscure and self-referential writing that plagues so much social science itself supports the forces countervailing against meaningful cumulation of knowledge. Most troublesome among these is the tendency to focus more and more narrowly on issues of interest only to restricted and self-absorbed intellectual constituencies.

By making one's ideas unintelligible to the skeptical, one does at least gain a certain protection against criticism. But the price, from any broader assessment, is prohibitive – the creation of a world where developments within any one theoretical niche are matters of indifference to everyone else. Thus my concern to assess all the ideas considered here from the standpoint of a theoretical "outsider" – a concerned thinker who begins with no prior stake in those ideas. And thus my effort to rely on language accessible to any thoughtful reader. If sunlight is indeed the best disinfectant in public affairs, as Brandeis had it, let us hope that something similar holds for the relationship between straightforward writing and scholarly communication.

In the years since beginning this book, I have enjoyed support and advice from many more sources than I can adequately acknowledge. My home institution, the State University of New York, Stony Brook, has provided sabbatical leave and other important local support. The Institute for Advanced Study at Princeton made a major contribution by appointing me as a Mellon Fellow for the 1992–1993 academic year. My particular thanks go to Professors Geertz, Scott, and Walzer of the Institute for making possible this indispensable period of intensive research and reflection. The Russell Sage Foundation has provided crucial support for the final editing and organization of the mansucript.

Other debts are less institutional. Above all, Stephen Cole, my colleague at Stony Brook and my contemporary at the Institute for Advanced Study, read and criticized much of this manuscript in various stages of its preparation. In addition, I have received important critical support and advice from Robert Alford, Said Arjomand, R. Douglas Arnold, Stephen Brush, Lewis Coser, Cynthia Epstein, Scott Feld, Steven Finkel, Debra Gimlin, Mark Granovetter, Melissa Grogan, Leslie Irvine (coauthor of Chapter 6), Nilufer Isvan, Michael Kimmel, Larry Laudan, Rachel Laudan, Doug McAdam, James Rauch, Ian Roxborough, Barrie Thorne, Charles Tilly, Axel Van Den Berg, and Dennis Wrong. Alford, Cole, Roxborough, Van Den Berg, and Wrong have labored over the entire manuscript, going over some parts more than once; if there is an editorial equivalent of the Purple Heart, they surely deserve it. Needless to say, none of these thoughtful people could possibly endorse all the positions taken here, and some would take exception to nearly all of them. But all have helped me to make these observations and arguments as strong and as clear as they can be.

Aniane, Herault, France
Summer 1996

Introduction:
Progress: Formal and substantive

Anyone who delves deeply into the literatures of theoretical social science must eventually sense that the reach of our disciplines exceeds their grasp.

On the one hand, the concerns that impel people to reflect on social life have unmistakable validity. People are moved to understand the dynamics of war and peace. People yearn to comprehend the causes of economic growth and stagnation. People want to grasp the processes by which human personality is formed. People seek to comprehend the forms taken by social inequality, and their relations to other social conditions and arrangements. People want to understand the origins of deviance, or of the causes of civil upheaval, or of the changes in family structure now sweeping the world. And on and on.

There is nothing mysterious about the reasons for such concerns. They arise directly from the realization that the forces and processes implicated in them *matter* for widely shared human interests. People have no choice but to act in response to some assessments of these forces or remain at their mercy. They are things that people *need to know about* in any reflective effort to make the most of social life. Academic social science may sometimes turn away from such concerns. But the result is only to leave them to others to ponder.

Of course, professional social scientists often *do* strive to address such issues in their work. The problem is that the resulting formulations rarely seem as forceful, or as enduring, as the original concerns. The specialist literatures offer many points of departure for thinking about these questions. But what social scientist would dare to propose a list of succinct, persuasive theoretical answers to them – answers that could be claimed to command wide assent among informed observers?

I scarcely mean that present-day social scientists, individually, have nothing to say about such important issues. The situation is more the opposite: a cacophony of rich but often mutually antipathetic responses. Indeed, on politically charged theoretical issues like those cited above, the doctrines of social scientists often sound suspiciously like abstracted versions of the conflicting prejudices of nonspecialists.

What is worse, nonspecialists who turn to current social science literatures for insight on questions like those noted above are apt to feel that their original concerns have been lost in the intellectual shuffle. State-of-the-art discussion on these and other specialities is often so arcane as to mystify outsiders. And disappointment will be all the more acute should the uninitiated reader stray into the domain of "pure theory" – studies of the basic logic of human capital theory, or rational choice thinking, or network analysis, hermeneutics, ethnomethodology, or any other generic way of knowing social reality. Here one enters a world of theoretical obsessions whose relevance to the concerns of outsiders is apt to seem utterly obscure.

Thus, a tension that forms the central theme of this book. On the one hand, we have an array of questions and concerns whose moral and intellectual legitimacy is hard to miss. On the other, we have specialist literatures whose "answers" rarely seem altogether satisfying in relation to the questions. Indeed, it often seems that what counts as an answer – or as a reasonable effort in that direction – is highly context-dependent. That is, what makes any line of inquiry appear as a promising approach to basic issues – from social stratification, to international conflict, to personality formation – is apt to vary from moment to historical moment, and from one intellectual constituency to another. Such evident transience makes it appear that the theoretical imaginations of social scientists are governed by intellectual tastes far less enduring than the questions they address.

Let us be fair to social science. It is hard to imagine any systematic social inquiry that does not involve theoretical *programs* – extended strategies of inquiry oriented, perhaps quite indirectly, to long-term goals of enlightenment. Such programs, of the utmost interest for this book, range from agendas for the study of specific phenomena to grand designs for scientific inquiry. The trouble is that one can note so many more optimistic departures in these programs than successful arrivals, in the sense of settled conclusions to perennial questions. En route, our programs of inquiry often seem to turn in upon themselves. Instead of registering what any conscientious observer might recognize as *progress* in understanding civil upheaval – or declining productivity, or the origins of deviance, or any number of other widespread concerns – programs of inquiry often devolve into obsessions with issues of concern only to those indoctrinated to the program in question.

To be sure, other disciplines foster intramural debates no less arcane than those pursued by social scientists. Most of us would consider it no more than natural to find communication among specialists in molecular biology or systems analysis or seismology to some degree opaque to the uninitiated.

But there is a difference. In many fields, arcane theoretical debates are ultimately constrained by inputs from empirical inquiry. A space satellite is sent aloft and attains (or fails to attain) its expected orbit; a vaccine is developed that successfully creates immunity in a previously vulnerable population; or (we may someday hope) seismologists learn to predict earthquakes with accuracy. Such outcomes may uphold one theoretical position or another, no matter how obscure the debates en route may have been.

In the study of social life, few programs of inquiry can claim such vindication. Although social science produces many "findings," one must strain to identify what could legitimately be called social science "discoveries," or empirical observations by any name that decisively settle theoretical controversies. Such decisive results require a measure of agreement on the *significance* of empirical observations that appears much scarcer in our disciplines than in natural science.

All of this is hardly for want of attempts to invent, and reinvent, durable structures for interpreting empirical material. On the contrary, social science could shame Detroit with the regularity of its claims for theoretical "breakthroughs," "new syntheses," "reorientations," and, above all, "revolutions." But the very rapidity of such changes illustrates a key contention of this work – that ways of interpreting and ascribing significance to empirical material are enormously vulnerable to the shifting winds of theoretical fashion. Thus the empirical "findings" that strike professional social scientists as being full of significance at one point may presently appear as nonfindings or even embarrassments to those who follow. Without a more stable theoretical context, the interest they hold is as volatile as the price of speculative issues on a stock exchange.

Consider the succession of theoretical visions that have preoccupied social science in the English-speaking world in the second half of the twentieth century: structural-functionalism; behaviorism in its many forms; network analysis; game theory; symbolic interactionism; and countless varieties of Marxism, "structuralism," and hermeneutics, to note just a few of the more prominent. And within the subdisciplines focusing on organizations, international conflict, development economics, public policy, religion, political upheaval, deviance, the family, or the like, one could identify many other theoretical twists, most of them equally short-lived.

Contemplating the passing array of such innovations, one cannot shake the impression that they reflect nothing other than a constantly varying intellectual *taste*. And insofar as such transitoriness represents the *only* pattern shaping theoretical change in our disciplines, compelling answers to enduring human concerns about social, political, or economic life would appear to be a utopian prospect. The long-term results of our work might then be better characterized in terms reserved for pure fashion: always changing but never improving.

True, proponents of each new theoretical wrinkle are apt to claim that their favored vision will be different. *Our* new framework, they will insist, finally captures the fundamental realities of social life. It at last focuses on the "core concepts," "basic processes," "deep structures," or the like that represent the royal road to any and all meaningful understanding. Thus it finally puts our enterprise on the proper analytical footing and, by so doing, sets the stage for authentic, enduring progress.

Such claims increasingly generate a sense of déjà vu. The half-life of new theoretical projects in social science, it would appear, is considerably shorter than that of volatile radioactive substances. The "progress" that they achieve, it becomes increasingly clear, often registers as such only from within the worldview that theoretical enthusiasts create for themselves. Once the social context supporting that vision shifts, one suspects, the "fundamental" status of its concepts or findings, the progressive lustre of its accomplishments, are bound to fade.

And in light of such transience, is anyone safe in imagining that the theoretical preoccupations of today – including one's own – will prove more enduring than earlier ones? Can we reasonably expect that the next fifty years of our intellectual history will describe clearer lines of intellectual progress than the last? Or will future developments in our disciplines simply resemble what we are familiar with to date: a succession of short-lived visions, each satisfying a specific and ephemeral theoretical taste?

What *would* constitute authentic intellectual progress, then? Obviously, any understanding of this slippery notion has to identify, not so much a quality inherent in any particular idea, but rather a *relationship* among ideas. What marks any idea as progressive, in other words, is something about where it leaves us in relation to where we started. For the purposes of this book, an idea embodies progress when it can be shown to be a necessary stepping-stone to understandings of value to subsequent analysts. Ideas may be progressive, in this view, even where those whose thinking depends on them are unaware of their role. The notion that life-forms do not generate spontaneously – as flies were once thought to do from decaying flesh – may not be a salient concern to life scientists today. Nevertheless, I would count the rejection of the spontaneous-generation model a progressive step in the history of today's life sciences; for that rejection helped to constitute necessary premises for subsequent lines of thought.

Were this the only criterion of progressive status, however, nearly every program of inquiry could claim to exhibit it. For every such program develops its own intellectual agenda – including its own standards of accomplishment and strategies for pursuing such accomplishments. And every intellectual program succeeds, at least to a degree, in pursuing its own agenda; each can point to accomplishments registered strictly in its own terms. That much can be claimed as readily for now abandoned and apparently irrelevant intellectual systems – say, Scholastic philosophy or Stalinist economics – as for the flourishing intellectual traditions underlying theory and practice, say, in today's life sciences.

Thus it is essential to distinguish between *formal* and *substantive* progress. Every theoretical system in our disciplines registers formal progress, simply by pursuing those intellectual directions that it sets for itself. The question is, do these strictly "local" accomplishments matter in any way to the concerns of the broad public of "outsiders" to the theory? The ability to make such a difference amounts to what I term *substantive progress* – the development of analytical tools that subsequent thinkers "cannot afford to do without," regardless of their identification (or lack of it) with the theoretical program that gave rise to them.

In focusing on this distinction between formal and substantive progress, I am embracing a distinctive (and anything but uncontroversial) theoretical position. No view of theoretical success or failure, I hold, makes sense without some vision of the ultimate interests guiding inquiry. By my lights, those interests have to be identified with the challenges and strains of social living itself – with action dilemmas experienced by the widest potential intellectual constituencies. These concerns, which include those noted at the beginning of this Introduction, are at once theoretical and practical. When understandings arise that provide a better grip in dealing with such issues, it is no exaggeration to say that they leave the overall state of social understanding improved. To say the least, not all formal accomplishments registered within programs of inquiry can lay claim to such status. But when such broadly shared analytical interests are served, one can speak of substantive progress.

Judging substantive progress is obviously an enormously interpretive business. I do not for a moment pretend that even the most scrupulous observers could easily agree on specific instances. But the principle that I invoke should nevertheless be clear. Expansion of the fund of insights that the widest constituencies of analysts *need to know* amounts to substantive progress.

To expect this much of any idea – any generalization, any finding, any analytical concept or strategy, and so on – may seem like a tall order. It is. Yet one can point to cases where it is amply fulfilled – though more readily outside of social science than within. Ideas on the role played by tectonic plates in the production of earthquakes, for example, are foundational for seismology today – including both "pure" theory and the practical mobilization of theory, as in efforts to predict earthquakes. It may well be that today's working seismologists have only the foggiest idea of the intellectual context out of which prevailing theories arose. Perhaps, for example, the alternative formulations that had to be rejected in order to embrace these ideas have long since been forgotten by today's researchers. But today's concepts appear to be things that any analyst *needs to know* who wants to understand and deal with earthquakes and related movements of the earth's crust.

Is it possible to identify such substantively progressive ideas in social science? Possible, I think, but anything but easy. A key problem is the difficulty of agreeing on what constitutes what "any analyst" would or would not "need to know" about any subject. One reason for these difficulties is the volatility of the intellectual sex appeal surrounding the formal claims of programs of inquiry as they flash across the intellectual stage. For a time, enthusiasts of every ascendant mind-set are apt to tout their distinctive analytical achievements as "steps ahead" sub specie aeternitatis. The question is, which of such claims can legitimately promise to retain their force in any longer historical assessment? Judgments of such staying power are a key aim of this work.

In the attempt to make such judgments, I seek to approach each theoretical program considered here from the standpoint of a theoretical "outsider" – someone who begins with no special stake in the short-term appeal that momentarily surrounds every ascendant theory. And in doing so, I try to make my language reflect the attitude I adopt. When I invoke the editorial "we," I mean to express the view of a distinterested theoretical "outsider." For each analytical accomplishment claimed by enthusiasts of any particular theoretical program, I want to ask "What's in it for us?" – with the "us" understood as referring to the broadest community of those seeking to understand and deal with social, economic, and political life.

My concern here is with *theoretical* knowledge, as distinct from the *techniques* of inquiry. The distinction is crucial for this book. In the strictly technical aspects of our work – indeed, as in the technical side of art, music, and literature – progress is unmistakable. By almost any standard, today's means for assembling, organizing, and analyzing relevant information are far more effective than those of earlier periods – indeed, even than those of a decade ago.

By technical improvements, I mean much more than just increased sophistication in computerized data management and statistical analysis, important as these things are. I also have in mind such things as compilations of comparative ethnographic data, techniques for transcribing and analyzing conversations, methods of content analysis, and a host of other ways of bringing analytical attention to bear on relevant data.

These successes count to the enduring credit of our disciplines. They demonstrate both the intellectual virtuosity and the practical utility of social science. But technique is not theory. Today we have statistical and survey techniques far superior to Emile Durkheim's for analyzing such things as suicide, crime, and divorce. But definitive judgment of Durkheim's broad doctrines – say, on the relationship between moral authority and deviance – is more elusive. I do not mean by this that Durkheim's position is forgotten, or should be; on the contrary, it has shown far more staying power than most theoretical doctrines in our discipline. I simply mean that informed thinkers continue to disagree as to how right Durkheim was about key theoretical points – for example, the relative importance of moral authority versus other forces in ensuring compliance with normative standards.

When I speak of theoretical work, I mean analytical ideas of applicability extending beyond any single case: not just the causes of a single strike, but those of a wave of strikes or a category of similar strikes; not just an account of the social forces underlying Hitler's rise to power, but an analysis of shifts from pluralist to extremist politics in a variety of settings. I have in mind both representations of particular slices of empirical material that are given in theoretical terms – for example, comparative analyses of suicide rates – and also the conceptual and strategic rationales that frame such investigations. All such heterogeneous intellectual productions form part of our effort to make theoretical sense of the social world.

Strictly one-of-a-kind, idiographic investigations unquestionably and legitimately command our interest. The effort to understand the chain of events that brought Hitler to power, after all, has a claim on our imaginations quite independent of any parallels to similar processes elsewhere. Moreover, many utterly nontheoretical investigations lead to insight of much practical value – for example, by charting the spread of an infectious disease or showing how to reach voters susceptible to particular electoral appeals.

But few students of social life, I suspect, can altogether resist what one might call the *theoretical yearning* – the temptation to draw from analyses of specific situations implications for the understanding of others. What does an analysis of the transmission of AIDS in a particular population suggest about the spread of the same disease elsewhere or about that of other diseases altogether? Like many another yearning, the appetite for theoretical inquiry is hard to suppress, once aroused. Most of us cannot resist the temptation to consider what implications processes observed in one setting may have for understanding material from other domains.

Note something distinctive about theoretical as distinct from strictly idiographic work. The intellectual appeal of theoretical work depends enormously on the promise of the larger, unrealized structure of enlightenment that it implies. The perceived virtues of theoretical work, in other words, lie not just in the light it sheds on a particular case but also in our assessment of the larger intellectual enterprise which it supposedly helps to further. It depends, in other words, on shared perceptions of where our broader enterprise is going – and of where it has been.

Thus the intense interest surrounding work successfully portrayed as "paving the way" for new and compelling forms of enlightenment – work construed as "breaking new ground" or "opening the path" to "new vistas" of theoretical understanding. The first functionalist account of urban graft, or the first feminist account of the rise of modern science, or the first network account of job markets thus generate keen excitement. The attraction stems not just from what such studies have to say about the specific materials reported in them but from the broad sense of intellectual direction that they convey. Even work that strikes outsiders as utterly arcane or obscure – and sometimes especially work of this kind – may assume intense theoretical interest, if only its enthusiasts see it in this light.

And thus the extraordinary premium, in theoretical work, placed on the proclamation of "core concepts," "basic processes," "deep structures," and the like. Any theoretical view whose proponents succeed in convincing the scholarly public that it focuses attention on issues somehow logically or strategically *prior* to other concerns is bound to reap great success.

The trouble with all this is hardly that such "deep structures" are not there to be discerned, but that the study of social life admits of so many of them. What appear as the most fundamental of considerations at one intellectual moment, or to one intellectual constituency, may appear as irrelevancies and distractions elsewhere. The conviction that a particular insight represents an indispensable step in some ordained progression of expanding enlightenment is an indispensable ingredient in the constitution of theoretical fashion. But it is hard to point to many such convictions that have endured.

Or, to put matters a little differently: The possibilities of theoretical abstraction in our fields are infinite. There is simply no logical limit to the theoretical agendas that could conceivably serve to animate our work – and, in so doing, form bases for judgments of strictly formal progress. The question is, which of such formal achievements will impress the intellectual public, at any one moment, as consequential or worthy of attention? The difference between compelling, widely adopted theoretical programs and others lies in the ability to command a sense of *meaningfulness* – to convince intellectual "consumers" that the aspects of social life on which they focus are ones that matter, that deserve our attention. And much of this ability turns on our perception of the directions of theoretical movement or progress. Hence the vast energies devoted to portraying each bit of theoretical work as an essential step in some far-reaching process of progressive enlightenment.

Some readers will no doubt find this judgment excessively harsh. But how else are we to account for certain unmistakable features of theoretical communication in our disciplines? Everyone recognizes the standard incantations, at the beginnings of books and articles, invoking supposedly unimpeachable sources of theoretical meaning. In sociology, these claims are apt to take the form of insistence that the intellectual problems one is addressing in fact go back to Marx, Weber, and/or Durkheim. Other disciplines will invoke their own totems of theoretical authenticity – from Adam Smith or Schumpeter to Machiavelli, Murdoch, Aristotle, or Burke. And in concluding our works, of course, we reemphasize the theoretical "centrality" of the questions to which we have sought to "contribute." We insist that "more research is necessary" to illuminate these questions fully – thus inviting the sort of continued attention that would imply that our own contribution represents a step ahead in some common pursuit. If the directions of intellectual movement were indeed self-evident, such breast-beating would hardly be necessary.

Thus the key preoccupation of this book: To what extent do the often transitory preoccupations of theoretical social science generate insights with the potential to outlive the context of their origins? When, if ever, do the accomplishments registered by theoretical programs in their own terms include insights potentially constituting substantive progress? Do professional social scientists today in any meaningful sense know *more* than their intellectual ancestors a generation or a century ago? Is it accordingly reasonable for present-day social scientists to seek – as I suspect we all do – to create in their work a "contribution" to some relatively enduring, larger structure of enlightenment?

I believe that such questions are even more important than we generally acknowledge. If one's aim is to create insight whose value can be reckoned only from within a single theoretical project, the irrelevance of the results to "outsiders" should be of no concern. But for anyone with more far-reaching aspirations for his or her work, it becomes necessary to raise the pressing question: Why should anyone on the outside *care* about these intellectual exertions? What reason is there to believe that any particular insight from any particular program will matter to future thinkers, once the short-term glamour of the program has worn off? What prospect is there that any such insight might achieve the status of *reliable means* to *enduring analytical ends* – and by that token constitute an authentic contribution to social science wisdom, a manifestation of substantive progress? Such questions, taken seriously, impose a rigorous constraint on any approach to social inquiry.

Can we identify any theoretical insights from the social science literature that meet such demanding criteria? Questions of this kind, it seems to me, trigger self-deprecating chuckles in social scientists' off-the-record discussions. The very discomfort evidenced by such reactions, I suspect, may account for the scarcity of systematic attention to the issues involved.

Yet there is really no need to shy away from these questions. Indeed, there are certain advantages to posing them at this stage in our intellectual history. For by now we have seen enough theoretical doctrines come and go to grow wary of the more extravagant claims made for their enduring accomplishments. We ought to be able to mine our own meandering intellectual history for insights into the long-term prospects for theoretical understanding of social life.

In pursuing such aims, I want to avoid focusing exclusively on the formal claims of theoretical doctrines – claims to identify the unique and indispensable "deep structures" or "core concepts" of the subject matter, for example. Such claims typically amount to exhortations on the value of particular forms of insight over others. Often it is asserted that one or another set of such assumptions is the only viable long-term basis for successful elaboration of social understanding – which is to say, the only hope of authentic intellectual progress.

For the purposes of this book, I start with quite a different assumption. Any number of conceptual systems or research strategies, I want to argue, could in principle serve to organize the work of social inquiry – and produce results that embody what I have termed formal progress. The question is, for any particular theoretical program, *is there any reason to believe that the insights so generated would long engage the theoretical yearnings of social scientists?* In short, have we any reason to believe that the knowledge yielded by any theoretical approach will continue to serve the analytical needs of future generations?

To answer such questions, one must concentrate on what might be called the *intellectual ecology* of theoretical work – that is, the empirical realities of shifting theoretical taste. What is it about particular doctrines, at particular historical moments, that makes them seem so compelling? And what has changed when (often only a little later) they appear to have lost all meaning? To what extent are the salient theoretical "victories" of any particular approach meaningful only in the terms of the doctrine itself? And where, if at all, do particular theoretical visions yield insights that justly command attention even from those with no initial affinities to the school in question?

Theories of Civil Violence opened consideration of these questions by examining debates on one of the longest-standing themes in theoretical social science. Most major schools of thought in the various disciplines have at one point or another offered some theory of the origins of civil upheaval. If there was a case to be made for intellectual progress, I felt, one should be able to make it here.

Yet the case that I ended up arguing was cautious and qualified. For *Theories of Civil Violence* demonstrated the tenuousness of identifying what constitutes theoretical success. Theories that succeeded for one generation and one constituency often had no such allure elsewhere. When certain theoretical ideas gave way to others, it was often easy to identify reasons for the shift in terms of social and political context – for example, a change in political identifications among the community of analysts. But to demonstrate that the "best" theoretical ideas, according to some overarching standard, were the most likely to survive was a much more problematic matter.

Conundrums of this sort, I argue, present themselves in countless instances where one might seek to judge the progressive status of theoretical shifts. And if such judgments were difficult in *Theories of Civil Violence,* they are all the more so for the purposes of this book. For here I aim to assess the progressive status of the broadest theoretical currents, not just in relation to the origins of civil upheaval or any other relatively delimited question, but *in general.* Such questions are extremely subtle. But turning our backs on them ultimately places us in a far more troublesome position than confronting them.

Any successful confrontation, I will argue, requires consideration of two contrasting principles for the elaboration of theoretical work. I call these *expressive* and *coping* criteria for theory – theory as evocation of social experience versus theory as a guide to constraints and possibilities posed by social forces for human interests. These two criteria have quite divergent implications for our efforts.

No one should be surprised that a single slice of reality may legitimately and successfully be portrayed in more than one way. We simply expect something different in an artist's rendering of a building, for example, from what we expect in an engineer's drawing of "the same" building. The former succeeds by capturing the inner experience of the viewer – or, at least, by capturing one form of experience, according to one set of artistic conventions. The criteria of success or failure of the artist's work are aesthetic, like those applicable to poetry, fiction, music, or dance.

By contrast, the engineer's drawing may evoke the experience of no one; indeed, such a drawing may give little satisfaction in the contemplation. It succeeds by providing a guide to characteristics of the building likely to matter for one human purpose or another but which have nothing to do with aesthetics. These coping considerations might include the strength of the beams supporting the structures, for example, or the materials used inside the walls, or the normally concealed locations of electrical, water, and sewer lines. The virtues of this second kind of representation lie in the ability to identify forces that potentially bear on our interests, but which may form part of no one person's experience of the building when the drawing is made. Insofar as we deal with social forces or facts that exercise constraint over us, we need such coping representations for guidance in dealing with them.

I hardly mean to suggest that any particular theoretical idea could or should be exclusively bracketed, once and for all, as coping or expressive. The distinction between the two principles has to do with the criteria that make ideas attractive or valuable to particular thinkers at particular moments; it is not something inherent in ideas themselves. Thus a given idea may be a success both as a vehicle for expression and as a basis for coping. Consider, for example, Gunnar Myrdal's analysis of the Jim Crow ideology and institutions of classic American racial segregation in *An American Dilemma*. One of his salient contentions was that these hierarchical arrangements, far from being consensual, comfortable institutions for all concerned, were in fact regarded with unstated ambivalence and distress by many citizens, both black and white. This idea had great expressive appeal to those who found segregation distasteful – including those who had sponsored Myrdal's famous research. At the same time, it appears to have been more accurate as a basis for dealing with the racially polarized situations addressed by Myrdal than with the segregationist ideas that it challenged.

But it is also true that a given idea may succeed by the one criterion and fail by the other. Many intellectually comforting or aesthetically satisfying notions, including entire programs of inquiry, may nevertheless prove utterly useless or misleading as bases for coping. In everyday life, for example, some people insist on espousing a theory to the effect that everyone they meet is fundamentally good at heart – or, for that matter, fundamentally evil. Such theories obviously succeed in giving satisfying expression to a certain mental attitude. But as bases for coping with the full range of human personalities, a more nuanced model is surely preferable.

Insofar as social analysis is governed solely by expressive criteria, I will argue, we should not expect progress of other than a formal sort. For the ingredients of success in expressive terms are extremely dependent on context. Different historical moments, different social contexts produce aesthetic projects oriented to very different standards. Thus, no one should imagine that American abstract expressionism represents an effort to improve upon, say, German social expressionism, any more than Shakespeare's tragedies should be judged as attempts to improve upon those of classical Greece. The aesthetic vision underlying any line of expression, from Romanesque churches to Elizabethan sonnets, may be more or less competently realized in specific cases. But success and failure in these respects can only be judged in terms internal to the guiding vision itself.

Aesthetic worldviews also do more than just satisfy preexisting intellectual or perceptual yearnings. They ultimately *create* perceptual yearnings that only they can satisfy. Early impressionist painting (or free verse or Bauhaus architecture) may strike the uninitiated public as jarring if not repellent. But when such insurgent principles win out, they shape our expectations to such an extent as to seem "natural." The greatest victory that a school of painting or fiction or music can have is to create a public who want, and ultimately "need," perceptions that only that school can gratify.

Many theoretical dynamics in social science clearly follow this pattern. Successful theoretical visions in our disciplines clearly do succeed in instilling intellectual "needs" that set a new standard for successful analysis. When this occurs, no analysis can be deemed theoretically satisfactory unless it takes account of the "deep structures," "underlying principles," "core concepts," or the like identified by the theory – whether these be the insights of dialectical materialism, or indexical nature of everyday concepts, or the implications of the analysis for women's interests. The process of embracing new theoretical visions of this kind is apt to resemble religious conversion more than intellectual persuasion.

In the extreme case, fidelity to the demands of a theoretical asethetic may be all that is considered necessary for successful analysis of a particular subject. In such a case, there can be no analysis that is true to the logic of the theory but *wrong* – wrong, that is, in terms of failure to provide accurate guidance for action. Instead, the theoretical "aesthetic" is an end in itself, much as in art or literature. Thus analytical success would be defined solely in terms set by the theoretical worldview itself – that is, in terms of the ability to evoke exactly "what really matters" in the material at hand.

By contrast, consider the notion of theory as a coping, rather than aesthetic, activity. Here criteria for success are framed in terms of an ability to solve problems whose validity could as readily be recognized by theoretical outsiders as by enthusiasts of the theory. For a pure case, one might think of the search for a needle in a haystack – or, to make the example more theoretical, an effort to develop a system for locating any needle in any haystack. Differences there may be as to which, among contending approaches, appears most elegant or intellectually exciting. In the absence of definitive solutions of a pragmatic sort, aesthetic considerations may have everything to do with which approach attracts more followers. But ultimate success – a formula that enables any competent analyst to locate any needle in any haystack – is unmistakable to all concerned and enhances the credibility of the theoretical approach that produces it. The accretion of such successes, if all concerned indeed agree in identifying them as such, would surely imply a case for the progressive development of knowledge. For if a reliable formula did in fact exist for locating needles in haystacks, any reasonable person would want to employ it in any such search.

I hardly mean to suggest that the ends of theoretical inquiry in our disciplines could ever be so succinct and straightforward as those of a search for a needle in a haystack. We know, on the contrary, that analysts seek extremely different rewards from the study of social, political, and economic life. Yet this diversity is hardly infinite. Indeed, I hold that the nature of social experience generates certain predictable commonalities of analytical concern, commonalities that we can reasonably expect to govern thinking well into the future. Thus, knowing more about the causes of war and peace, or the conditions of economic growth and stagnation, or the origins of civil upheaval promises to leave us in a better position to *cope* with these things. And insofar as our shared coping abilities are indeed enhanced – in the very broadest assessment – we can reasonably claim to have made substantive progress in our grasp of our subject matter.

Again, I stress that this essentially pragmatic view of theoretical "success" is anything but a consensus position. For many social scientists, theoretical growth or progress has little or nothing to do with social practice. Instead – to take just one alternative possibility – theoretical growth might be seen to lie in the ability of inquiry to penetrate the most fundamental levels of social reality, to mobilize the "core concepts" or chart the most basic of "deep structures." Examples of such claims are quoted from proponents of a number of theoretical programs discussed in the following chapters.

I have no doubt that such visions may inspire programs of inquiry capable of animating intellectual work over long periods. My reservations about them simply have to do with their sheer multiplicity. The theoretical history of our disciplines amounts to a long succession of proclamations of new core concepts, deep structures, fundamental processes, and the like, with attendant efforts to reorganize inquiry to focus on the targets so identified. The trouble is that the theoretical enthusiasms fueling such efforts are evidently so transitory. If we are to expect any stability of interest in theoretical work over time, it would appear, the best place to look for it is in issues associated with enduring action dilemmas of social living itself.

At issue here is the distinction between theories of social life as *means* (for dealing with the constraints imposed by social facts, forces, and processes) versus theories as expressive ends in themselves. Such assessments confront us with the question of what, ultimately, we expect of theories. Is it the ability to highlight, emphasize, or dramatize those aspects of social reality that matter most to a particular public at a particular moment? Or the ability to afford guidance for coping with forces, conditions, or processes that pose enduring problems for practical social action?

A little of each, many readers will respond. The response is accurate as far as it goes, but it leaves the most profound sorts of questions unanswered. For the demands of expressive versus coping strategies in theory making are often antipathetic, and the organization of our intellectual work often requires choice between them.

Perhaps this moment in the history of social science offers a special incentive to consider this choice. Sociology, especially, seems at a low ebb in public esteem in the last decade of the twentieth century. One reason appears to be precisely the lack of persuasive and consensual theoretical conclusions that can be drawn from sociological work. For many, it would appear, sociology and its sister disciplines have failed to yield long-awaited "answers" – however vaguely such answers are conceived. Or, worse, the answers generated by the discipline often seem little more than abstracted expressions of the *partis pris* that sociologists bring to their work in the first place.

And yet, from one perspective, theoretical work should never be expected to do more than give expression to such predilections. If theoretical analysis aims essentially to express, to evoke, to convey a vision of the social world that "fits" the sensibilities of those attracted to it, then no one should object to results of a self-affirming kind. And, if not, what other sorts of results can we reasonably expect from our work?

Thus this book seeks to pose, for each program of inquiry considered here, the following question: *What would be lost, in the broadest assessment, should this line of inquiry simply be stricken from the intellectual record?* What interests or values shared by the broad publics of "outsiders" to the theory in question stand to be served by its pursuit? Should the distinctive successes, accomplishments, or "advances" registered by the program be expected to *matter* to those who do not embrace its distinctive worldview? In short, can the world afford to get along without the insights distinctive to this approach?

Introduction

Our interest in questions of this kind is by no means purely abstract. Underlying the public skepticism of social science since the 1970s appears to be a profoundly mistrustful perception – to wit, that rather little of value *would* be lost if social scientists' pursuit of their theoretical programs were simply suspended. This is a harsh view, but that is no reason not to take it seriously. If we social scientists are prepared to defend our work, we should certainly have some account to give as to what its long-term results offer to nonspecialists.

If the reader feels that answers to these questions are self-evident or simple, then I have not effectively made my case. For I maintain that virtually any position one might take runs the risk of intellectual anomalies or absurdities. Most working social scientists, I suspect, implicitly embrace divergent and even contradictory commitments on these questions – though normally without reflecting on it. And these unresolved conflicts, I will argue, help to account for the inconclusive, erratic character of theoretical development in our field, and for our uncertainties about such basic matters as its progressive character.

Yet I am sure that we stand to gain by confronting these perplexities frankly. Indeed, we have an important advantage in such confrontations simply in the historical record of theoretical change in our disciplines thus far. By juxtaposing the formal claims of various theoretical approaches against the empirical realities of changing theoretical taste, we open the way to a more realistic, less self-indulgent understanding of our work.

Consider purely aesthetic or expressive views of theoretical work. Descriptively, such models provide an accurate guide to vast ranges of theoretical change in our disciplines. No one could deny that our work is substantially governed by something like theoretical tastes, and that such tastes are as subject to change in our fields as they are in art or literature.

The question is, are such processes *all* that govern theoretical change – or should they be? Is the ability to capture the imagination of the intellectual consumer the only reasonable or worthwhile criterion for theoretical success in our fields? Here an affirmative answer is the first step on the journey to solipsism. For if the experience of the thinker is indeed the *only* test of the satisfactoriness of theoretical ideas, then the "theories" of the paranoid schizophrenic are as valid as those of the most attentive analyst of empirical evidence. Such strictly internal criteria of theoretical adequacy not only preclude anything like intellectual progress; they offer no hope of any theoretical correction or revision through empirical inquiry or critical reflection.

Few proponents of any theoretical view are content to offer their style of analysis simply as a matter of arbitrary taste. Instead, they invoke what I call an "or-else clause": arguments, expressed or implied, as to what any reasonable thinker stands to lose by ignoring the unique insights afforded by their approach. Such arguments inevitably imply judgments of two broad kinds: on the nature of the intellectual needs or interests that theoretical inquiry should be expected to serve; and on the workings of social, political, and economic processes as they impinge on such needs.

And in so doing, these arguments shift the terms of discussion, however imperceptibly, toward some form of coping model of theoretical work. For they imply that even the most diverse theoretical worldviews should be expected to address a core of common analytical concerns. Insofar as this is true, we must conclude that the success or failure of theoretical systems in the study of social life is not to be judged purely in terms internal to the systems themselves.

True, the rewards that different thinkers, from different social viewpoints, seek from the study of social life will always be in some degree incommensurable. Special intellectual "tastes" will always emerge to captivate one theoretical public or another for a time. But these variabilities are not infinite. And the fate that awaits strictly idiosyncratic intellectual quests is the same as that which has overtaken so many other such predilections in the past: relegation to the rarely visited museum of theoretical anachronism. Meanwhile, the record of commonalities in theoretical interest is there, if we wish to read it; doing so can enable us to anticipate what sorts of insights show most promise of durability.

Thus I seek to judge the "staying power" of various forms of theoretical insight and the implications of such judgment for our expectations of intellectual progress. This task requires attention to a wide gamut of analytical programs. Many of these approaches are so deeply different from one another that some readers may find it strange to treat them together. Yet I hope that a hard look at their very dissimilarities will help answer the question of what commonalities, if any, these heterogeneous manifestations of theoretical yearnings share.

Clearly the sort of "hard look" I have in mind will not please all readers. The intellectual passions that grip enthusiasts of virtually all theoretical worldviews often leave no room for nuance or qualification. For anyone who sees in one of the theoretical positions considered here the royal road to analytical salvation – or in this case, to authentic intellectual "progress" – any systematic attempt to weigh its virtues against those of other theories will appear suspect. At worst, such efforts may appear tantamount to an effort at reconciling the demands of God and Mammon. I would accept this characterization, if only the parties could be identified less tendentiously. Against efforts to uphold any One True Faith, the position taken here is overtly polytheistic.

Or, as one prepublication reader of this book acutely commented, "What you're aiming for here is the 'swing voter.'" Indeed. Basic to my argument is the assertion that no one genre of theory of the sort considered here can reasonably claim to yield the full range of insights required for our analytical needs. The best case for progress in the understanding of social life lies in what I see as the expanding fund of insights and understandings derived from a wide variety of theoretical inspirations. Moreover, I shall argue, every theoretical program is prey to the tendency to fruitless obsession with issues of relevance only from within its own frame of reference. Nothing ages faster than such "second-order questions," when changing expressive contexts undercut the claims of the program in question to *meaningful* status.

Thus, if we have any interest at all in the prospects of theoretical ideas to endure, we cannot afford to embrace any one program exclusively. We all need, in this case, to be "swing voters" – to demand relentlessly, for every theoretical project, which of its elements promise to retain analytical usefulness once the expressive appeals that originally brought it to prominence subside.

I cannot write these words without vivid anticipations of the allergic reactions they will spark in some readers. Some of these reactions will reflect authentic differences. But other objections will undoubtedly involve misreadings of my positions. Although it may not do much good, I would like to distinguish in advance a few points that I do and do not intend to argue:

1. I do not argue that "progress" – however understood – is the only reasonable goal for social inquiry. I do hold that few students of social life are really indifferent to the prospects of their own ideas, or any others, to outlast the immediate context of their creation.
2. I do not deny – on the contrary, I emphasize – that different schools and categories of thinkers are oriented to different forms of theoretical "success." But I do consider it both feasible and valuable to identify analytical interests shared by thinkers of contrasting and even opposing approaches.
3. I hardly doubt that many theoretical worldviews win success precisely in the same ways that myths succeed – that is, simply by *constituting* for their believers the reality that they appear only to describe. Thus the very diffusion of rational-choice thinking, for example, appears to make the theory more "true," insofar as it leads people who would not otherwise do so to experience their own lives in calculative terms. But I do argue that few students of social life would be satisfied to embrace mythmaking in this sense as the *only* criterion of theoretical success.

4. I by no means deny that theoretical ideas may serve as vehicles for moral and political messages of compelling import. I do insist that it is feasible, and important, to judge the analytical usefulness of theoretical ideas independently of such value.

5. I do not dispute that a vast variety of theoretical programs may offer a comprehensive agenda for the organization of intellectual work. In this sense, any number of theoretical systems may "succeed" by occupying the minds of investigators and registering their own variety of formal progress. My concern is simply to judge which programs will generate insights likely to *matter* to future thinkers, once the expressive vogue of the original program has faded.

Thus I offer a skeptical, eclectic, and – from my point of view – optimistic argument. At least in this work the reader need fear no manifesto for still another "theoretical breakthrough," "reorientation," or "revolution." My ambition is rather the opposite – to vaccinate theoretical discussion against the need for constantly making and responding to such sweeping claims, with their attendant demands to reconstitute theoretical knowledge from the beginning. Instead, I want to consider how we might develop criteria for identifying the potential for enduring usefulness in ideas from the most diverse theoretical origins.

Either we should regard the merit of the endless array of theoretical programs that compete for our attention as matters of arbitrary predilection, in which case we need only ask whether they suit our inner sensibilities, our expressive mind-sets. Or we should strive to judge them according to standards of analytical usefulness likely to matter to thinkers from the most diverse social and intellectual contexts, both present and future. And this means seeking to assess their ability to address certain perennial issues – issues whose hold on the theoretical imagination is evident in the historical record. Here reasoned judgment, though difficult, is surely possible.

My aim in the pages to follow, then, is the same as that which underlay *Theories of Civil Violence*: to narrow the gap between the aspirations we profess in the study of social life and what we may actually hope to deliver.

PART I

1

Dilemmas of intellectual progress

There are certain moments that few social scientists cherish. One of these comes on being asked to specify the historical achievements of our work as a whole. What fundamental questions about social life can we confidently say we have resolved? Which of our theoretical reflections, which research discoveries, are most apt to endure – or, more importantly, deserve to endure? In short, have we any reasonable basis to claim progress in theoretical understanding, any grounds for belief that our understandings are at all more profound or comprehensive than those of our intellectual predecessors?

The unsettled state at the theoretical core of our disciplines has a variety of symptoms. One is our troubled relationship to our own intellectual past. As Merton noted long ago, the ways in which students learn social science differ fundamentally from those in which "hard" science is learned. Training in our subjects always requires some acquaintance with certain classic texts. No student of revolution or social stratification, for example, no matter how technically sophisticated, can afford to ignore the original writings of Marx. Somehow, our intellectual heritage is never fully encapsulated in textbooks. Perhaps because we are so divided or so ambivalent about what deserves to endure from our past, we cannot leave it to others to codify that past for us.

Another manifestation of our troubled theoretical life is the arcane, contested, and transitory quality of what are promoted as "state-of-the-art" lines of inquiry. Apparently unsure of where the disciplines are headed, we are subject to a steady stream of false starts. Nor do we readily agree about what constitutes the state of the art at any particular moment. Exotic specialties arise from time to time to dazzle certain sectors of the theoretical public, then abruptly lose both their novelty and their appeal. But though the appeal of such innovations may be intense for some, other subcommunities remain indifferent or even hostile to the intellectual "revolutions" that give rise to those claims.

23

To such discomfiting observerations one routinely used to hear a simple rejoinder: The systematic study of social life is simply too young; once it has had the time required for maturation and testing of its key ideas, a clear direction of progress will emerge. But our disciplines are not really *that* young. A number of their current concerns go back well into antiquity – to Aristotle's *Politics,* for example. Some themes, like the quest for the origins of civil violence, have received relatively sustained attention from major thinkers for centuries. One has to conclude that something other than just more time would be required to alter the inconclusive intellectual performance of our fields.

Another variant of the "give us more time" response has been to identify some crucial intellectual ingredient allegedly missing to date in our theoretical work. "If only the field could get straight on *x,*" one hears, "things would really begin to plunge ahead." Sometimes this elusive insight is perceived as methodological, sometimes as theoretical.

But such assertions become suspect in light of our meandering theoretical history. The revolutionary developments of any one intellectual moment all too quickly attract no more than antiquarian interest. Thus it is embarrassingly hard to agree on what enduring difference, if any, debates over doctrines and issues like the following have made to the theoretical wisdom of social science today: classic structural-functionalism in sociology and anthropology; economists' debates over whether capital can meaningfully be aggregated; Pareto's theories of derivations and residues; pluralist theories of American political process; or ethnomethodology. This list (which could be extended at length) now has an anachronistic ring. Yet all these preoccupations have constituted the "state of the art" at one point or another in our recent history.

Some readers will find these criticisms too severe. Aren't the net accomplishments of our work manifest, they might ask, in the rich theoretical *literature* that makes up our common intellectual heritage? Can't we at least claim consensus on the importance of key writings from the pantheon of our past – say, from Aristotle, Hobbes, and Marx through twentieth-century classics such as the works of Park, Gramsci, or Schumpeter?

Consensus of a rough sort we indeed have on the greatness of these and other key figures. But where we cannot so readily agree is on what, precisely, deserves to endure from their work. Admirers of Marx, for example, may vie with one another in their praises of the master; but they disagree bitterly about how to apply his insights to their current intellectual agendas. Moreover, many of the intellectual antinomies among our classical ancestors seem as strong and as little resolved today as ever. Disputes between Marxian and Hobbesian views of how to account for such things as revolt and revolution are as basic among today's students of these subjects as they ever have been. Perhaps that is why we dwell so much on our intellectual history – because so much of it in fact continues to set the terms of current debate.

And yet, pretentions to progress are pervasive in the images we project of our work. Conferences are convened, and volumes of studies commissioned, purporting to extend the "frontiers" of knowledge in one or another domain. Yearbooks are published documenting "advances" in the discipline. Journal submissions, books, and doctoral dissertations are assessed in terms of whether they constitute "contributions" to existing knowledge. Such language obviously presumes movement in the direction of fuller, more comprehensive, more *advanced* understanding. The very notion of a "contribution" implies not just the sheer addition of another book, article, or research report to an ever-lengthening bibliography, but a meaningful step forward in a direction shared by all. And claims to participate in such advances, I hold, are central to the justifications most of us would put forward for our work.

A common reaction to such perplexities, it would seem, is simply to turn away from them. Many empirically minded social scientists would no doubt acknowledge the ambiguous theoretical state of their disciplines yet nevertheless deny the relevance of such things to their own work. Where theory as a whole is headed, it is said, is a conundrum perhaps never to be resolved; in the meantime, let's just get on with our efforts to do *good, solid research.*

Obviously there is everything to be said for doing good research. But what we *mean* by good research often turns on just those theoretical assessments where consensus is so difficult. What constitutes an important research problem rather than a trivial one? What lines of inquiry promise to help advance the discipline, and which will presently appear irrelevant or even bizarre? Any study with theoretical pretentions must address such questions, and they are never easy. And yet any assessment of what I have termed "substantive progress" requires that such judgments be made.

THEORETICAL PROGRAMS AND CLOSURE

Endless dispute prevails among students of social life over how "theory" should be conceived. But attention to the ways in which the term is actually *used* reveals one commonality. Whatever else we may also have in mind, we mean by theory the processes by which individual facts, findings, observations, or analyses are organized into larger intellectual structures.

Any vision of progress in our disciplines assumes some theoretical assessment – some assumption as to how various intellectual elements are to be fitted into their "appropriate" relations to one another. Theories are our way of *registering* progress, of ordering various inquiries into some larger, meaningful whole. Without theory, as George Homans once put it, social inquiry offers "just one damn finding after another."

Indeed, I contend that issues of cumulation and progress are implicated in *all* theoretical debates in our discipline. I hardly mean by this that all such controversies are somehow disguised debates over how to define "progress," though I believe that many of them are. But I do assert that any response to standard theoretical questions in our disciplines cannot help but bear potent implications for how individual "contributions" might be expected to comprise larger structures of knowledge.

Central to these concerns is what I call "closure" in theoretical work. As used in gestalt psychology, this term refers to basic mental structures by which sense-data are organized and interpreted. For present purposes, I mean "models of closure" to indicate *the assumptions relating individual elements of analytical work to the larger intellectual wholes they are supposed to help form.* Every program of social inquiry, every theoretical vision, I suggest, implies some model of closure, some sense of how individual bits of insight fit, or fail to fit, into some larger project of enlightenment.

Principles of closure organize work at a variety of what theorists like to term "levels of analysis." By this I simply mean that some such principles apply strictly to the study of specific ranges of empirical phenomena – for example, the workings of the American presidency or processes of influence within small, face-to-face groups. At the other end of the scale, some closure principles are far more abstract and encompassing, shaping broad approaches to the study of the most disparate material. Examples here might be the vision of science as the quest (as discussed below) for universal, law-like relationships, and the concomitant effort to explain specific phenomena in deductive relation to such principles. Thus we might think of more encompassing forms of analytical closure embracing many smaller, more specific ones. The important point is that such expectations, from the most general to the most specific, are indispensable for the organization of theoretical work. Without some sense of what can be asssumed, what remains to be discovered, what constitutes meaningful understanding and what does not, intellectual communities would be incoherent, unable to organize their members' efforts.

In other fields of endeavor, individual performances may stand or fall purely on their own, in terms of the immediate satisfaction they afford to "direct consumers." A plate of chicken Kiev or a performance of a Mozart piano sonata may be evaluated in this way – in terms of how well they appease a single consumer's immediate physical or aesthetic hunger. And indeed, many representations of the social world are "consumed" on just these terms – as when newspaper readers absorb results of surveys on, say, the distribution of sexual practices throughout the population. Here the consumption of titillating, invidious, or reassuring "facts" is presumably an end in itself, rather than a step toward realization of some larger pattern of enlightenment.

But the virtues that we publicly proclaim for our theoretical work more likely have to do with their perceived status as steps – however modest or indirect – toward some larger goal. Thus our obsession with defining our work as a "contribution" to some broadly attested, wider form of enlightenment. To this end, we invoke sacred sources of authority for the problems we pursue, seeking to portray our work as a necessary stepping-stone in a long journey whose endpoint is beyond question. Such rhetorical tics betray the sensitivity of both writer and audience to the fact that the work in question can claim significance only as part of some larger context.

Nonetheless, such rhetorical flourishes do not necessarily offer a complete guide to the principles of closure that may be shaping the work in question. The real force of such principles, I am convinced, is often unconscious. As a competent speaker of one's mother language, one has a subtle sense of when sentences one hears are appropriately generated, when they are a little "off," and when they are quite defective. Yet one often cannot articulate the rules one is responding to in making such judgments. I believe that something quite similar is true of our sensitivities to theoretical work – both our own and others'. Individual "contributions" – articles, books, talks, reviews, and so on – are in fact governed by principles of closure of which both consumers and producers are only imperfectly aware.

Thankfully, a few especially naive ideas on these subjects have been almost universally discarded. Today hardly anyone would hold that sheer *accumulation* of knowledge is tantamount to progress. All publications no doubt accumulate somewhere – in bibliographies, libraries, and the like. But *cumulation* requires that new work somehow meaningfully incorporate and build upon earlier work. One may think of individual contributions as "bricks to the edifice of knowledge." But bricks that enter into no particular structure, or those fitted into structures soon abandoned, scarcely contribute to anything. Indeed, a distinctive theoretical feature of social science seems to be the sheer variety of potential structures – all offering programs for elaboration of inquiry that are viable in their own terms, and none exercising anything like a permanent hold on the theoretical imagination. Under these circumstances, it should hardly be surprising that the shape of a growing edifice of understanding is difficult to discern.

Some would deny the appropriateness of the construction metaphor altogether, along with any expectation of progress or cumulation in our theoretical work. Those who take such a view are often inclined to see the study of social life as more akin to literature or art than to natural science.

But even such nonprogressive models of social inquiry appeal to models of closure. Even in the purest of art and literature, evaluations of individual works turn to a considerable extent on the relations of the work in question to other "contributions" to the genre. To claim value within any artistic or literary tradition, a work must achieve a certain tension between the realization of a given aesthetic standard and the requirements of originality. Once we have *The Iliad,* for example, a second quasi *Iliad* is simply derivative.

Moreover, all artistic and literary traditions eventually reach a point of saturation. At some point the community of artistic or literary consumers come to feel that everything to be said within that tradition has been said, and it is time to pass on. A contribution that successfully forges adherence to a new aesthetic is considered a great success; a contribution to an aesthetic that has lost its grip on the collective imagination is no contribution at all.

THREE MODELS OF CLOSURE

Again, principles of closure often work like those of grammar in our native speech – that is, without our being able to articulate why the "right" choice is indeed correct. But obviously that is not the whole story. We do agonize publicly, after all, about how theoretical inquiry ought to be organized, and these debates do have at least *something* to do with the ways in which social inquiry goes on. Indeed, the models of closure conveyed in formal theoretical doctrines often shape the practice of social inquiry in far-reaching ways.

Consider three relatively comprehensive models that exerted vast influence in the postwar generation of North American social science: the classic structural-functionalism of Talcott Parsons; George Homans's model of theory building as deductive explanation; and the view of theory as a program of criticism from the political left articulated by figures like C. Wright Mills and Barrington Moore, Jr. From roughly the 1950s to the early 1970s, these three programs dominated the theoretical map – above all, in sociology, but in other social science disciplines as well. The contrasts among them, from the distance of a generation, are instructive.

Parsons's "system," in its full-blown form, exhibited all the characteristics of a model of closure. It offered above all a vision of the social *whole* –

a catalogue of the features of social systems that *mattered,* along with a rationale for their relative importance. This catalogue implied its own agenda for intellectual work – for example, through the extension of Parsons-style thinking to new areas of social life. Theoretical analysis, in this program, became a matter of showing how subject matters previously uncharted, or studied only from the vantage point of other theoretical systems, could be rendered into terms derived from Parsons's system.

Parsons's claims for the importance and centrality of his model of closure grew with his eminence. By the 1960s, as Chapter 4 notes, both Parsons himself (e.g., 1961, p. 31) and many others had come to see his theoretical program as the consensus position of social science. Yet, like nearly all comprehensive models of closure, the sweeping appeal of Parsons's worldview dissipated more abruptly than anyone could have expected. The perception of his distinctive concepts and analytical strategies as meaningful or relevant largely dried up in the 1970s. Specific ideas of his remain well known. But few if any social scientists today would consider it sensible to do what Smelser did to such widespread acclaim in *Theory of Collective Behavior* (1962) – "retheorize" an existing literature by casting it into categories derived distinctively from Parsons.

George Homans, of course, was Parsons's Harvard colleague and a kind of theoretical counterweight. For Homans, Parsons's program for closure through conceptual comprehensiveness amounted to massive conceptual hypertrophy. Homans's model of closure, developed very much in opposition to that of Parsons, derived from key doctrines in the midcentury philosophy of science – notably, those of Carl Hempel (1965), Ernest Nagel (1961), and R. B. Braithwaite (1953).

For these exemplars, and for Homans, what assured the basic order of the universe was the *lawful* quality of all that occurred there. All events, from the motion of galaxies to elementary social behavior, are governed by laws, and the role of science is to discover these and demonstrate their applicability. Scientific progress occurs as more and more individual phenomena and categories of phenomena come to be understood as governed by such laws. *Explananda* are understood by citing the laws governing them and the conditions under which the law operated.

For Homans, as for Hempel and Nagel, the world of social events and processes required explanatory strategies of the same form as subjects studied by natural scientists. Successful theory in social science, as in "hard" science, required subsuming *explananda* in deductive systems that specified them as lower-order manifestations of prevailing laws. Thus we have Homans's rendition of Durkheim's famous theory of suicide:

1. In any social grouping, the suicide rate varies directly with the degree of individualism (egoism).

2. The degree of individualism varies with the incidence of Protestantism.
3. Therefore, the suicide rate varies with the incidence of Protestantism.
4. The incidence of Protestantism in Spain is low.
5. Therefore, the suicide rate in Spain is low. (1964, p. 951)

Durkheim does what every authentic theorist must do, Homans contends: He explains the particular (the low rate of suicide in Spain) as an instance of the general principle that governs it. If general principles and the specific conditions under which they operate are cited with sufficient rigor, the *explanandum* should follow syllogistically. By contrast, Homans held, "theories" that account for phenomena simply by describing them in terms of one conceptual scheme or another are no theories at all.

Homans's view has all the characteristics of a model of closure. It offers a way of *taking stock* of what is and is not known. It ascribes *meaning* to different bits of knowledge, for example, by locating them in the process of theory building and explanation. And it provides an *agenda* for analytical work, in the quest for more and more complete explanation of the *explananda* that make up the social scientist's subject matter.

Both Parsons's and Homans's models of closure, however antipathetic in other respects, are in a sense *formal* models. Follow these rules, arrange your descriptions and findings according to this scheme, they assure us, and the positive results will ultimately be apparent to all in the form of theoretical progress. For many on the political left, such doctrines amounted to renunciation of the analyst's most compelling intellectual responsibilities.

Against such formalisms, C. Wright Mills, Barrington Moore, Jr., and others offered strikingly different claims for their model of closure. The point of theory building, they held, was not to follow any particular model of logical or conceptual form. It was instead to build hard-hitting, critical analyses that challenged unsatisfactory social conditions, showing the discrepancies between what is and what ought to be. The organizing principle of good analytical work – the standard of closure, in other words – was not the logical form of the analysis, but its *political relevance*.

The overarching aim of social inquiry, in this view, was to create understandings which, if widely absorbed, would lead directly to ameliorative change. Here proponents of the model obviously drew from Marx's famous dictum on the importance of not simply understanding the world but changing it. Thus Barrington Moore, Jr., in an essay he named "Strategy in Social Science," disparaged what he saw as the pointless conceptual maunderings of Parsons: "Abstraction is not an end in itself," he wrote (1958, p. 129). Nor did the search for scientific generality of the sort espoused by Homans appeal to him: "In human affairs the mere fact of uniformity or regularity, expressible in the form of a scientific law, may be quite trivial" (ibid.).

Like other models of closure, this one offers above all a criterion for *meaning* in theoretical work. It puts forward a basis for distinguishing between what is worth knowing and what is trivial. It implies an agenda for inquiry, with the most unjust and destructive social conditions presumably targeted for first attention. And it implies a criterion of intellectual progress as the informed indictment of unacceptable social conditions grows more complete.

The predominance of these three programs had clearly dissipated by the 1970s, when they relinquished center stage to a much wider array of theoretical possibilities. But some more recent writers do actively continue to draw inspiration from models closely related to these three. Consider a thoughtful article by Wagner and Berger (1985) upholding a model of closure akin to that of Homans. Entitled "Do Sociological Theories Grow?" this study answers its own question affirmatively, and in so doing seeks to cast doubt on a variety of accounts skeptical of progress in the discipline. Contra the skeptics, Wagner and Berger identify a variety of logical processes by which growth, as they understand it, is manifest – for example, in terms of what they call "theoretical branching."

The authors give many examples of how such processes have occurred in their own domain of special interest: social psychological studies of justice in interpersonal comparisons. In the case of branching, they describe the development of

a new theory [that] incorporates consideration of both expectations for task performance and expectations for reward allocation, specifying structural conditions under which these two types of expectations become interdependent. . . . Thus it becomes possible to talk about the effect of reward expectations on task expectations and the effect of task expectations on reward expectations.

The expectation states program is a branching program. Each branch represents the application of the basic underlying principles of the program to a new explanatory domain. . . . In other words, each branch represent a theory proliferation. (p. 716)

"Do Sociological Theories Grow?" is replete with instances of such patterns of logical elaboration of theoretical ideas. For the authors, such examples make the case decisive that theories do indeed grow.

And indeed they do, so long as the particular model of closure that these authors embrace continues to strike some identifiable community of scholars as meaningful. But what about the many other communities following different models of closure? Wagner and Berger give no reason why anyone should embrace their particular scheme for making such connections in preference to others. And if models like theirs should altogether lose the ability to convey a sense of meaning – in short, if people simply cease to *care* about the pursuit of closure along the lines that they pursue – what are the implications for any understanding of theoretical progress?

At stake here is the tension between what I have called formal and substantive progress. One can imagine the community of those embracing the model of closure shared by Wagner and Berger "moving ahead" indefinitely along the lines described above – generating and substantiating new hypotheses, extending established insights to new domains, and so on. Or, one can equally well imagine the demise of that model of closure simply because no one continued to pursue it. In either case, it is reasonable to ask *what difference* the "accomplishments" registered within this program make for those on the outside. The mere fact that the theory "grows" in its own terms – as do theoretical programs of the most various sorts – tells us nothing about the potential of insights generated within it to afford reliable means to enduring, widely shared analytical ends.

Imagine the theoretical exertions of a hypothetical investigator determined to create a general theory of *bottlecap dispersion.* As a graduate student, she had noted certain deep structures in the distribution of bottlecaps on the streets of New York City – with Perrier predominating on the Upper East Side, expensive beer from the People's Republic of China on the Upper West Side, and less distinguished brands near the Bowery and in the outer boroughs. In time, she developed an elaborate multivariate model, based on rigorously deductive reasoning. Treating characteristics of bottlecap populations as dependent variables, she related them to a variety of neighborhood variables: income, education, age and sex distribution, predominant forms of commerce and land use, and so on. So refined did the model become that it could reliably predict the results of bottlecap samplings from streets never before studied, simply on the basis of their background characteristics. The next step, one might imagine, would be to seek National Science Foundation backing to generalize the model by developing coefficients for other cities.

Is this an intellectual success story? Certainly the research pursued under this model of closure achieved formal progress. But whether the analytical victories registered in these efforts could be expected to matter to those not naturally intrigued by bottlecap studies is another matter. If the protagonist of this project had normal instincts of theoretical self-presentation, she would want to persuade the intellectual public that bottlecap dispersion actually provides the key to understanding matters of much broader import. Interpreting such claims is not always easy; they are rarely just an open-and-shut case. Yet it would be wrong to assume that we have no grounds for assessing them.

A follower of Mills or Moore would most likely scorn the bottlecap dispersion program as the epitome of the irrelevant formalism they deplore. Yet their model of closure has difficulties of its own. In "Strategy in Social Science," Moore criticizes at length an article, published in 1957 in *The American Sociological Review,* that he considered outstandingly pointless: "professional journals are full of similar articles where careful methodology is used on trivial problems. Unfortunately most of them are not as amusing as this one. If demonstration of uniformities like these were all that social science had to offer, it would constitute no more than an enormous diversion from more important problems" (1958, p. 130). But the study that Moore is disparaging here deals with rates of male sexual aggression against women, based on data from the victims – a subject redefined some years later as being of the utmost relevance!

Such twists of intellectual fate should remind us that relevance is a more ambiguous criterion than Moore and Mills allowed. Lewis Coser once wondered aloud what sociologists of the Moore–Mills persuasion would have made of the early preoccupations of Sigmund Freud, so absorbed in the (apparently psychosomatic) complaints of repressed, middle-class Jewish women in turn-of-the-century Vienna. His contemporaries might well have disparaged him for turning away from the urgent public issues of his day – the collapse of the Austro-Hungarian Empire, the approach of world war, the inequalities of Viennese society. Yet Freud's early work succeeded in doing what he had hoped – opening previously uncharted psychological processes so as to render meaningful and explicable a wide range of otherwise banal or anomalous phenomena. Who could say that these concerns were ultimately less relevant than more obviously topical ones?

As the epigram for "Strategy in Social Science," Moore cited Alfred North Whitehead: "The main evidence that a methodology is worn out comes when progress within it no longer deals with the main issues." No doubt each of us has had occasion for similar reactions. And no criticism of theoretical work is more devastating than the charge that a particular line of inquiry "leads nowhere" – that it has exhausted its ability to generate important insights, that its best accomplishments are in reality inconsequential.

But how are such claims to be assessed? How do we judge whether particular assumptions and strategies for inquiry indeed promise to address "the main issues?" And how is anyone to judge what really constitutes "the main issues" in those (by no means unusual) instances of fundamental disagreement on the subject? Proponents of programs like that of Moore and Mills in fact slide over a stubborn logical problem at this point. Conceptions, like theirs, of theoretical analysis as a direct attack on "urgent social problems" or "the great issues of the day" imply a transparency in such matters that simply is not there.

Moore and Mills wrote, after all, as self-avowed radicals. For them, the urgent problems were such things as inequality of power and privilege, or the failure of democratic institutions to fulfill their role, or the triviality of information conveyed in the mass media. But for analysts from the other side of the political fence, these "problems" might appear as nothing other than the inevitable symptoms of irreducible differences in human capacities, or the futility of trying to make the elite functions of governance open to the masses. To conservatives, the great problems of the day might appear as populist interference with policy-making or the stubborn persistence of "antinomian" ideologies.

My aim here is not to choose sides in clashes like these. I simply mean to insist that any judgment of what constitutes the most urgent problems for analytical attention implies some particular analysis of its own. One's own "gut reactions" to these matters are a reasonable point of departure in developing such analyses, but no more than that. Without reasoned justification, they have about as much persuasive power as flat assertions about one's likes and dislikes in art or entertainment.

THE USES OF INTELLECTUAL HISTORY

What form could such justification take? Some such judgment is essential if there is to be any assessment of what I have termed "substantive progress." And however one proposes to make such judgments, history clearly has to play a role. We need to judge what issues have most persistently intruded themselves into the reflections of social analysts, and which responses to such issues appear to promise the broadest "staying power," the widest analytical utility for future thinkers.

These were key concerns of my *Theories of Civil Violence*. That work examined the long pedigree of theoretical attempts to account for riot, rebellion, civil war, and other breaches of civil sovereignty – themes that have attracted "contributions" from most major theoretical approaches since the beginnings of social science. Surely, it was assumed, if the social sciences admit of anything like progress, it should be evident in some net analytical gain over the course of these debates.

That conspectus made it clear that, in the study of civil violence as much as elsewhere, different generations and different intellectual constituencies within generations often seem driven by different intellectual *interests*. The view of a subject that, to one group of intellectual consumers, illuminates precisely the most important issues often leaves the next group cold. When this occurs, a new way of seeing things seems necessary – and usually is quickly forthcoming. But the theoretical vision that satisfies these new intellectual needs may have no more permanent a claim on the theoretical imagination than the one it displaced.

Consider a case from North American social science in the 1960s. For decades, analysts had viewed civil violence as part of a genre of social processes known as "collective behavior." With its origins in the thinking of such figures as Tarde, LeBon, and Park, collective behavior theory pictured civil violence as a result of innovative, emotional, and basically nonrational mental processes on the part of its participants. Explaining instances of such events was accordingly a matter of citing how normal social process, with its cues sustaining "normal" forms of behavior, had broken down.

In the mid-1960s, these views gave way dramatically to insurgent theories that portrayed civil violence as normative, continuous with everyday social life, and ultimately rational on the part of its embattled participants. Led notably by Charles Tilly and William Gamson, proponents of these new views drew inspiration from intellectual traditions dating to Marx and, in some respects, back to Hobbes himself. Proponents marshaled a wealth of empirical material to illustrate the newly rediscovered rationality of militant group action, including some striking presentations of historical materials. The deeper they delved, the more instances they found where violent outbreaks served interests that participants had long experienced but had simply lacked the opportunity to do something about. Thus emerged a view of militant action as an eminently normal, if not necessarily felicitous, social process growing out of the same sorts of tensions and interests that underlie more peaceful collective action.

By the mid-1970s, these views had decisively eclipsed collective behavior theory. A new generation of researchers simply found little interest in the discontinuous or nonrational aspects of militant events. For most members of the new theoretical generation, the new way of looking at things was self-evidently a step ahead.

As a number of observers (Gamson and McEvoy 1972; Morris and Herring 1987) have noted, this striking theoretical shift could hardly have failed to be influenced by equally dramatic changes in the political and cultural contexts of intellectual work. The history of the 1960s, and the new generation of scholars who arrived on the scene in that turbulent period, seemed to require a different view of political upheaval. The previous generations of analysts of militant political struggle, it appears, had generally shared negative associations to their subject matter – Nazism and Stalinism abroad, McCarthyism and the lynchings of blacks in the United States. By contrast, for those who came of intellectual age in the 1960s, civil upheaval could hardly help but be associated with movements on behalf of peace and civil rights – in short, with causes to which social scientists were highly sympathetic. It simply would not do to embrace a theoretical view of such phenomena that cast them in an unfavorable light. Theories stressing their rationality, normality, and perhaps even their inevitability as responses to unjust conditions, by contrast, were made to order.

Was this theoretical shift *progressive,* in any overarching sense? True, proponents of the new views convincingly undermined some key tenets of the older theories – notably, the notion of drastic discontinuity between interests guiding action in militant situations and those underlying "normal" social existence. Yet, viewed from a certain intellectual distance, the newer theories also seemed to turn their backs on certain theoretically promising aspects of the older views. The idea that the rise and fall of militant action might be shaped by transient emotional states – perhaps governed by dramatic public events or other specifically interactional dynamics – is a salient example. Focusing on a longer time perspective, and ignoring the less calculative aspects of participation in militant events, the new theories simply had little to say about these forces.

Certainly the new theories afforded an understanding of what now appear as significant aspects of the subject matter – ones strikingly neglected by earlier views. And the technical improvements in methods for study that the new approaches brought with them are hardly less clear. But was it – *is* it – more important to consider the long-term, rational aspects of militant struggle or the short-term, episodic, emotional dynamics underlying such events? Indeed, do such questions admit of any strictly objective or categorical, once-and-for-all answer?

Such observations have significance that goes far beyond the study of civil violence or any other single topic. When we encounter a way of looking at things that seems to highlight just what, as we see it, *matters most* in a subject matter of interest, we are apt to praise the "power" of the new theory. Obviously more "powerful" theories are preferable to less "powerful" ones, so our affirmations implicitly endorse the sense that the theoretical change we are promoting is, in fact, progressive. But without some overarching standard for judging the importance of different aspects of our subject matter, our claims for "powerful" theoretical visions amount to little more than confessions of what matters most to us. Thus the complexity of seeking any Archimedean point for judgments of progress in theoretical understanding. Different eras, and different intellectual communities within each era, clearly seek at least somewhat different things in theories about "the same" subject matters. At best, it appears, bad ideas may be rejected when they repeatedly fail to accord with systematic empirical inquiry. But, at the same time, it appears that perfectly good, or at least highly promising, theoretical ideas get neglected or even forgotten for reasons having little to do with their strictly analytical merits.

An extended look at the theories of Hobbes in *Theories of Civil Violence,* for example, revealed all sorts of subtle theoretical implications – implications virtually ignored by generations of theorists influenced by the thinking of Parsons. Similarly, ideas of Pareto on the social composition of participants in civil upheaval appear to fit certain forms of evidence on participation in such events. Yet those ideas have been virtually neglected in the research traditions that have held center stage since the vogue of Pareto – most likely because antipathetic views, especially ones derived from Marx, have been more politically congenial to researchers.

Thus relatively transient intellectual needs clearly have an enormous impact on the perceived strength of theories. The qualities that analysts seek to account for in civil violence – or stratification, or economic development, or religiosity, or any number of other key subjects of theoretical attention – plainly shift with the times. And just as changing political and cultural contexts bring new and often persuasive analytical ideas to light, so similar changes seem to consign analytically promising theories to oblivion – at least until the tectonic shifts of intellectual life propel them back to the surface.

And yet, nothing in *Theories of Civil Violence* would suggest the impossibility *in principle* of casting doubt on weak theories, or of upholding good ones, on the strength of empirical evidence. A striking example was relative deprivation theory, a major theoretical inspiration that came to prominence on much the same wave of cultural enthusiasm that supported theories portraying militant collective action as rational or normative.

For many American analysts in the 1960s, it seemed almost self-evident that protest and other militant action stemmed from participants' sense of injustice or grievance relative to others. The protests of black Americans, to take the most notable example, were attributed to the fact that their position in American life was plainly inferior to that of whites. Relative deprivation theory simply generalized this observation: Shared indignation, according to commonly held standards, was seen as the key cause of all militant collective action. Note how well this doctrine served expressive needs for a morally positive view of the subject; civil upheaval represented nothing other than a symptom of universal strivings for justice.

But conscientious research over nearly two decades has cast much doubt on a key empirical implication of the theory: the expectation that, within any particular population, the most aggrieved or indignant should be most likely to take part in militant action. Relative deprivation theory had everything in its favor in terms of expressive appeal and of consonance with the social demands of the times in which it came to prominence. But these expressive advantages did not rescue it from theoretical disfavor stemming from repeated falsification through conscientious empirical research.

Such accounts – of which *Theories of Civil Violence* produced more than one – bear much reflection for the purposes of this book. They suggest that at least one form of theoretical progress – the enhanced "survival value" of theoretical tenets better supported by empirical inquiry as against those less well supported – is an authentic possibility. The relative rarity of intellectual verdicts as conclusive as those on relative deprivation theory does not seem to stem from limitations inherent in the subject matter or the analytical potential of social science. Rather, it appears to have much more to do with the instability of the short-term, context-bound interests underlying the organization of so much of our intellectual work.

RELATIVISM AND PROGRESS

For some thinkers, even these guarded conclusions go much too far. Authentic skeptics would consider any notion that systematic empirical inquiry could constrain the developement of theoretical understanding naive and unsophisticated – either in the study of social life or elsewhere. For similar reasons, they view any notion of theoretical cumulation or progress over time as a sham and a delusion. Every theoretical vision, in their view, entails its own standards of success – and succeeds in those terms. Intellectual history simply consists of the succession of fundamentally incommensurable theoretical visions, and with them their associated programs for empirical inquiry.

Nowhere is this view developed with greater verve than in Paul Feyerabend's *Against Method* (1975). Feyerabend devotes much attention to historic "scientific revolutions," seeking to show that the intellectual conquests of victorious theories always require connivance to change the rules by which evidence is interpreted. What Galileo "saw" with his telescope, in Feyerabend's account, was scarcely unproblematic "evidence" for his theories on celestial motion. Rather, Galileo had to indoctrinate viewers in *how* to look through the instrument – then a novelty – and how to mobilize such observations as bases for theoretical inference. The success of Galileo's efforts stemmed from his command of dramaturgy rather than on any constraint inherent in the objective realities of the situation. Feyerabend does not mince words in drawing conclusions from such accounts: "Propaganda is of the essence" in theoretical arguments, he insists (p. 157). Asked what a thinker should be required to demonstrate in order to win acceptance for a theory, Feyerabend would apparently advise, "Whatever works." Thus he espouses a kind of "survival-of-the-fittest" doctrine, in which fitness is determined by the theorist's ability to create the sort of superior propaganda likely to win the day.

But surely such a doctrine raises an embarrassing question: Are there no generalizations to be made about what sorts of propaganda are most likely to work? Don't theories susceptible to being properly advertised have *any* qualities in common to distinguish them from those unlikely to prevail, even with the benefits of propaganda? And wouldn't any such commonalities imply ultimate limits to thoroughgoing relativism à la Feyerabend?

I am not sure what response Feyerabend's supporters would make to these objections. But it should be clear, in any case, how important doctrines like his are for the concerns of this book. If all theories really do entail worldviews assuring their own self-justification, any objective reckoning of progress, any idea of selection of "better" theories over a long historical run, is out of the question. In Feyerabend's world, there are no standards of theoretical adequacy that outlast the life of theories themselves – no overarching criteria by which one could judge whether more is known now than before.

One can readily construct an account of any form of scientific change along Feyerabend's lines. Each new theoretical persuasion is seen as a self-contained worldview that lasts just as long as it continues to satisfy the sensibilities of its intellectual constituents. But how do the relativistic views of figures like Feyerabend fit what we already know about theoretical development in our own field?

None too gracefully, if *Theories of Civil Violence* is any guide. True, that work did underscore the weight of contextual forces in the currency of theories. One saw repeatedly how cultural, political, and social context focused extraordinary interest on some theoretical views, discouraged attention to others, and often reshaped prevailing standards of theoretical adequacy.

But, then again, nothing in *Theories of Civil Violence* suggested that things must work this way. Here and there, where collaboration of theorists and researchers has been steady enough, and research concerted enough, empirical inquiry has indeed afforded conclusions on important theoretical issues. In the case of relative deprivation theory, even the strong expressive appeals of the doctrine did not assure its continued currency. From this and other cases, it appears that repeated refutation of empirical expectations sometimes does undermine belief in the theory.

For someone like Feyerabend, of course, such conclusions merely reflect the sham of appearances. If every new theoretical view brings with it its own criteria for validation, then the empirical expectations of every theory are bound to be affirmed within the terms of reference of that theory. Thus the possibility that an idea might confront any facts, findings, or observations that might undermine its validity *from within the frame of reference of the theory itself* is always zero.

Yet that is just what we do not find in *Theories of Civil Violence*. Virtually all the theories considered there implied some empirical expectations which, if not met, would detract from their credibility. I could find no justification for viewing theories of civil violence as a series of doctrines walled off from one another by incommensurable metaphysical premises. Where theories had come and gone without much effect from the constraint of evidence, the reasons had much more to do with *the organization of intellectual work*. In other words, concerted empirical inquiry could well have yielded conclusions on the theoretical issues at stake, if only participants in the debate had taken the trouble to develop such a program of inquiry and stick to it.

Thus I see no reason why relativistic views need define our best hopes for the progress in social understanding. It is no doubt true that, for any item of evidence that threatens to shake a treasured worldview, *some* paradigm could be constructed that would rule such evidence out of court. Indeed, one can imagine ways of looking at social life in which *all conceivable* empirical data are interpreted so as to sustain one's overarching theory. The worldview of a sophisticated paranoid schizophrenic has this quality of total resilience against nonconspiratorial interpretations of events. And, of course, to the extent that we use theory in this way, it is ridiculous to seek anything like progress in theoretical social science. For, then, the most we could expect of any theory would be that it suits the needs of those who embrace it, whose number may well be limited to one.

But such uses of theory are not attractive to most of us. Ultimately, I suspect, most readers prefer to entertain theories with more informative content concerning a world that impinges upon our interests, and with which we are obliged to cope. And this means recourse to forms of theoretical analysis that admit of revision in light of empirical inquiry.

Thus we return to the question of such central importance for this work: What model of closure, what program of inquiry offers the best prospect for yielding understanding of enduring analytical usefulness? If we indeed seek theories susceptible to change in response to the encounter with empirical evidence, how do we direct our attention to empirical issues and material most likely to matter to analysts who come after us? These are obviously highly abstract questions – but unavoidable ones. And again, it is hard to see how they might be answered without considering a variety of previous historical efforts at theory building.

THE ENDS OF THEORETICAL INQUIRY

In 1913 Emile Durkheim, who had for years held the title of Professor of Educational Science, became the first holder of a chair in sociology in France. This was a step for which Durkheim, an ambitious academic politician, had long striven. The appointment in effect consolidated his academic success in positing the realm of the social as a logically distinct, sui generis subject matter. It also marked his success in a larger public arena, by persuading progressive politicians of the Third Republic of the indispensability of sociology as an instrument of social policy.

However the modern reader regards Durkheim's thought, it is hard not to be impressed by the unity of theory and practice that it embodied. His functionalist views implied both an agenda for social inquiry and imperatives for social and political action. If, as Durkheim insisted, social systems were indeed *organismic,* then each social or cultural element had a unique and unambiguous part to play in relation to all others. And in this case, Durkheim reasoned, the analyst's role demanded that he or she diagnose the ills of social life and specify the measures necessary to return the "body social" to a healthy state – even when this meant offering programs and policies, endowed with the authority of science, for resolving the political or moral controversies of the day.

Today, I suspect, few social scientists would hazard claims for their programs of inquiry as sweeping as Durkheim's. One reason, no doubt, is the sheer multitude of often discordant voices making up the theoretical chorus. The fact that analysts differ so widely among themselves as to the "needs" of society, and the fact that the spectrum of theoretical opinion on issues of public import so closely parallels the range of opinion among nonspecialists, makes it harder to claim that social science offers authoritative wisdom. Similarly, where theory has inspired practical efforts at social improvement, the results have rarely succeeded in transcending political partisanship as Durkheim might have hoped. Pace Durkheim, what should be considered a "healthy" state of social affairs is nearly as controversial among social scientists as it is among the educated public more generally.

But there are other reasons, too, why moral certainties like Durkheim's about the long-term payoffs of social inquiry no longer convince. One stems from the very success of Durkheim and other founding figures in securing an established place for social science in the academy. The fact that our disciplines now enjoy a relatively secure claim on university appointments surely insulates us to some degree from the need to justify our "contributions" to the broader public.

Durkheim's model of closure aimed at establishing sociology as a legitimate enterprise in an intellectual and political world not initially disposed to it. That model promised both an unambiguous agenda for inquiry and straightforward moral and political implications to be drawn from such inquiry. We have come a long way from the day when social scientists felt constrained to offer so much. Consider the apology for economic theory given by an eminent representative of that discipline:

In the flight of rockets the layman can see the marvel of physics, and in the applause of audiences the marvel of music. No one understands the marvel of economics who has not studied it with care. (McCloskey 1985, p, xix)

Judging from his words elsewhere, I do not believe that this passage conveys the only justification McCloskey would want to make for economic theory. But the more closely one considers the claims in this passage, the more striking they become. The virtues of economic analysis, it seems, are not to be judged by its ability to resolve questions that might occur to just any of us. Instead, those virtues lie in the ability to perform feats that cannot even be appreciated without special indoctrination.

Such a position can obviously be quite persuasive on behalf of a system of thought whose claim on public acceptance is secure. For neoclassical economics, at least in the English-speaking world at the end of the twentieth century, such assumptions are reasonable. Economists in this setting are so widely recognized as trading in profundities that many outsiders are willing to undergo considerable tutelage to gain access to its theoretical "marvels." But a Durkheim would hardly have dared to offer an argument like McCloskey's on behalf of a discipline struggling for public recognition. What appeal could there be to theoretical "marvels" whose marvelous qualities had no one to vouch for them? Instead, Durkheim had to hold out the promise that sociological analysis would help solve "social problems" whose troublesome nature was compelling to all – regardless of whether they found anything marvelous in the analytical structures leading to the alleged solutions.

The distinction between the two approaches is of great moment for the purposes of this book. Durkheim justifies the elaboration of his intellectual project as the only promising *means* to a supremely important *end*: the resolution of the political and social conflicts facing early-twentieth-century France. For McCloskey, by contrast, following the inner logic of economic theory is an end in itself – something worth doing regardless of practical consequences, or lack of them.

Durkheim's confidence in the beneficent practical results expected of his model of closure is unconvincing. But McCloskey's vision of theoretical success is ultimately unappealing. One would not wish to deny McCloskey the "marvels" that he detects in economic theory. The problem is, the list of potentially "marvelous" theoretical abstractions is, in principle, infinite. Accordingly, we have no choice but to develop some rationale as to which ought to command attention. Without some account of why the potential results of any model of closure, in however long a run, ought to engage the interests of "outsiders" to the theory in question, we are left in an embarrassing position. If every program for social inquiry is justified "in its own terms" – as an end in itself – different approaches are apt to devolve into utterly inward-looking, self-absorbed, and mutually incommensurable activities. Who can deny that work in our fields has often taken on this guise?

This view of theoretical social science as uniquely susceptible to a pre-occupation with arcane and inconsequential questions is hardly original to this book. Perhaps it was a vision of this kind that moved Lewis Coser, in his 1975 presidential address to the American Sociological Association, to score some influential models of closure. The title of the address was "Two Methods in Search of a Substance," and the targets were eth-nomethodology and status attainment studies:

our discipline will be judged in the last analysis on the basis of the *substantive enlightenment* which it is able to supply about the social structures in which we are enmeshed and which largely condition the course of our lives. If we neglect that major task, if we refuse the challenge to answer these questions, we shall forfeit our birthright and degenerate into congeries of rival sects and specialized re-searchers who will learn more and more about less and less. (1975, p. 698; emphasis added)

"Substantive enlightenment" – it is the sort of thing that no one would dare to oppose. But the trouble is, reasoned argument as to how to identify such enlightenment, and how to organize inquiry so as to achieve it, is no open-and-shut case.

Coser holds, in effect, that the models of closure pursued by eth-nomethodology and status attainment studies simply do not deserve a following. They *miss the point;* they fail to move us toward understanding the sorts of things about social life that it matters most to understand. The charge is devastating, if it convinces. Perhaps the most damning criticism of any line of work is that it "leads nowhere," that it mobilizes energies leading only to intellectual "dead ends" – just as the highest praise is to assert that a genre of inquiry yields "major advances" in the field, or that it "moves the field forward" or "breaks new ground."

One suspects that one knows in advance the response of proponents of doctrines subjected to criticisms like Coser's. The critic, they will insist, has failed to appreciate the theoretical "marvels" inherent in the project; or, perhaps, has failed to appreciate the ultimate rewards of pursuing it. Virtually every model of closure, I have argued, entails *some* means-to-ends assumptions, some more or less complex strategy in which incremental steps in intellectual work ultimately lead to powerful enlightenment. The temptation is always great to portray those who fail to perceive the virtues of such grand designs as simply unqualified to evaluate them.

Such responses cannot simply be dismissed out of hand. It was Lewis Coser himself who once defended the right to pursue lines of inquiry that might seem "irrelevant" in terms of immediate bearing on public events. One may feel confident that one "knows *substantive enlightenment* when one sees it," much as some people feel they know pornography. But, like

43

pornography and nonpornography, profundities that are unmistakable in the eye of the beholder may appear in quite a different light to other sophisticated observers. Models of closure that appear irrelevant or arcane at one point – or those that strike us as embodying the very state of the art or cutting edge of theoretical progress – may assume a different aspect with a shake of the historical kaleidoscope.

THE CRITIQUE OF CLOSURE

Let us give credit to Durkheim. At least he did not shrink from a nettlesome issue that is fundamental to any theoretical vision: the linkage between his program of inquiry and the value-relevance of its results in the larger scheme of human affairs. If his arguments now seem overly optimistic or indeed naive, we need to do better at the same task. Most of us, I suspect, are not satisfied to contemplate the continuing history of our disciplines as an unending succession of short-lived and incommensurable theoretical visions. Accordingly, we need to weigh our rationale for relating day-to-day theoretical work to our conception of the ultimate ends of social inquiry.

This is no easy task. Social scientists have well-worked-out terms for debating the finer details of their conduct of inquiry – the rules for relating evidence to conclusions, for example, or the exact relation of one concept to another. By contrast, we often find ourselves at a loss for language to weigh the far-reaching, context-forming issues implicated in the closure models that guide our work. In the face of uncertainties on these matters, it is hardly surprising that we confront such endless contention over what we should invoke as the "core concepts," the basic causal processes, or the most fundamental social relationships in our work. If differences on where we are going are indeed endemic, we should hardly expect easy agreement on how to organize the trip.

Should we ever expect things to be different? Are there any enduring standards, any perennial *analytical interests* that might form the basis for judgments as to whether our overall grasp in understanding the social world is growing? I believe that there are, and that these criteria are implicit in the existential tensions predictably generated by the exigencies of social life itself.

Because of these abiding tensions, our theoretical history is not only a catalogue of grandiose schemes for one or another now forgotten program of inquiry. It is also a record of analytical (and practical) themes that show commonalities stretching over generations. Intelligently interpreted, this record offers guidance to which concerns and insights are likely to animate those who come after us. In the study of civil violence, for example, one can point to themes and insights of interest from a wide range of historical and intellectual standpoints. While altogether less pretentious than the claims put forward for the ongoing stream of theoretical "revolutions," the record of these accomplishments offers something ultimately more important. It offers hope for a practice of social inquiry whose results could form the basis for meaningful cumulation over time – that is, for substantive progress.

This brings me to the pivot of my argument. *I hold that no program of social inquiry – no model of closure – will long claim attention if it fails to address a core of historically enduring questions. These questions occupy a special place in the theoretical life of our disciplines because they emerge predictably from certain endemic tensions of social life itself.* I call them *first-order questions.* Consider a few examples:

What causes deviance? How do we explain varying levels and forms of deviance across social systems?

What social influences – from family constellations to community milieux to political institutions – shape the development of adult personality? What essential personality characteristics are indispensable for a vital civic culture?

What conditions favor economic growth? What mixtures of institutions, economic resources, attitudes, and practices provide the best chance of fostering increased wealth?

What conditions foster international peace, and which lead to war and other forms of conflict?

What are the limits to the changes in family organization that are now sweeping the world's most prosperous societies?

How much social stratification, and what forms of it, are necessary to ensure productive and cohesive social relations in complex societies? How equal might social systems be, in other words, without jeopardizing other important values such as social order, prosperity, and diversity?

Where does civil violence come from? To what extent is it endemic in all social life? What kinds of social and political arrangements are apt to foster or contain it?

These questions are substantively quite diverse. But they share something of the utmost import in terms of their origins: All arise directly from recurrent and abiding strains and perplexities of social life itself. Thus we have reason to believe that such questions will be posed wherever people have to confront the demands of living in a world marked by such things as deviance, international conflict, stratification, and the like. And authoritative answers to such questions, if we could ever grasp them, would clearly make a difference in social practice.

Let me stress what I do *not* assert about these first-order questions. First, it should be obvious that the list is not exhaustive, nor even a representative sample of some larger universe. Nor are such questions utterly eternal. One can imagine, with a bit of effort, worlds in which stratification, or civil upheaval, or economic growth simply no longer impinge on human interests. But such worlds, it must be said, are far removed from those that have given rise to the traditions of social inquiry in which we situate ourselves; it is unlikely that anything like them will form the context for such inquiry in the immediate future. As long as social relations take certain familiar forms, questions of the sort noted above will continue to matter.

We can thus view such first-order questions as the social equivalents of certain basic questions in ethics: for example, "What are my most fundamental obligations to others?" or "How does one weigh quality of life against its duration?" or "When is one obligated to speak one's conscience, even in the face of threatening consequences?" Indeed, first-order questions are deeply implicated with basic ethical issues, since any response to them is apt to reflect directly on the goodness or badness of various courses of social action. *They are the kinds of questions that draw people to study social life in the first place, and that are constantly raised anew in the minds of nonspecialists seeking reasoned bases for action in the face of endemic social tensions.*

First-order questions in this sense offer one possibility for a meaningful criterion of progress. One of the most embarrassing things about our transitory agenda for inquiry is the frequency with which issues once considered of paramount importance plummet into obscurity. Yet what I call first-order questions are unlikely to do this, much as specific approaches to answering them may fall into and out of fashion. Their very centrality to enduring dilemmas of social action promise that students of social life will return to them again and again. To the extent that we can claim to know more about such issues, we can be said to achieve what I have called substantive progress – advance within a common analytical enterprise.

None of this is to suggest that such questions could be answered in any definitive, once-and-for-all fashion. As Chapter 8 argues at length, responses to such questions turn on the understanding of systems that are in varying degrees *historical* – that is, which operate somewhat differently at different points in time. Thus we have good reason to believe that the conditions of economic growth at the end of the twentieth century are different from those in the middle of the nineteenth, for example – just as they differ for countries with different economic and social characteristics at present. But I hold that the causal systems targeted in first-order questions are at least stable enough so that insight gained at one point enhances our prospects for coping with similar processes elsewhere. By my lights, this amounts to progress.

I do *not* suggest that only first-order questions matter, or that only they should be studied. I *do* hold that no agenda of theoretical inquiry, no model of closure, can long to hold the theoretical stage unless it promises to address such questions. But not all theoretical questions, and certainly not all important ones, are of this kind. Consider some other broad thematic questions that most readers will also find familiar:

Do white-collar workers engage in "production" in the same sense as workers who produce *things?*

Are all institutions in an apparently harmonious society necessarily "functionally integrated" with one another?

Is it legitimate to use parametric statistics for inferences about relationships where population distributions have not yet been demonstrated?

Was Poland at the end of the sixteenth century part of the "periphery" of Europe, or of its "semiperiphery?"

The difference between questions like these and those in the first list "jumps in your eyes," as the French say. These questions are scarcely direct outgrowths of social experience. Rather, their interest arises strictly out of analytical structures created by social scientists. Call them *second-order questions.*

Some readers will inevitably conclude that I mean this term to designate questions that are somehow of secondary importance. This is far from what I have in mind. No genre of intellectual work known to me can proceed without concentrating attention on questions of this kind. By way of analogy: Every thoughtful citizen must wonder at times whether particular laws really serve some higher standard of justice. Yet few can become deeply interested in the technicalities that legitimately absorb legal philosophers in pursuing such questions in a more systematic way. Similar examples could be given for all areas of intellectual inquiry. One can identify certain profound puzzles or problems that represent enduring *ends* of inquiry and, no less characteristically, other analytic conventions or strategies developed as potential *means* to such ends.

Yet social science seems afflicted by a particular slippage in the relations between its first- and second-order questions. Even where there is a measure of agreement on the forms of enlightenment worth having – as I hold there is, in the case of first-order questions – disagreement widely reigns as to what intellectual strategies show the best promise of delivering such insight.

Worse, *our second-order questions all too readily become obsessions of such proportions as to represent ends in themselves.* Once a particular model of closure has gained a certain credibility and a cohesive group of followers, theoretical enthusiasts can insulate themselves from any need to justify its special preoccupations. Thus followers of any ascendant model of closure are apt to find themselves increasingly absorbed in questions of less and less interest to the uninitiated. The problem is not that such questions appear obscure to those on the outside; that much is standard, and often unavoidable. The problem arises instead when such questions are pursued past the point where any answers to them could possibly matter, directly or indirectly, to the uninitiated. Can any reader deny that such conditions are widespread in theoretical work in our disciplines?

Enthusiasts of one or another model of closure are rarely content to advance their favorite theoretical obsessions simply as idiosyncratic matters of taste. Instead, they typically seek to show how their chosen list of second-order questions represents indispensable means to ends that anyone could subscribe to. In the term used here, they invoke "or-else" clauses: "Pay attention to our ways of understanding," proponents of every theoretical vision in effect insist, "*or else* you will fail to grasp something you urgently need to know, strictly in your own interest."

Proponents of virtually all models of closure, all programs for social inquiry, imply or assert such rationales. They maintain, in other words, that the second-order questions peculiar to their theoretical program are indispensable to the resolution of first-order questions. This is true both for the most self-consciously "relevant" of approaches, like that of Moore and Mills, and for utterly academic theories like network analysis.

Throughout this book, I seek to pay special attention to such "or-else" clauses. Sooner or later proponents of every model of closure must respond to questions like: Why does anyone *need* the sort of insight provided by this project; How do these insights help us cope with a world that impinges on our interests, regardless of our theories about it? Responses to such questions, and the degrees of their explicitness, are enormously varied. Yet, if we hope to weigh the prospects of any line of inquiry for producing insight of enduring value, we need to take a hard, critical look at them.

Thus, for a variety of theoretical programs – all of them manifestations of striking theoretical progress, at least to their enthusiasts – I want to subject the underlying model of closure to serious scrutiny. What prospects has this model of closure, if pursued conscientiously in its own terms, of contributing to the understanding of first-order questions? How likely are the insights it generates to be useful to analysts whose mind-sets have been shaped in quite different expressive contexts from those which originally brought the theory to prominence? What, in short, are the chances that these ideas will appear in retrospect as a step forward, a "contribution" to some common, relatively enduring fund of theoretical understanding?

2

The reckoning of progress

The criterion for theoretical progress developed above is clearly a *pragmatic* one, having to do with the ability of different forms of understanding to support efforts at *coping* with practical dilemmas of social living. This is far from being a consensus view. Proponents of alternate views would argue that each theory generates its own criteria of success, and that such criteria need have nothing to do with what I have termed coping. In this light, the analytical accomplishements of any theoretical program, and certainly any "progress" achieved by it, can only be judged in terms defined by the theory itself. The implications of such views for the study of progress – indeed, for the idea of progress – are far-reaching.

This chapter seeks to explore some of these implications. The main focus is the sociological study of science. Proponents of the two main currents in this subdiscipline, the Mertonians and the constructivists, have put forward what most would see as quite opposing views of progress. Yet I argue that, for some purposes, these two views actually converge in a kind of shared antipathy to a conception like the one embraced in this book.

What sense do such different views make of theoretical change in social science? To address this question, I consider the life cycles of ethnomethodology and Balesian small-group studies – two theoretical projects whose meteoric rise and dramatic decline hold special interest. Once widely regarded as the very embodiment of increased theoretical sophistication, these programs have experienced fates ranging from partial to total eclipse. My question is, what interpretation do different notions of intellectual progress have to offer for such apparent contre-temps in the forward march of knowledge?

THE SOCIOLOGICAL STUDY OF SCIENCE

The founding of the empirical sociological study of science can be dated with an exactitude possible in few other specialties. It came with publication of Robert K. Merton's *Science, Technology and Society in Seventeenth Century England* in 1938, shortly after its completion as his Harvard doctoral thesis. Merton's analyses of the social forces behind the efflorescence of English science during this period defined the terms for an entire literature that sprang up in its wake. And in so doing, it raised the question never adequately answered in that literature: how to reckon progress, or the lack of it, in science.

Merton was hardly the first to imagine that state sponsorship, economic conditions, religious ideas, or other social arrangements might shape such abstract pursuits as science. But Merton mobilized such notions as bases for empirical accounts of the origins of specific changes in scientific institutions and in the content of scientific work. Today, his book is best known for its portrayal of Puritan ideology as a stimulant to seventeenth-century English science. But the work also examines such issues as the role of military and population factors in shaping these same developments.

The spur to Merton's original interest was presumably the dramatic progress made by English science during the period in question. But how do we know that science did, in fact, "advance" at this point? For Merton, the question posed no theoretical problem. He documented the rise of science by showing growth in the numbers of persons pursuing scientific work, for example, and by citing the rise in "important discoveries and inventions" (1938, p. 40) during the period.

For the purposes of this discussion, such evidence has to be considered problematic. How do we know that the people identified as scientists were really doing "science?" What reason have we to believe that "discoveries" are indeed equivalent units, objective milestones in the forward march of knowledge? How do we know, for example, that what registers as a discovery in the mind of one enumerator will have the same significance in the mind of the next or that the discoveries of one decade or era are comparable in import to those declared elsewhere?

It seems unlikely that the young Merton gave such questions much thought. In the 1920s, and for decades thereafter, the distinctive and progressive quality of science was considered self-evident. Moreover, Merton, like most of his contemporaries, found reinforcement for this view in the role of science in solving practical human problems. One reason for the rise of science in seventeenth-century England, Merton posited, was the press of new "needs" generated by the growth of the British population (1938, p. 215). Because science fulfilled human needs, he reasoned, the rise of such needs conduced to growth in science. This view continued to inform Merton's understanding of scientific advance in later writings:

The increasing comforts and conveniences deriving from technology and ultimately from science invite the social support of scientific research. They also testify to the integrity of the scientist, since abstract and difficult theories which cannot be understood or evaluated by the laity are presumably proved in a fashion which can be understood by all, that is, through their technological application. Readiness to accept the authority of science rests, to a considerable extent, upon its daily demonstration of power. Were it not for such indirect demonstrations, the continued social support of that science which is intellectually incomprehensible to the public would hardly be nourished on faith alone. (1973 [1938] pp. 260–261)

Thus Merton gives a simple and reassuringly affirmative view of the progressive nature of science and its social outputs. The practice of science produces increased understanding of the natural world; and scientific understanding yields technologies that satisfy human needs. The more science flourishes, the more human needs stand to be satisfied. And in this increase in need satisfaction, the great public at large quite properly sees evidence of the success of science and the justice of its claims on scarce social resources.

This analysis fits gracefully with the broader structural-functional model of social life that came to infuse Merton's later thinking. In this view, every social arrangement and institution in a stable social system has its distinctive contribution to make to the "health" or "efficiency" of the social whole. Science was thus seen as claiming its proper place in the social order as a source of social benefit. And, in a distinctively functional view of stratification, rewards for scientific "contributions" were to be graded in direct relation to the extent that each article, monograph, discovery, or career actually helped science to fulfill its larger social function.

This view helped inspire a research program that has animated Mertonian sociologists of science ever since. If science is indeed "functional" for "society" at large, then what social arrangements are most conducive to its fulfillment of the functions assigned to it? More specifically, what sorts of norms of scientific conduct promise to elicit the most productive science? What systems of reward are most promising to this end? How, in short, can science best be cultivated to produce all the good things, all the "functional contributions," of which it is capable? These questions – and particularly those concerning relations between social *rewards* and scientific productivity – have underlain the inquiries not only of Merton himself, but also of such influential followers as Stephen Cole, Jonathan Cole, Harriet Zuckerman, Lowell Hargens, Jerry Gaston, and many others.

THE REVOLT OF THE CONSTRUCTIVISTS

In the 1970s, the Mertonian dominance of the sociological study of science came under sharp challenge. The challengers, mostly British and European, shared the Mertonian concern to chart the social arrangements and processes shaping scientific work. But they differed on a most fundamental point: the nature of the "discovery" process in science and the role of strictly social forces in that process. The intellectual insurgents viewed not only the rate and the social auspices of scientific work but also the *content* of scientific discoveries as subject to sociological explanation. Social forces were seen as accounting not only for how scientists went about their work, but also as explaining the nature of what they found when they did. The picture of the world generated by scientific inquiry was thus as much an imprint of social forces as the representations offered by artists, dramatists, or novelists. The truths enshrined by scientific progress were not so much *discovered* as they were, to use the phrase adopted by the insurgents themselves, *constructed*.

This is of course a relativistic position. For Merton and his followers, the truths that science sought to represent were somehow always "there"; the question was, what social conditions and arrangements facilitated their discovery? For the constructivists, the natural world had no one story to tell. Scientific truth consisted simply of what scientists *agreed* to be true at any specific moment. The task of the sociology of science was to show how different sorts of truth get to be "constructed" according to the social forces prevailing on particular scientists at a particular moment. Thus the "truths" established by scientific inquiry were factitious and arbitrary. It is a view that could well have been inspired by Feyerabend's characterization of scientific authority as being won by those who deploy the most splendid propaganda in the theoretical war of nerves.

It is not clear that Feyerabend was an inspiration for the constructivists. But one such inspiration was certainly ethnomethodology, particularly in the fine-grained concern of that specialty with folk techniques for making sense of everyday life. A particular knack of the constructivists was to apply close observation to the work of scientists *as it actually unfolded,* not as it was later reconstructed and presented in talks, laboratory reports, journal articles, or textbooks.

This approach has yielded a rich literature on the role of imagination, negotiation, interpretation, and, ultimately, more or less friendly persuasion in the creation of scientific "truth." Karin Knorr-Cetina titled her study of laboratory research, *The Manufacture of Knowledge,* an eminently appropriate choice in light of what she reports of the process of "discovery":

Methods and results are dependent upon each other in a very simple way. For example, when I asked a scientist if some value he had obtained in a previous experiment weren't proven wrong in the light of results from a new method he had tried, I was told:

> "You have to stop thinking in absolute terms. The water content of a substance depends on the method chosen, on the time, the temperature, and so on. In general, you dry for 3 to 5 hours at 105 (degrees); if drying is done for 30 hours at 150 (degrees), then you get a higher water content. . . ."

The lesson was that results are always the result of specific methodological selections. . . . Methods were chosen with a view to the anticipated or intended results, just as results were rejected because of the methods used to obtain them. (1981, p. 122)

The heterodox, debunking quality of such analysis is obvious. Like a film set, what at first appears solid and normal is in fact constructed for effect. The difference is that, unlike film production, the constructions made by scientists ultimately convince their makers and the professional community themselves, as well as lay "consumers" of science. Such conclusions in turn appear to uphold a key claim of ethnomethodology: that seemingly regular, predictable, and settled features of social life are as though imposed, via a procrustean bed of interpretation, on a reality that is inherently unformed and devoid of unique significance.

The revolt of the constructivists in the sociology of science seems to have ridden the same cultural waves that reverberated throughout Western university culture in the 1960s and 1970s. In this period, intellectual orthodoxies, like many another form of authority, came under bitter attack throughout social science (see Attewell 1984, pp. 1–5). New generations of analysts in fields as diverse as political economy, deviance, communications studies, social movements, and economic development all took aim at established theoretical views they considered overly complacent. The Mertonian view of science as progressive, authoritative, and bountiful could hardly have been a more natural target.

To be sure, the constructivists scarcely denied the *experience* of scientists of participating in a progressive enterprise. Latour and Woolgar, key figures in this tradition, put matters as follows:

The result of the *construction* of a fact is that it appears unconstructed by anyone; the result of rhetorical *persuasion* in the agonistic field is that participants are convinced that they have not been convinced; the result of *materialization is that people can swear that material considerations are only minor components of the "thought process"; the result of the investments of credibility, is that participants can claim that economics and beliefs are in no way related to the solidity of science; as to the circumstances, they simply vanish from accounts, being better left to political analysis than to an appreciation of the hard and solid world of facts!* (1986, p. 240; emphasis in original)

Thus, whereas the Mertonians ask "What norms and social arrangements help discovery of scientific truths proceed as rapidly as possible?" the constructivists ask, "What social conditions led to the 'discovery' of these 'truths' rather than others?"

Do theoretical worldviews stand or fall according to analytical virtues of enduring significance or by their ability to persuade us that the criteria they entail are *the* criteria that define theoretical success? The position of constructivists on these questions could hardly be clearer: The practice of science consists simply and exclusively of rhetorical combat, with the mantle of truth being awarded to the contestants whose intellectual propaganda proves most persuasive.

One trouble with these doctrines is that, like all radical forms of relativism, they ultimately undermine themselves. If we can properly exercise no standard for judging the quality of scientific understanding apart from how well it resonates with the inner sensibilities of the thinker, then the same principle applies to the constructivist view itself. The worth of the doctrine of relativism should be reckoned strictly in terms of how many participants in the relevant scholarly communications find the position congenial – regardless of their reasons for doing so.

As Latour and Woolgar write, in the closing pages of *Laboratory Life* (1986):

In a fundamental sense, our own account is no more than *fiction*. But this does not make it inferior to the activity of laboratory members: they too were busy constructing accounts to be launched in the agonistic field, and loaded with various sources of credibility in such a way that once convinced, others would incorporate them as givens, or as matters of fact, in their own constructions of reality. . . . The only difference is that *they have a laboratory*. We, on the other hand, have a text, this present text. By building up an account, inventing characters (for example, the observer of Ch. 2), staging concepts, invoking sources linking to arguments in the field of sociology, and footnoting, we have attempted to decrease sources of disorder and to make some statements more likely than others, thereby creating a pocket of order. (pp. 257–258)

These authors have indeed created their own "pocket of order" – that is, a coherent way of looking at the work of scientists, endowed with its own logic and rhetorical appeal. But what claim does their view of things have on the beliefs of anyone who simply lacks a taste for the particular brand of order that they offer? Certainly they would not wish to point to any *evidence* for their view of things; for standards in the evaluation of evidence, they must hold, are themselves simply matters of theoretical taste.

There can be no doubt that constructivist studies have illuminated some noteworthy processes in scientific work. The tentative, negotiated, hortatory quality of communication at the grass roots of science is indeed filtered out in all sorts of official accounts. Yet the notion that the collective imagination responds only to its own inner dynamics – that is, that no constraints from the empirical world of events, facts, or processes need be posited in accounting for change in scientific thought – leaves us with a rather special view of science, to say the least. Essentially, it is a view that draws no distinction between the representations of the world yielded by science and those produced by works of the pure imagination – in dreams, for example, or in drama, or in music. All such productions are governed by their own criteria of success, but these standards involve representation of an inner, rather than an external, reality. One wonders whether such a view is wholeheartedly embraced by the constructivists themselves, or at least all of them.

Just decades ago, poliomyelitis was a major preoccupation both of the medical research community and the general public. The disease was held responsible for thousands of deaths and crippling injuries around the world every year, mostly among young people. In 1950, more than 33,000 cases were reported in the United States, with roughly 20 percent of them resulting in death or paralysis. By the early 1950s, a number of teams were pursuing research programs aimed at perfecting a vaccine. Controversy swirled at the time as to which approach to these efforts was most promising, and indeed as to whether a vaccine was even theoretically possible.

By 1954, however, the "killed virus" vaccine developed by Jonas Salk had won wide confidence and was widely administered to children in field tests. The numbers of cases reported in the United States dropped drastically.

No doubt, during the race among researchers to produce a safe and effective polio vaccine, many contested interpretations were resolved through strictly rhetorical processes. What approaches were "in," which were "out," whose results looked compelling and whose uninteresting, whether a particular animal trial appeared promising or not – such issues must have been decided much as the ones described by Latour and Woolgar or Knorr-Cetina.

But, in the end, anything offered as a polio vaccine faced an evidentiary test: Would it provide immunity against polio? Note that the "theory" necessary for evaluating such results was not identical to the theories involved in interpreting various interim results on the way to the development of a vaccine. Once any proposed vaccine reached the field-testing stage, it faced evaluation according to criteria that one did not have to be a scientist to apply: Were those who received the vaccine indeed immunized? Did they, to put it in the simplest possible terms, develop the symptoms identified as those of polio infection, and suffer subsequent crippling and death? Surely the test to which the Salk vaccine was subjected, and passed, in these terms was more than just rhetorical.

I suspect that some authors of constructivist analyses of science might be willing to concede this much. But not all of them, evidently. In a noted study in the constructivist tradition, Bruno Latour (1988) describes the processes by which Pasteur perfected his vaccine against anthrax and won acceptance for it from the livestock owners who were to represent the ultimate consumers. Latour's central concern is the process by which the vaccine came to be authoritatively constructed as efficacious. This was nothing so simple as public recognition of changes in the currency of a destructive disease, Latour insists. Instead, Pasteur engineered something more like what symbolic interactionists would call a new *definition of the situation* – a definition that could only have been brought about by mobilizing the authority of French state officialdom. He writes:

Like an experiment in the Pasteur lab, statisticians inside the office of the agricultural institutions are able to read the charts of the decreasing slopes that mean, so they say, the decrease of anthrax. In a few years, the transfer of the vaccine produced in Pasteur's lab was recorded in the statistics as the cause of the decline of anthrax. Without these institutions it would of course have been utterly impossible to say whether the vaccine was of any use, as it would have been utterly impossible to detect the existence of the disease to begin with. (p. 153)

At first impression, Latour may appear to be saying no more than that official record keeping helped make it possible to recognize the decline of anthrax. But on closer examination his claims appear much more sweeping. He seems to believe that efforts at coping based on scientific insight can "succeed" only if pursued with the same mind-set as that which gave rise to the insight in the first place. This amounts to something very like the notion that the success of theories can only be reckoned in terms established by the theories in question. A few pages after the passage quoted above, he writes:

Most of the difficulties associated with science and technology come from the idea that there is a time when innovations are in laboratories, and another time when they are tried out in a new set of conditions which invalidate or verify the efficacy of these innovations. . . As this example shows, the reality of it is more mundane and less mystical.
  First, the vaccine works at Pouilly le Fort and then in other places only if in all these places the same laboratory conditions are extended there beforehand. (p. 155)

By these lights, Pasteur's vaccine had no special properties other than those imparted to it by the social processes that he helped to orchestrate. Presumably, the same sort of conclusion would be offered for the success of the Salk vaccine.

Perhaps it is ultimately impossible to *prove* the reality of a world that exists independently of our beliefs about it. But for most of us, other possibilities are simply not credible as bases for daily practice. Most present-day social scientists would probably grant that we can never know the outside world·in any definitive or comprehensive way. But most of us prefer a view of theoretical inquiry that promises to help us distinguish between more and less accurate guidance for dealing with an exterior world. Even the most earnest constructivists, one suspects, operate on that assumption when they have to decide what to do about symptoms of appendicitis in themselves or inoculating their children against polio.

Doctrines of the relativists notwithstanding, I believe that the history of science does hold many points, like Salk's development of the polio vaccine, where evidence offers dramatic conclusions on fundamental theoretical issues. The criteria by which we recognize such success are essentially pragmatic, having to do in this case with the ability of the insight involved to sustain efforts to cope with the threat of disease.

Today we know that flies do not generate spontaneously from decaying flesh; we know that meteorites are of extraterrestrial origin; we know that blood circulates, and in the course of doing so supplies the body with oxygen; we know that bombarding the nuclei of certain atoms can result in the release of large amounts of energy. There were times where such ideas were theoretically antipathetic to prevailing worldviews. No doubt all of them stand to be revised in one way or another on the strength of future inquiry. But it is difficult to believe that these beliefs will be reversed in their essentials so long as human interests continue to be engaged by the processes depicted in them.

The question is, can one point to any comparable achievements in the study of social life?

THE QUANTIFICATION OF PROGRESS

The clash between the two approaches to the sociological study of science sheds a fascinating light on the question of progress in the study of social life. For the constructivists, of course, any notion of an overarching standard of progress reflects the sham of appearance. The task of the sociology of science, in this view, is to analyze the process of intellectual *change* and to demonstrate how such change is successfully packaged as progress. Implicit in this program is the assumption that progress has no existence other than in the minds of those who "construct" it. For their part, the Mertonians have largely held to the line established in *Science, Technology and Society in Seventeenth Century England*, where scientific *discoveries* are taken as direct manifestations of progress. "Scientific advance," writes Stephen Cole in a recent work, "is uniformly defined as the number of significant scientific discoveries" (1992, pp. 207–208). Thus the affirmation of an objectivist view: that there is something "out there" to be discovered, and that the discovery process may progress more or less rapidly.

This latter view, I have noted, brings conceptual problems. How does one know that one discovery is indeed comparable in import to the next? The earth apparently harbors at least 300,000 species of beetles, most of them still unclassified by entomologists. Is each new classification a discovery, in the same sense that Pasteur's work on anthrax was a discovery? Presumably not, for hardly anyone would consider the two equally "significant." But how do we reckon different degrees of theoretical significance, in this sense? It should be clear that any attempt to rank the significance of discoveries is fraught with the imponderables and context-dependency that relativists would be the first to point out.

The assessment of discoveries in science is crucial for any sociology of science, and not just because it offers an index of progress. For certainty of what constitutes a discovery would also afford judgments on the quality of individual "contributions." Items of scientific work that can be seen to "contribute," however indirectly, to the discovery program have a claim to be accorded greater significance than those which "lead nowhere," which play no part in the production of discoveries.

The sociology of science, in its Mertonian version, seems to crave some quantitative measuring rod for reckoning the success of scientific work. After all, if the key theoretical question is how and how rapidly scientific "advance" occurs, then some ready index of such advance is essential. And for this purpose, the enumeration of "discoveries" presents problems. Authentic discoveries, even if they were easy to agree on, are relatively rare. Some more clear-cut, measurable quality of scientific efforts had to be made available for assessment.

The response to this practical research problem came in 1961 with the development of citation analysis. In this now well-known technique, citations – references to other scholarly work in scientific literature – in all major scientific journals are scanned and all citations compiled. In analyses based on these compilations, citation totals are used as a kind of geiger counter of scientific import. The rationale is simplicity itself. Everyone, it is said, agrees that more "important" work is cited more frequently; it would be difficult to imagine a work that matters greatly in scientific thinking yet is never acknowledged in print. Or, as Jonathan and Stephen Cole stated their position in their influential *Social Stratification in Science*:

One of the most significant ways in which scientists are rewarded is by having their work used by other scientists. Thus, the number of citations a scientist receives may be taken as an indicator of the amount of recognition his work has received. (1973, p. 34)

Or, as Stephen Cole wrote in an earlier article:

the *Science Citation Index (SCI)* provides a useful measure of the impact or quality of scientific papers and their diffusion. By looking at the number of citations to papers, we can roughly judge their quality. (1970, p. 288)

By extension, the frequency of citation to a particular idea, intellectual program, or school of thought should likewise index its intellectual import.

This position would appear eminently consistent with the Mertonians' view of science. Science is a process of discovery, their argument might go, and those who contribute the most to the discovery process are bound to win the most attention, in the form of footnotes.

Formalization of these assumptions, through compilation of the *Science Citation Index,* helped fuel a kind of Weberian rationalization of scientific work. For it offered funding agencies, university deans, and others concerned with the administration of science handy and unambiguous tools for judging the "productivity" of "investments" in various forms of inquiry. And, for similar reasons, the additive, easily quantifiable nature of footnotes has made their analysis a natural vehicle for the quantitative inclinations of the Mertonians – in contrast to the more ethnographic approach of the constructivists. And, again, a major theme in these quantitative investigations has been the very issue brought to the fore by Merton's functionalist vision: What social arrangements enable science to play its functionally optimal social role? How is scientific "productivity" recognized and encouraged, through awards, appointments, grants, and the other rewards presumably necessary to elicit the needed "contributions" from the ablest scientists.

Thus, in *Social Stratification in Science,* Jonathan and Stephen Cole argue for the essential universalism of science. They demonstrate positive associations between the frequency of citation of scientific work and the quality and quantity of awards, appointments, and similar forms of honorific and tangible recognition accorded to scientists. This theme, and the citation methods used to buttress it, suffuses the work of other key researchers in the Merton tradition. And they have continued to espouse citation counts as indices of the import of academic work.

This position has consistently evoked skepticism from those outside the Merton tradition. And, indeed, everyone who attends to the creation and consumption of scientific literatures can offer examples of citations attesting to everything from authentic intellectual dependence to the most opportunistic sorts of intellectual log rolling. Sociologists of science outside the Merton tradition have developed such criticisms systematically, as in the study by David Edge (1979). Drawing on detailed case analysis from astrophysics, Edge shows how enumeration of citations exaggerate certain kinds of intellectual dependencies and obscure others. Citation statistics, he concludes, "offer subsidiary means towards the attainment of some traditional aims – but only if used critically, with care, and in context" (p. 127).

For the purposes of this book, such questions of "context" matter enormously. Frequency of citation may well serve to distinguish among authors in terms of whose words are receiving the most current attention. But whether citation statistics can tell us more about the progressive status of scientific ideas, other than the extent to which they currently are in the "public eye" in their literatures, is another matter. In social science, these questions become acute when we seek to assess the significance of strains of thought that command much attention at one historical moment, then drop substantially or entirely from intellectual view. How are we to interpret such sequences? Does the work in question embody high quality at one moment, then lose that quality a few years later?

THE RISE AND FALL OF INTERACTION PROCESS ANALYSIS

In the 1940s, the young social psychologist Robert Freed Bales conceived an idea that was to animate a long and distinguished career. In observing the interactions of a variety of primary groups – that is, face-to-face encounters among people with relatively enduring relations to one another – he sensed the existence of certain recurrent patterns and sequences. These patterns struck him as basic social units, elementary building blocks for all sorts of larger social processes. Surely they warranted systematic study.

To this end, Bales invented and perfected one of the few machines that can be characterized as distinctively sociological in purpose: the Interaction Recorder. This device facilitated the systematic observation of face-to-face groups, normally from behind one-way mirrors installed in laboratories constructed for this purpose. The machine constantly moved a specially marked band of paper across its open face, enabling the observer to note and code every action of participants in the groups under observation. These markings facilitated coding of the interaction into Bales's basic categories. These are the categories:

1. *Shows solidarity,* raises other's status, gives help, reward
2. *Shows tension release,* jokes, laughs, shows satisfaction
3. *Agrees,* shows passive acceptance, understands, concurs, complies
4. *Gives suggestion,* direction, implying autonomy for other
5. *Gives opinion,* evaluation, analysis, expresses feeling, wish
6. *Gives orientation,* information, repeats, clarifies, confirms
7. *Asks for orientation,* information, repetition, confirmation
8. *Asks for opinion,* evaluation, analysis, expression of feeling
9. *Asks for suggestion,* direction, possible ways of action

10. *Disagrees,* shows passive rejection, formality, withholds help
11. *Shows tension,* asks for help, withdraws out of field
12. *Shows antagonism,* deflates other's status, defends or asserts self

As a junior faculty member at Harvard, Bales began applying this analytic mechanism to a variety of different groups, eventually incorporating the method into an undergraduate course. Sometimes the groups were given written materials to discuss. But Bales and his associates increasingly encouraged participants to discuss the inner workings of the groups themselves. As years passed, ideas from group psychotherapy, and particularly from psychoanalysis, seem to have increasingly informed the design and interpretation of the Bales studies.

Bales's work benefited from support from the RAND Corporation in its early years. But its reception would almost certainly have been much more muted without the attention of Bales's senior colleague, Talcott Parsons. In an inspiration to incite envy from assistant professors everywhere, Parsons saw in Bales's work theoretical significance more far-reaching than Bales himself had ever claimed. Indeed, Parsons held that the interaction processes disclosed by Bales's studies demonstrated the applicability of Parsons's own theories in altogether new domains. As Parsons and Bales wrote in *Working Papers in the Theory of Action* (1953):

> We have long believed that . . . the theory of action . . . has been converging toward a general theoretical scheme which was applicable . . . all the way from the smallest samples of experimentally controlled animal behavior to the analysis of large-scale social processes. (p. 63)

Indeed, their extended considerations of the deeper significance of Bales's small-group findings led them to the brink of what they anticipated to be truly extraordinary insights:

> If all this . . . is correct, then it would seem likely that there is a very important analogy between the scheme we have developed in this paper and the classical mechanics. If this supposition stands up to critical testing of a variety of sorts, it is evident that it should turn out to have far reaching implications in that it should open up possibilities of quantitative as well as qualitative systematization which are far beyond those which the sciences of action have yet attained. (p. 102)

Coming just as Parsons was reaching the apogee of his influence, such statements could hardly detract from the attention directed to Bales's project.

From the early 1950s to the mid-1960s, Bales and his students produced a steady stream of studies of small-group process. Some of these studies won very wide scholarly attention, notably Philip Slater's "Role Differentiation in Small Groups" (1955). This article put forward what was probably the best-known finding to issue from the research. In Slater's words:

the most fundamental type of role differentiation in small experimental groups is the divorcing of the task functions from social-emotional functions. Presumably, the ideal leader of a small group would be . . . a high participator, well-liked, rated high on task ability and eventually [a] chosen leader.

Such individuals are rare. . . . (p. 308)

Thus the distinction between the instrumental leader and the social-emotional leader entered the lore of American social science.

In 1955 Bales was promoted to associate professor at Harvard. By the end of that decade, his work had become a "hot" specialty – for many, the cutting edge, the state of the art in the linkage of macro- and micro-processes in social life. Besides the aura of association with Parsons's thinking and with psychoanalysis, it had the virtue of generating quantitative depictions of a reality that had hitherto been studied only qualitatively. At Harvard, and then at other universities, T-groups (that is, Bales-style "training groups") became the bases for many courses. At Harvard, Bales's Social Relations 120 had by the 1960s become one of the most talked-about institutions of undergraduate life.

By the same time, Bales's work had also begun to percolate into American culture outside the research community. What psychoanalysis had done for the individual quest for meaning in life, the study of group process was doing for the experience of group participation. The self-obsessed conventions of T-group conversation began to pervade cocktail parties and other gatherings of college-educated Americans. Retail establishments around Cambridge offered various items of Balesian kitsch, including at one stage a T-group coloring book.

What commends Bales's theoretical project to the concerns of this book is the decisiveness with which it crashed. In a matter of a few years, beginning in the late 1960s, it simply lost its hold on the theoretical imagination – lost its ability, one might say, to invest research findings with meaningful status. By the time of Bales's retirement from Harvard in 1986, as far as I have been able to determine, no other researcher was pursuing investigations in the Balesian line. Defined as occupying the avant-garde of theoretical advance around 1960, his enterprise found itself becalmed in theoretical apathy no more than fifteen years later.

Reading through Bales's studies, it is hard not to be impressed with the pains he and his associates took to achieve scientific rigor in their work. Coders were carefully trained in the method, and careful statistical checks of intercoder reliability applied. Equations were developed for describing various states and sequences of group process, and statistical techniques were honed for locating different personality types within the broader constellation of the group. Clearly his efforts succeeded in introducing statistical exactitude in matters that other sociologists and psychologists had represented only in more experiential or qualitative terms. But these facts seem to have done nothing to avert the brutal collapse of the program's theoretical potency.

What are we to make of this collapse? One could construct any number of plausible stories demonstrating that Bales's approach lacked some crucial ingredient necessary to qualify as an enduring theoretical contribution – or, at least, a *more* enduring contribution. One could point out that its association with psychoanalysis or with Parsons's theories were inopportune, in that both lost favor in the social science of the 1970s. Or one could point to the relentlessly group-centered character of the data generated by Bales's studies, whereas social psychologists' interest was shifting at this point to individual-level data. Or one could question the relevance of studying the virtually content-free, inward-looking group discussions orchestrated by Bales and his associates for understanding groups in the real world.

But against these stories, it seems to me, one could just as well juxtapose any number of others as to why Bales's work should have been destined to continue its path across the theoretical firmament. After all, it was quantitative. And it did focus attention on the linkages of micro- and macrosocial processes – a theoretical obsession of the 1980s and many another era in the history of social thought.

Nevertheless, observation of phases in the lives of groups preoccupied mainly with their own inner processes has today lost its grip on the theoretical imagination. This is hastily not to deny that work of this kind might one day be successfully repackaged or rehabilitated. Then, perhaps, Balesian explorations would once again be defined as occupying the "cutting edge" in theoretical advance. But this story should certainly give pause to anyone inclined to portray the history of our disciplines as one of steady movement toward a stable set of intellectual goals.

THE RISE AND DECLINE OF ETHNOMETHODOLOGY

Many of these same questions are raised by the unusual theoretical career of ethnomethodology. To be sure, there are differences. For one thing, ethnomethodology was always more widely practiced than Bales's specialty, and its decline has been less complete. For another, in contrast to the conventional scientific logic of Bales's work, the initial epistemological stance of ethnomethodology was flamboyantly heterodox. It grabbed the theoretical imagination by offering a stunningly different way of knowing about the social world.

But the two enterprises share a quality of much interest for the purposes of this book. Both rose meteorically and declined abruptly, for reasons that leave one wondering about the nature of their enduring "contribution."

Ethnomethodology grew out of, and in opposition to, the symbolic interactionist tradition. The two schools shared the view that seemingly "solid" elements of social life – institutions, processes, relationships, and so on – are in fact products of the dynamic interchange of human actors. For both, social reality was forever *emergent*, continually in the process of innovation in light of the parties' unfolding impressions of one another and their never totally predictable signals in return.

But ethnomethodology went considerably further than symbolic interaction in its critique of other forms of sociological inquiry. Beginning in the early 1960s, and led initially by Harold Garfinkel, ethnomethodologists attacked the epistemological claims on which, as they saw it, all other forms of sociology reposed. The "facts" that other sociologists study, the ethnomethodologists charged, were in reality *factitious*. Instead of being the trustworthy, rock-solid elements that scientific-minded sociologists (that is, *all other* sociologists) thought they were, social facts really were nothing of the kind. To miss this point was to accept at face value the very mystifications of everyday life that sociologists ought to unmask.

Thus ethnomethodologists insisted that ordinary social events, episodes, understandings, and arrangements are the products of complicated social processes by which ordinary actors actually "create" social reality. Both the language and other media of communication involved in such creation is *indexical* – that is, particular words, gestures, conventions, and the like have meaning only in relation to the entire social context in which they occur. Yet it lies in the nature of social life – and, alas, of sociology itself – to obscure or deny these processes. As Garfinkel wrote:

> For the purposes of *conducting their everyday affairs,* persons refuse to permit each other to understand "what they are really talking about" in this way. . . . Persons require these properties of discourse as conditions under which they are themselves entitled and entitle others to claim that they know what they are talking about, and that what they are saying is understandable and ought to be understood. In short, their seen but unnoticed presence is used to entitle persons to conduct their common conversational affairs without interference. Departures from such usages call forth immediate attempts to restore a right state of affairs. (1964, p. 229)

Following Garfinkel's early publications, ethnomethodology quickly branched into several not always congenial schools. Yet all variants shared the drastic critique of other forms of sociology. They held, explicitly or implicitly, that there could be no proper study of social life that failed to interpret the complex processes by which the stuff of everyday existence was constituted. If one could not show how ordinary people agreed on what they understood as a conflict, a job, or a family, Garfinkel and his followers seemed to claim, sociologists had no business carrying on as usual, studying conflicts, occupations, families – or any other standard topic of inquiry. As Cicourel wrote:

Social structure remains an accountable illusion . . . unless we can reveal a connection between the cognitive processes that contribute to the emergence of contextual activities, and the normative accounting schemes we use for claiming knowledge as laymen and researchers. (1973, p. 7)

Strong words. It is difficult to appreciate, nearly an intellectual generation later, the seriousness with which these ideas were taken – or the extent to which they appeared to threaten conventional sociology. I do not mean by this that the claims of ethnomethodology ever enjoyed anything like majority assent across the discipline. But, for a time, the development of ethnomethodology was watched with extraordinary, and often uneasy, attention.

Consider the "official reception" accorded Garfinkel's book, *Studies in Ethnomethodology* (1967): a review symposium in *The American Sociological Review* (1968), with lengthy discussions by three eminent figures, Guy Swanson, James Coleman and Anthony F. C. Wallace. The reviews were critical in varying degrees, but the message was unmistakable: The revolutionary doctrine was an intellectual presence to be reckoned with. For some years, ethnomethodology enjoyed the status of one of those high-sex-appeal insurgent theoretical specialties that periodically grab the center of the intellectual stage.

It is hard to avoid the conclusion that ethnomethodology rose on that wave of upwelling distrust of established arrangements and institutions that swept America and Western Europe in the late 1960s. For many, ethnomethodology was the ultimate debunking doctrine, the most thoroughgoing repudiation of the claims of sociological orthodoxy. If its very ways of knowing reality were faulty, its most basic assumptions no better than participation in a shared delusion, then better to start again, giving no credit to those who have gone before. Although these sentiments may not have been recorded in so many words, it is hard to miss the theme in the following statement. Here a British proponent lists the shortcomings of conventional sociology that ethnomethodology was supposed to rectify:

. . . A view of methodology as a set of techniques to be used to catch the unchanging properties of a "solid" factual world.
. . . A reliance on the unexplicated assumptions of commonsense knowledge expressed in a preparedness to impute "reasonable" motives to actors and to make phenomena non-problematic in terms of "what everybody knows."
. . . An absence of philosophical sophistication in focusing on "things" taken to be unquestionably obvious within a world through which our mind can roam at will. (Silverman 1972, p. 2)

In opposition to these deficiencies, ethnomethodology developed its own model of closure: a program of investigation aimed at demonstrating how shaky the taken-for-granted aspects of everyday social reality really were. These included studies of decision making by juries (Garfinkel 1967, chap. 4), verbal and nonverbal communication among the deaf (Cicourel 1973, chap. 5), or consultations with fortune-tellers (Wedow 1974). Many differences notwithstanding, these studies shared a common theme: The confidence that we have, as lay actors and sociologists alike, in the facts of the world as it appears is misplaced. We cannot hope to do justice to social reality unless we somehow decode the complex social processes by which that reality is created in the everyday world. Only then can a truly veridical social analysis begin.

Paul Attewell, in discussing the work of Harvey Sacks, put the matter well. Attewell notes:

a basic property of the phenomenological sociologies: their general belief that a truly scientific analysis is possible only if we first do X. X varies from individual to individual. Sacks, with his interest in language philosophers, believes that if we first understand language we may then attempt a social science without presuppositions (or at least a social science where all the presuppositions are consciously known). . . . (1974, p. 189)

The statement applies to ethnomethodology quite broadly.

Yet it is never clarified what, precisely, that missing X is; nor are we permitted to glimpse how one would apply the crucial insight to the established agenda of sociological concern. The ethnomethodologists succeed in convincing us that social arrangements ranging from evanescent verbal exchanges to enduring institutions presume complex structures of understanding and communication. *But they never ultimately succeed in making good on the claim that no worthwhile analysis can proceed without somehow dwelling on such complexities.*

The decline in the fortunes of ethnomethodology was as abrupt as its rise. By the mid-seventies, its revolutionary claims were heard less and less, and less heeded when heard. Yet though the fortunes of ethnomethodology have drastically declined, the specialty is not dead. It continues to have a number of practitioners among established sociologists throughout the English-speaking world. Certain concepts from the doctrine – indexicality, reflexivity – have entered the common parlance of sociological analysis, though they have hardly had the revolutionary effects that the founders expected. Moreover, ethnomethodology has informed certain of the constructivist studies of science noted earlier in this chapter (e.g., Knorr-Cetina 1981). And thinkers influenced by ethnomethodology have continued to publish studies of conversations and other interactional subjects, studies recognizably inspired by the founders of the specialty.

Nevertheless, by the time of this writing, the decline of ethnomethodology has been drastic. Work by its more recent proponents has the unmistakable ring of a rearguard action. Despite the fact that the specialty is "radical in an intellectual sense and irreducibly distinct," one of its proponents writes, ethnomethodological writings have been "absorbed into the sociological mainstream of the substantive areas in which [their authors] . . . work" (Boden 1990, pp. 186–187). Nevertheless, the author insists, "ethnomethodology is well and truly abroad in the sociological landscape" (p. 187).

Clearly, no such insistences and qualifications would have been necessary in 1970, when ethnomethodology was widely perceived as an active threat to virtually all other theoretical programs in sociology, and was treated as such by the sociological establishment. Unlike the works of its mainstream-oriented exponents today, the claims of the founders of the specialty were clearly revolutionary and exclusive. They purported to supplant standard ways of knowing about social reality with something fundamentally different.

With the abrupt decline in credence of those expectations, ethnomethodology has simply undergone sharp routinization of what was once white-hot intellectual charisma. Its techniques are simply one variant in the array of qualitative tools for studying human interaction. If its proponents consider themselves a threat to standard forms of sociology, they are very reserved about it. Surely this is a striking development for a movement that jarred the scholarly establishment a few decades ago with its claim to subvert the very foundations of social science.

How are we to account for such a dramatic reversal of fortunes for a specialty whose "contributions" to sociological insight had been so highly touted? As with Bales's program, it would be easy to invent narratives retrospectively to explain the decline. Some, for example, might cite the difficulties of ethnomethodologists in defining a program of inquiry that went beyond pure criticism of other sociological work. But I do not believe that such difficulties had to be fatal. Other specialties have embodied contradictions and anomalies no less grave, while still commanding a following.

Ethnomethodology could have gone on indefinitely to register what I have termed formal progress – had the theoretical taste of the 1970s and 1980s simply continued to match that of the late 1960s and early 1970s. But by the 1990s, the formal program of ethnomethodology does not appear to offer many insights that serve present-day analytical needs. And insofar as notions like indexicality have indeed entered such a common armamentarium of conceptual tools, they have done so discretely, rather than as part of any permanent revolution in theoretical worldview.

THE SOCIOLOGY OF SCIENCE: REPRISE

What are students of science to make of the curious life cycles of theoretical programs like those of ethnomethodology and Balesian small-group studies? Does the upsurge of interest in such new forms of knowledge represent "progress?" And if so, how are we to interpret their equally rapid fall from scholarly grace? Such questions compel hard thinking, regarding not only the specialties themselves, but also our understanding of progress in the study of social life.

For those in the constructivist tradition, the cases in point would seem to pose no problem. For a time, it would be said, proponents of these theoretical views succeeded in creating and defending their particular "pocket of order." But these pockets of order simply collapsed, as perhaps all scientific worldviews are bound to do sooner or later. Did their rise, then, represent intellectual progress? Perhaps, a constructivist might say, but no more than did their demise. For this viewpoint recognizes no standard of achievement in intellectual life that outlasts the lifetime of a particular theoretical worldview. The "best" ideas, the most compelling theoretical programs, are simply those that best serve the needs of the moment – and such needs are constantly changing.

For students of science in the Merton tradition, the two cases pose a more complicated problem. Merton's original pronouncements, let us recall, reckoned the march of intellectual progress in terms of the pace of "important scientific discoveries." In the case of natural science, such discoveries won approval from the broader public by affording life-enhancing technological innovations. But what interpretation does this view imply of intellectual innovations like the schools founded by Garfinkel or Bales – "discoveries," if we can call them that, which lost most of their interest within a few years? Can the Mertonian tradition make sense of such apparent kinks in our theoretical life and still preserve a basically progressive view of social science?

There are several possibilities. One might, for example, liken these two intellectual departures to "dead ends" in the search for authentic discoveries – like once promising leads in the campaign against polio that ultimately failed to yield an effective vaccine. This would preserve the idea of social science as a basically progressive enterprise while picturing the specialties in question as failed efforts to realize progressive aims. Or, one might argue that these two schools did in fact make important contributions to a progressive or cumulative enterprise, only to have these contributions forgotten through their incorporation into the common store of accepted sociological knowledge. Such a fate is said to be normal in the natural sciences, as key discoveries become so widely accepted that they are no longer alluded to (or cited).

A third interpretation would be that these two theoretical programs were simply agendas for the pursuit of short-lived intellectual tastes. The theoretical "marvels" that they embodied were held to be marvelous for a time, in this view, then lost their grip on the imaginations of working social scientists. Such sequences – and our discipline abounds with them – remind us that innovations held to be highly progressive at one moment, that even seem to represent the wave of the future or the cutting edge, may quickly appear as abandoned outposts when prevailing directions of theoretical interest shift.

Such observations in turn raise questions about the interpretation of citation statistics and other behavioral measures of quality in scientific work. If a particular work or genre of work is first widely heralded (and cited) but then drops from intellectual attention, leaving scarcely a trace, what conclusions are we to draw concerning its "quality?"

Or, to put the matter more abstractly: Are counts of citations to be considered important because they represent *indices* of some other reality of ultimate import – contribution to real or potential scientific discoveries, for example? Or are citations (or other forms of behavior associated with scientific recognition) *themselves* the intellectual reality constituted by scientific activity?

To be consistent, writers in the tradition of Merton's *Science and Society in Seventeenth-Century England* would no doubt hold to the first alternative. That is, they would want to argue that the importance of citations lies in their role of acknowledging work constituting objective scientific accomplishment. And what if a work that appears in retrospect to bear great importance is originally ignored? In that case, it might be allowed that occasional "mistakes" can occur, glitches in the recognition process that leave a discovery at least temporarily "undiscovered." Such arguments might be advanced, for example, in the case of Mendel, whose work indeed seems to have been neglected for some time after its publication. Perhaps cases like this might be seen as the obverse of those depicted above, where a line of work enjoys much acclaim for a time, then drops from intellectual view.

But such a solution poses problems of its own. For if an important discovery can be temporarily neglected, it is at least theoretically possible that discoveries could also be neglected permanently. Such "nondiscoveries," after all, would ipso facto remain hidden from the attention of investigators. If such neglect is possible, one would have to ask what accounts for the difference between "discoveries" that are properly recognized as such, and the other "undiscovered" discoveries. And if one holds that the difference lies strictly in the social processes by which discoveries and nondiscoveries are brought to the attention of the intellectual community, then one has begun to edge closer to a constructivist view. Perhaps, after all, only those discoveries attended by the proper intellectual "propaganda," to use Feyerabend's term, can be expected to count as such.

Other followers of Merton seem to go even further toward the constructivist position. Consider Stephen Cole's defense of citation enumeration:

Although . . . the "quality" of scientific work cannot be objectively assessed, extensive past research indicates that citations are a valid indicator of the subjective assessment of quality by the scientific community. The number of citations is highly correlated with all other measures of quality that sociologists of science employ. As long as we keep in mind that research of high quality is being defined as research that other scientists find useful in their current work, citations provide a satisfactory indicator. (1992, p. 221)

Here, it appears, the accomplishments of science are isomorphic with scientific communication; science is, by implication, what scientists do, or at least what they say in print about what they do. Ideas, works, and authors are taken to have succeeded in their scientific tasks to the extent that they figure centrally in the literatures of the disciplines concerned.

Such a view, of course, makes it impossible to conceive of theories that are widely acclaimed but *wrong* – wrong, for example, in the sense of providing poor guidance for practice or coping. In Cole's view, the sheer expression of scholarly attention, as judged through citations or other behavioral measures, represents the best if not the only criterion of theoretical success. As he notes at another point:

There are no objective criteria that allow sociologists to conclude that social network analysis is "more important" or of "higher quality" than ethnomethodology. Such a question is a matter of subjective opinion. (1992, p. 181)

All opinions are subjective *perforce*. But are there *reasons*, grounded in criteria independent of the theory under consideration, for evaluating one theoretical program more highly than another? Or are the expressions and opinions of those identified (by whatever social processes) as scientists to be understood as *the* subject matter of the study of science?

If the only criterion of scientific success is the amount of supportive attention paid to a particular doctrine within the scholarly community, then the position is really indistinguishable from that of the constructivists. In that case, *there can be no such thing as a "mistake" in attribution of credit via citations.* For the attention of the community – at whatever moment in time the investigator chooses – is the only criterion of the goodness of scientific thinking. In short, any "contribution" that attracts a given amount of attention within the scholarly community has to be considered as successful as any other.

"I've gotten to the point," a literary critic tired of the slack response to his work once confided to me, "where I'd rather be interesting than be right." A thoroughgoing constructivist need never worry about making such a choice. From that perspective, what attracts interest (in the form of citations or any other indicative behavior) is ipso facto successful. The question is, is this really the only, or indeed the main, criterion of theoretical success that we wish to entertain? If citation establishes the status of an author, an idea, or a theoretical program in "communal knowledge" (to use a term favored by sociologists of science), can we do without a concept of "communal error?"

The words of the exasperated critic attest to a criterion of analytical success quite different from that which underlay, for example, the quest for a successful polio vaccine. No doubt it was true that, as researchers sought to perfect a vaccine against polio, various approaches rose and fell in current "intellectual sex appeal" within the research community. It would come as no surprise to find that such fluctuations were reflected in various behavioral measures, including citations to articles reporting work carried out in the various approaches. But, ultimately, any proposed vaccine had to meet a simple and basic test – that of safely providing immunity from the disease. Similarly for those who sought to create the first artificial nuclear fission, or those who held that space satellites of human design could be set in orbit. At some point, results were produced that could be evaluated even by those who did not start by embracing the original theory. In the social sciences, such clear verdicts are in short supply, to say the least. Given their scarcity, it is hardly surprising that we set so much store by the sheer extent of attention accorded theoretical ideas.

But we cannot afford to forget how profoundly different the two criteria of intellectual success really are. Imagine an investigation of theories of personal misfortune in seventeenth-century New England. Obliged to explain crop failure, marital disharmony, malicious gossip, financial straits, and other frustrations of everyday life, many observers – both intellectuals and others – invoked witchcraft. Consensus on the danger posed by witches and on the telltale signs by which they could be identified seems to have been broad indeed during this period. Had one enumerated the frequency with which such ideas were affirmed, either aloud or in print, the victory of the witchcraft theory might have seemed complete.

But, of course, the fact of consensus in this critical social construction could not possibly help us to answer a question of compelling import for coping with the action dilemmas of the day – namely, whether the activities designated as witchcraft were, in fact, responsible for the results attributed to them. And if this question held little interest for the most reputable authorities of seventeenth-century Massachusetts, we are obliged to conclude that these authorities were wrong.

CONCLUSION

From my vantage point, it is hard to see how any notion of intellectual progress can make sense if it is predicated only on the consensus of a particular intellectual community. There must be room, in other words, for the possibility that the community of authoritative opinion is satisfied but mistaken. Failure to make this distinction would threaten to leave the study of science in a position like that of epistemologies that make no room for the concept of error.

What are the implications of this position for the curious life cyles of ethnomethodology and Balesian small-group studies? Did the rising crescendo of interest in these programs entail progress? And if so, what significance are we to attribute to their decline?

The simplest account of these developments would be simply to conclude that these two models of closure responded to transient theoretical tastes. Such an observation is certainly true as far as it goes; clearly each doctrine served some sort of intellectual "need" that simply passed, wholly or in part. But the question remains whether the insights of either program might, in some overarching perspective, ultimately be reckoned as contributing to substantive progress. Do these doctrines indeed *deserve* the relative obscurity in which they now find themselves – or do they offer analytical tools that could reasonably be expected to provide reliable analytical means to enduring, widely shared ends, if only people would recognize this utility? Such judgments are obviously speculative and interpretive, but I am convinced that we have both the need to make them and the grounds for doing so.

In the case of ethnomethodology, I am inclined to think that the accomplishments of the theory will remain, let us say, a rather special taste. One does not doubt the premise that familiar macro-social realities presuppose microprocesses governed by special cognitive patterns. But one does wonder why students of the former need necessarily dwell on the latter in order to get on with their legitimate analytical work.

The case of Bales's project is more mysterious. I can see no a priori reason why insights that did, or could, issue from Balesian studies might not prove valuable to analysts with no preexisting stake in that model of closure. A good example is the model of instrumental and social-emotional leadership in face-to-face groups. If the need for such a division of labor were indeed borne out in any significant range of cases, the insight could be useful for all sorts of analytical and practical purposes.

The trouble is, we are apt never to know whether the model has any such applicability unless interest in the program miraculously revives.

I present these judgments in simple, thumbnail fashion here. In the chapters to come, I seek to make a more detailed assessment of the potential staying power of insights from four theoretical projects of more immediate current interest.

PART II

No one familiar with the history of our disciplines would deny that something very like fluctuating "taste" plays a vast role in our theoretical life. And as in art, literature, and other domains of pure expression, the rise and fall of such tastes often bear obvious links to social experience. Thus, if ethnomethodology fit the mind-set of certain thinkers in the 1960s and 1970s, one might conclude, no one should be surprised to find that different needs set the terms of theoretical work a generation or so later.

Some would insist that we should expect no more of theoretical social science than this – that is, the ability to capture the distinctive perceptions or sensibilities of a particular era or constituency. But doesn't such a position leave certain basic and utterly legitimate expectations unsatisfied? Are there indeed no valid criteria of analytical success or failure other than those set by the theories themselves?

The alternative – vastly more fruitful, by my lights – is to conceive of theoretical inquiry as an effort to fashion tools for responding to certain very broadly shared analytical needs, however abstractly conceived. These needs arise from the challenge of making sense of, and responding to, nearly universal perplexities of social life – dilemmas for action associated with such widespread conditions as social stratification, deviance, international conflict, poverty and prosperity, and so on. These concerns form the bases for what I term first-order questions. Such questions are bound to be posed by thoughtful participants in social life, whether social scientists choose to address them or not. They focus, one might say, on things that people predictably *need to understand*, even across vast differences of social perspective. We can accordingly expect such concerns to reassert themselves again and again, even as the expressive appeals of particular theoretical approaches come and go.

If one grants the authenticity of such first-order questions, I hold, one must acknowledge at least the *possibility* of long-term intellectual progress. For if the ends of theoretical inquiry are stable – even to a modest degree – across changes of theoretical fashion, one might reasonably hope that "contributions" in one existential context will prove useful to those who grapple with the same issues from different social perspectives.

One can consider these issues as matters of pure principle – as abstract possibilities for knowing the social world. But they also point to questions that are altogether empirical. Assume, for a moment, that judging the accomplishments of theoretical programs by some overarching, common standards is indeed logically possible and analytically feasible. The question then remains as to whether the actual work of social inquiry indeed exploits such possibilities. Does our work in fact generate insights of the sort likely to show lasting value – that is, to constitute means to enduring analytical ends? We can take for granted social scientists' conviction that they are "moving the field forward" by pursuing the distinctive insights of their favorite theoretical programs. But can we identify specific insights emerging from their work that have the potential to endure once the expressive climates that fostered them have altered? Only a hard, empirical look at intellectual history can afford answers to such questions.

Such a look is the aim of the following four chapters. Each provides a brief overview of a theoretical program influential in the last decades of the twentieth century. The programs are rational-choice thinking; Jeffrey Alexander's retooling of Parsons's "general theory"; network analysis; and feminist social science. Like the programs from an earlier generation considered in Chapters 1 and 2, each of these four embodies a distinctive model of closure, including a logic for the elaboration of social understanding and a vision (if only implicit) of analytical success. And each asserts or implies its own claims to illuminate just those domains of social life that most urgently need to be understood – in effect, claims to embody a "step ahead" in overall understanding. These claims will bear special attention.

The four programs are about as diverse as possible in terms of the forms of knowledge they endorse and the styles of inquiry they foster. Indeed, some readers, including some proponents of the theories involved, may consider these differences so profound as to render any analytical comparisons among them meaningless. But the heterogeneity is intentional. The very fact that the aims and methods of the four approaches are so different should help to highlight certain crucial commonalities. For each of these programs aspires in its own way to illuminate *what matters most* in the subject matter – at least, as their proponents see it. Each, in other words, combines forms of analysis with affirmations, explicit or not, about what kinds of understanding most appropriately fit our most pressing analytical needs.

Those claims require sober judgment, critical thinking about the forms of understanding constituting the central focus of each theory. Do these concepts, relationships, processes, or the like indeed answer to analytical needs beyond those fomented by the theory itself? Obviously, every theoretical community generates a certain amount of ingrown communication – that is, preoccupation with second-order questions. My question is simply whether, at their best, these programs promise to do more: to generate insights that may continue to command the attention of analysts even when the expressive appeals that originally brought the theory to prominence have faded.

Clearly these are highly interpretive judgments; any of them will inevitably be subject to thoughtful dispute. But it would be as absurd to deny the necessity of making them as it would be to neglect the bases for doing so. For each of the four programs, I want to note the expressive elements of its appeal – the features, often quite obvious, that make it attractive to a particular intellectual constituency at a particular historical moment. Having allowed for these, I then want to identify what I call the "or-else clause" implicit (or sometimes explicit) in the theory. By this I mean the case made by proponents for what would be lost should the distinctive insights of their favored theory be neglected. Without such a case, any theoretical school must simply present the analytical rewards it seeks as a matter of pure taste – something that few theoretical enthusiasts are prepared to do.

Thus, I want to look at each of these four programs from the standpoint of a theoretical outsider. In each case, I want to ask, "What's in it for us?" By "us" I mean all those who begin with no stake one way or another in the aesthetic or expressive appeals of the theory. What ideas does the theory generate, I want to ask, that one cannot afford to do without, whether one finds their expressive valences congenial or repellant? To put it another way: To what extent does the theory tell us things that we need to know, rather than simply affirming perceptions that its adherents find agreeable to entertain?

Inevitably, some readers will be dissatisfied with the accounts of their favorite theories given here. Some will surely maintain that my remarks are not nearly exhaustive enough to do justice to the virtues of the theory in question. Those virtues can only be properly appreciated, it may be said, through exegesis of the full canon of its literature. Only then will it be apparent, for example, that what appears at first as sterile preoccupation with second-order questions really unlocks the door to enlightenment of universal consequence.

But it should be clear that my purpose here is highly selective. Exhaustiveness is out of the question for literatures as rich and as continually evolving as these. Moreover, telling "everything" about these theories, even if it were possible, could hardly benefit the current task. What I want to show is that all four of these programs, their profound differences notwithstanding, raise parallel issues and face homologous problems. All, if they are to yield insights with the potential to endure, must do two things. First, they must demonstrate that they provide a coherent design for resolving a particular kind of analytical puzzle. Second, they must convince us that the puzzles so resolved are likely to engage the analytical interests of thinkers yet to come – thinkers presumably unmoved by the contextual appeals that originally brought the theory to prominence.

These requirements are formidable. Yet here and there, I argue, they are realized. And when this occurs, we have the beginnings of a case for our work as a progressive enterprise.

3

Rational choice

Rational-choice theory represents an obvious choice for attention in this book. For its greatest enthusiasts, the doctrine offers the best – and perhaps the only – hope for meaningful progress in social science. The eminent rational-choice scholar William Riker, for example, attributes the "disparity in development" between natural and social science to the fact that the latter "has not been based on rational choice methods" (1990, p. 177). Underlying statements like this is the conviction that the special insights of the approach tap the most fundamental levels of social reality – or, as another noted theoretical enthusiast states, rational choice thinkers embrace "the least unrealistic assumptions a theorist is called upon to make" (Moe 1980, p. 14). From this viewpoint, rational-choice thinking is not simply one set of theoretical tools among many, but rather a sine qua non of theoretical success.

Today's vogue of rational-choice thinking also illustrates another key fact of life in social science: Our theories not only come and go; they often also come back, suitably repackaged, for return engagements on the theoretical stage. The historical pedigree of present-day rational-choice thinking is very long, stretching back at least to Hobbes and the utilitarians. Since then, the theoretical fortunes of the doctrine have ebbed and flowed many times. The essential doctrine has been counted out of the theoretical sweepstakes more than once – most notably, perhaps, in Parsons's attempt at definitive dismissal in *The Structure of Social Action* (1937). Yet even at the height of Parsons's influence in the fifties and sixties, a variant of rational-choice thinking exerted much influence among psychologists in the form of behaviorism, only to crash abruptly in the 1970s. And in political science, sociology, and other social science disciplines, a new synthesis of classic rational-choice doctrines has once again gained ascendance since the 1980s. This recently reborn doctrine is the focus of this chapter.

Clearly a major impetus to this resurgence is the stunning ascendancy of neoclassical economics. This body of theory, also a direct descendant of utilitarian thought, has waxed without cease, at least in the English-speaking world, since the middle of the century, when it displaced institutional approaches to the subject (Yonay, forthcoming). The acclaim accorded it has had a profound effect on theoretical relations with its neighboring social science disciplines. Among economists, it has fostered imperial ambitions, inspiring some noted studies of such phenomena as crime (Becker 1968), social movements (Olson 1965), and marriage (Becker 1973, 1974). Among many political scientists, sociologists, and anthropologists, it has engendered a desire to emulate the example of their apparently more successful neighbors.

THE ESSENTIAL DOCTRINE

The version of rational-choice thinking flourishing among social scientists in the 1990s does not draw inspiration only from contemporary economics. Among its immediate theoretical ancestors is social-exchange theory as articulated in small-group studies of the 1950s and 1960s by scholars like Thibaut and Kelley (1959), George Homans (1961), and Peter Blau (1964). In the 1990s, the influence of rational-choice thinking is greater among political scientists than it is in sociology or anthropology. One senses that many sociologists view the approach as a direct attack on the theoretical identity of their own discipline, whose origins after all lie partly in efforts of figures like Marx, Weber, and Durkheim to develop positions distinct from those of economists.

What theoretical articles of faith distinguish current rational-choice thinking? There are of course many variations, but I would identify the essential tenets of the doctrine as follows:

1. Human action is essentially *instrumental,* so that most social behavior can be explained as efforts to attain one or another, more or less distant, end. For individuals, as for larger social units, these ends or values are organized in relatively stable *hierarchies* of preference or utility.
2. Actors formulate their conduct through *rational calculation* of which among alternate courses of action are most likely to maximize their overall rewards. The actor's access to relevant information plays a vast role in the outcomes of such calculation.
3. Large-scale social processes and arrangements – including such diverse things as rates, institutions, and practices – are ultimately to be explained as results of such calculation. Successful explanation of this kind may require tracing the (often unintended and nonintuitive) second-, third- or *n*th-order consequences of such choices.

Rational choice

A particularly crucial claim for enthusiasts of rational-choice thinking turns on this last point. This is the insistence that the doctrine provides the indispensable analytical tools for relating aggregate events and processes to the microworlds of face-to-face interaction and individual decision making.

There are of course many refinements on the tenets listed above. Coleman, for example, assigns a central place to rational actors' control over what he calls *resources,* sources of utility that can be conferred by one actor upon another (1990, p. 33). An example is his analysis of interactive control relationships between teachers and students, in which grades represent resources allocated by the former, and approval or popularity the resources allocated by the latter. Thus, his version of the theory focuses both on human and collective actors and on the things these actors control.

Rational-choice thinkers also differ in terms of the nature and complexity of the psychological models they invoke. Some, for example, have sought to account for the forms and nature of satisfactions that rational behavior yields to individuals. Homans, for example, characterizes the excess of rewards people experience in relation to their expectations in social interaction in terms of *profit* (1961, p. 71). But other analysts take much less interest in psychological states; for them, the experience of individual actors is irrelevant to the task of the theory. The question is, do actors, individual or collective, *behave as though* their actions were guided by rational calculation of consistent preference hierarchies? As Milton Friedman wrote in a much noted statement (1953), the rational model may fail to describe individual behavior in some crucial respects but still earn its keep by leading to accurate predictions of aggregate events.

Rational-choice analysts also vary in their assumptions on the *content* of human motives. In general, proponents of the doctrine show at least an elective affinity toward a narrowly self-interested view of human motivation. But there is no logical reason why the three tenets given above *require* a selfish view of human motivation. So long as human beings pursue stable preference hierarchies according to more or less accurate calculation (or at least act as though they were doing so), and so long as complex, large-scale social realities can be explained as results of these pursuits, the essential requirements of the model are fulfilled. The utilities being maximized might be as selfish as one's own lifetime financial worth or as altruistic as saving the whales. But so long as enduring preference hierarchies are pursued consistently on the basis of more or less rational assessments, the model stands.

THE EXPRESSIVE APPEALS

Like all theoretical doctrines, of course, rational-choice thinking bears distinctive expressive valences. That is, in addition to the formal content of its formulations, it exerts intellectual attractions through its perceived ability to dramatize, highlight, or uphold certain aspects of social reality over and against others. Such attractions are hard to miss, but are always more difficult to document than formal tenets like the three stated above. Moreover, we have no reason to assume that these appeals are constant over time or across constituencies. On the contrary, we know that theoretical doctrines, like other idea-systems, are subject to change in their "social identifications" – vide the case of mass society thinking, originally politically reactionary in its associations, then later linked to the defense of liberal democracy.

Among social scientists at the end of the twentieth century, however, it is safe to say that rational-choice thinking bears expressive associations that are liberal in the classic European sense of that term. The doctrine projects a view of the social world as composed of calculating, utility-maximizing actors pursuing ends that are essentially *divisible* – that is, capable of being attained without regard to the utilities of other actors (see Rule 1988, p. 33). Thus the doctrine does not highlight or dramatize such forces as identification of personal interest with the well-being of larger social aggregates or with abstract principles. The idea that any individual citizen, for example, might have a positive stake in the well-being of fellow community members – or in the ecological well-being of future generations or distant populations – even in the absence of objectively shared interests, does not come naturally. For some rational-choice thinkers – by no means all – sensibilities of this kind lead to a libertarian ethical position. Such a view posits no responsibility on the part of any social actor for the choices or social circumstances of any other.

The strictly ethical doctrines associated with rational-choice thinking, either in its libertarian version or others, are not the central concern here. But for the purposes of this chapter, we must not ignore the effects of the intellectual self-image of rational-choice thinkers on the currency of the doctrine. Many clearly take pride in viewing themselves as hardheaded analysts willing to write off conventional ethical considerations as sentimental obstacles to scientific judgments on human affairs. Among the forces thus disparaged, it seems, are actors' attachments to holistic principles of moral authority like those identified by Durkheim and others as bases for any viable social system. In a telling turn of phrase, Alan Wolfe describes this attitude of libertarian proponents of rational choice as a " 'naughty boy' tone, as though morality were of concern only to sissies"; from the perspective of the "Chicago school" of rational-choice thinking,

Wolfe comments, "there is no behavior that is *not* interpretable as economic, however altruistic, emotional, disinterested, and compassionate it may seem to others" (1989, p. 32).

Again, by no means all social scientists inspired by rational-choice thinking embrace these views. But it would be hard to deny that such expressive associations add to the attractions of the doctrine for many of its adherents and contribute to the currency of the theory.

The articulation of these expressive affinities, moreover, seems ultimately to have an effect on those exposed to doctrine. Social-psychological studies comparing the conduct of students of neoclassical economics (the analytical first cousin of rational-choice thinking) and those in other specialties have turned up some striking differences. Students of economics appear markedly less cooperative, less likely to identify issues of normative principle in situations requiring cooperation, and more inclined to exploit their fellows than students in other disciplines (Frank, Gilovich, and Regan 1993). The differences appear *after* the study of economics, suggesting that they are not attributable to self-selection to the discipline. Moreover, academic economists appear less likely to donate to charities than members of other academic specialties (though their incomes are generally higher). It seems that the rhetorical content of theories is forceful, at least to those immersed in them.

The expressive messages conveyed by rational-choice thinkers are not lost on outsiders to the theory. If enthusiasm for the doctrine indeed derives its currency from the expressive associations mentioned above, so does distaste for it. Detractors of the doctrine are often clearly inspired to oppose the very values or social arrangements that supporters see themselves as upholding. Some expressions of these opposing sentiments are noted below.

SUPPORTING CASES: THE "OR-ELSE" CLAUSE

How are we to judge the often sweeping formal claims made on behalf of rational-choice analysis? Perhaps we should begin with the simplest sort of test: Can we point to any important social phenomena that appear to be conspicuously consistent with its tenets?

It would be hard to deny that we can. Indeed, both the conduct of everyday social life and its systematic study would appear impossible, were the first two tenets of the doctrine given above not at least substantially realized. We base all sorts of analysis and practical decision making, for example, on the assumption that people's actions are governed by relatively enduring hierarchies of preference. We can often afford to assume that people oriented today, in varying degrees, to the acquisition of money, status, intimacy, or godliness are apt to pursue much the same hierarchies of rewards tomorrow. No less reasonable is the assumption that people weigh different courses of action, altering their behavior when changed strategies give better promise of producing the desired results. Thus, if someone finds new means for achieving long-standing ends, we expect his or her behavior to change.

True, such judgments are far from universally accurate. Sometimes people show abrupt changes in preferences, or even yield to consummatory actions like temper tantrums or outbursts of candor – behaviors counterproductive in relation to preferences implicit in their actions in other contexts. But the disruptive and extraordinary character of such events itself attests to the importance of rational calculation of enduring interest in rendering much social process at least minimally predictable and understandable.

Many noteworthy aggregate social phenomena, moreover, appear to show the effects of such calculation. People calculate about their careers, often trading off short-term advantages in matters like pay against such long-term rewards as job security and the inherent interest of the work. People calculate in their domestic economies, reducing spending and increasing savings when the larger economic picture appears threatening. Indeed, people evidently calculate in the often spontaneous realm of sexuality, if we can believe recent statistics on changed practices in the face of the AIDS epidemic.

Thus it seems easy to produce examples consistent with the elementary model of human behavior as the outcome of rational calculation. Yet one critique of rational-choice theory stresses the systematic *distortions* of human rationality. As Robert H. Frank writes:

> Economists are well aware that it would not be rational, let alone possible, for customers to make decisions on the basis of complete information. . . . What many economists have been slower to recognize, however, is that we often make very poor use of the information that we have right at our fingertips. The problem is not just that we make random judgment mistakes; rather it is that our judgmental errors are often systematic. If people are asked, for example, whether there are more murders than suicides in New York State each year, almost everyone confidently answers yes. And yet there are always more suicides. (1990 p. 54)

In developing his arguments, Frank relies heavily on the well-known studies of Tversky and Kahneman (e.g., 1974). Such research makes it plain that failures of rationality are not just random aberrations, but are virtually built into human cognitive process.

Do such observations undermine the credibility of rational-choice thinking? Certainly human powers of calculation are fallible, and, as the critics insist, these failings are predictable. But if these were the only objections, I believe that the claims of the doctrine would remain substantially intact. For we would still be left with a view of human action as being guided by *roughly* rational calculations in a wide variety of ordinary settings.

Consider the analogy to vision as a basis of orientation to the physical world: It is well known that certain misperceptions are inherent in human vision. Objects under water appear displaced from the standpoint of a viewer above. Or, a series of still images flashed in quick succession may appear to move, as in a cartoon or a movie. One can point to many similar examples. But for practical purposes – for example, in explaining how people get from one place to another for most everyday purposes – we can accept that most people, most of the time, *do* orient themselves more or less effectively by vision.

What about the third of the tenets listed above, which concerns the explanation of large-scale social and political processes as direct or indirect effects of individual rationality? Here, too, it would be hard to deny that many cases can be found to fit. Consider the social characteristics of marriage partners: One rarely encounters marriages in which one spouse is wealthy, high-born, personable, attractive, healthy, and well-educated, whereas the other is the opposite of all these things. Or consider what appears to be a basic reality concerning American colleges and universities: The amount of work expected and obtained from students appears to vary directly with the level of competition for admission. Such durable social realities seem to reflect consistent choices to make the most rewarding use of scarce resources of one sort or another.

Or, consider some cases noted by Jon Elster:

In traditional China, many poor families practiced infanticide of girls. The result was a surplus of boys, and a substantial number of unmarried young men who were excellent material for recruitment by bandits. The victims of banditry were mainly landlords and well-to-do peasants, who did not practice girl infanticide to the same extent. Predation on the rich was an unintended consequence of the self-defenses of the poor. When trade unions insist on job security for their members, they don't have the interest of the firm in mind. Yet as an unintended consequence lower turnover rates increase productivity. Mechanisms such as these are the stuff of social science. (1989, pp. 97–98)

Rational-choice enthusiasts take special satisfaction in tracing such nonintuitive connections between large-scale social realities and rational calculation. Thus, in *Foundations of Social Theory* (1990, p. 12), Coleman entertains the argument that changes in sexual morality can be attributed to demographic imbalances via assumptions of rational calculation. He cites a study by Guttentag and Secord (1983) positing that periods when larger numbers of females are "in the market" for smaller numbers of males lead to "looser standards of sexual behavior for women." Because both males and females gravitate toward relationships in which the male is about two years older, the males in relatively small age cohorts enjoy a "buyers' market" when the immediately younger cohorts are larger. These situations tend, according to this analysis, to produce more permissive standards.

Such accounts, if backed by persuasive evidence, produce a special kind of impact – like that generated by Durkheim's linkage of suicide rates to social affiliation, or the finding that military groups who received fewer promotions were nevertheless more satisfied with promotional possibilities. What impresses us in such cases is that the connection between the thing explained and the explanatory factor would not have been suspected but for the theory. When the theory that reveals the connection purports to identify the basic forces governing *all* social process, the effect is especially tantalizing.

THE CLAIMS TO GENERALITY

Some analysts working in the rational-choice tradition do not go nearly this far. For them, the theory is simply one source of analytical or explanatory possibilities among many, to be adopted or ignored according to its applicability to the specific case. In the words of one such theoretical pluralist:

> the point of rational actor models is not to find out whether they are "true" or not – they are axiomatically true and logically sound if the deductions are valid. The point is, rather, that they enter the theoretical depository of the sociologist – that is, the set of logical or theoretical constructs that he can draw on. . . . (Hernes 1992, p. 425)

Were claims like this the strongest ever made for rational-choice analysis, one doubts that its place in theoretical social science would be so controversial. Such a "weak" reading would be much easier for outsiders to the doctrine to accept, but also less inspirational to insiders.

By contrast, proponents of what one might call the "strong" version of the doctrine would want to insist that processes of rational calculation somehow represent the *ultimate* social reality and that they must accordingly play a role in any theoretical analysis. Such a view obviously claims for rational-choice thinking a special, central status among theoretical approaches – a status implicit in Coleman's characterization of rational choice as "one paradigm in social science that offers the prospect of greater theoretical unity among the disciplines than has existed until now" (1989, p. 5). In their purest form, such claims imply that all insights and accomplishments of alternate theoretical traditions could be better, more fully rendered, in rational-choice terms.

An analogy might be the use of digital technology for the reproduction of sound. Anything audible, we are told, can be reproduced by information stored in the proper combination of electronic "dots and dashes" (or plusses and minuses, or whatever). Thus though our *experience* of a symphony played from a compact disc may register nothing like the constituent digital elements, we recognize digital analysis and its related technologies as having captured the *basic building blocks* of sound as we experience it. The strongest claims for rational-choice thinking seem to assert something analogous: that all social processes and arrangements, including those which appear to have nothing to do with rational calculation, can actually be "fully" analyzed in its terms. This may seem like a sweeping claim, and it is. But I doubt that the strongest proponents of rational-choice thinking would be satisfied with less.

Can such claims be defended? Perhaps the easiest way of doing so is by reducing them to trivial truths – for example, by insisting that all social behavior must ipso facto represent the result of *some form* of rational calculation, and hence must be explainable in such terms. Such determination to defend the rational-choice vision at all costs leads enthusiasts to bend the doctrine out of all recognizable shape when confronted by discordant empirical findings. As Green and Shapiro point out (1994), the empirical literature abounds with instances of this kind. Among the most conspicuous failures of these collisions are attempts to explain voting in terms of rational choice – not voting for particular candidates or parties, but the fact that people vote *at all*. Given the extreme unlikelihood that one's own vote could alter the results of most elections, the theory would logically lead us to expect zero participation in elections. Green and Shapiro characterize as follows the efforts of two noted rational-choice theorists to make sense of the fact that people do, in fact, turn out to vote,

Riker and Ordshook . . . widened the purview of the theory to include the psychic gratification a citizen derives from going to the polls. These include five sources of 'satisfaction': those of 'complying with the ethic of voting,' 'affirming allegiance to the political system,' 'affirming a partisan preference,' 'deciding . . . for those who enjoy the act of informing themselves' and 'affirming one's efficacy in the political system.' . . . (1994, p. 53)

In the absence of evidence to the contrary, any and all forms of social action can in principle be explained as performed for the consummatory satisfactions they afford. But recourse to such an all-purpose escape hatch represents a departure from the fundamental rational-choice view of social and political behavior as instrumental. The insight that people do certain things because they find them satisfying in themselves is simply not theoretically distinctive. It might as well be derived from any number of approaches – for example, the normative or value-integration theories often disparaged by rational-choice theorists (e.g., Hechter 1987, pp. 19–29).

Part II

THE LIMITS OF RATIONAL-CHOICE ANALYSIS

However else we conceive the distinctive tasks of theoretical social science, those tasks indispensably include identification of what might be called "contingencies" in social life. Any theoretical representation of the social world, in other words, must specify how elements of that world "hang together," how they depend on others. Such contingencies take an almost unlimited variety of forms. Analytical connections requiring attention from theoretically minded social scientists range from demographic variability, to the evolution of idea systems, to technological change, to the organization of political power – and on and on.

Given this extreme variety, most arguments for theoretical generality would seem to face an uphill task. Any notion that one single genre of social force, process, or fact can provide the basis for any and all accounts or explanations legitimately required in our disciplines appears prima facie implausible. Yet the propensity to view the world in such categorical terms is clearly widespread. One result is the frequent insistence that contingencies posited in terms of theoretical visions other than one's own are better translated into the one, true theoretical language – much as though the theorist were a recording technician, translating the richness of a symphony into its elemental dots and dashes.

It is hard to credit such sweeping claims on behalf of any one theoretical scheme – rational-choice very much included. At their best, rational choice arguments succeed in demonstrating nonintuitive connections between aggregate social states and processes of individual choice. But such analyses cannot necessarily tell us much about *how particular options for choice come to be available to particular actors at particular junctures*. The point is not, of course, that calculative pursuit of enduring interest is irrelevant for action. It is simply that having an interest in acting a certain way is inherently of no greater importance as a basis for explanation than other conditions that make action possible.

Consider an example from current politics. At the time of this writing, the United States has just witnessed a spate of high-visibility confrontations having to do with relations between men and women. Some of these have been political in the institutional sense of involving struggles over elected or appointive office, as in the controversies over sexual improprieties attributed to a male Supreme Court nominee by his female former protégée. But even where the parties to these controversies have not been public officeholders, the struggles have clearly had political implications. At contest is the public definition of proper conduct between the sexes, with all the implications of such a definition for power relations between males and females, both in public and private.

These shifts in public consciousness have brought about far-reaching changes in electoral campaigns. For one thing, the (mostly male) candidates are being subjected to scrutiny in terms of a variety of what are now termed "women's interests," a notion that clearly does not have the same meaning ascribed to it in years past. In the current political climate, these interests are construed to include both policy questions like parental leave from jobs and subtler matters of what used to be considered candidates' strictly personal relationships with female staff or associates. One result is that candidates and other public figures are obliged to subject aspects of their lives and actions to public scrutiny in new ways – ways that would hardly have been thought necessary in periods when the behavior in question was assumed to be a strictly an offstage, "private" matter.

None of these profound shifts alters the fact that players on the political stage engage in calculated actions aiming to maximize their advantage. As always, for example, office seekers strive to present themselves publicly as showing "good character" in circumstances bearing on their public roles. But the *content* of the standards defining good public character is never fixed. Every so often, periods of intense public dramatization like the one described above bring about redefinitions of such standards, creating new (though usually unstated) ground rules for political process.

It may be possible to *describe* such changes – or at least certain aspects of them – in terms drawn from rational-choice theory. One might say that the distribution of utility functions had shifted among the electorate, for example, and that calculations and ensuing actions by political actors are changing accordingly. Such a reformulation would be true as far as it goes. But it would neither explain nor fully describe the processes of meaningful reinterpretation and revaluation effected by recent public dramatizations of gender issues in America. Any approach that neglects such processes perforce misses crucial categories of social forces that are responsible for far-reaching, highly value-relevant consequences.

Since Mancur Olson's celebrated book (1965), many enthusiasts of rational-choice thinking have seen in their doctrine a royal road to the conquest of political analysis. And there can be no mistaking the role of rational calculation in all sorts of important political processes. Anyone seeking to explain how trade associations and other lobbyists distribute their largesse among those they seek to influence, to take just one example, would ignore rational calculation at great risk. But political life is multifarious in the processes, forces, and causal connections governing outcomes of interest. To imagine that all of these can somehow be translated into the language of rational calculation is overweening.

Consider the analysis of a slump in the stock or commodities market. One description of the events – and, by this token, one promising category of explanations – might focus on changing calculations by self-interested actors. But another, potentially no less valid, explanation might lie in emergent changes in the shared mind-set of participants. Actors may simply lose their "taste" for risk, for example, regardless of the objective signals available to them from the market. True, once the attitudes of other participants in market situations become evident, it also becomes rational for each player to calculate in terms of those attitudes. But where do such attitudes arise in the first place?

The force of such "definitions and redefinitions of situations" in shaping potentials for public action is vast. One could characterize the period of social effervescence in the United States in the late 1960s as a time when many Americans were willing to entertain a great variety of social experiments, both in personal relations and in public policy. In contrast, public opinion in this and other Western democracies in the 1990s appears far more averse to risk. Again, such states of public opinion provide bases for all sorts of rational calculation on the part of those who must act under their constraints. But it would be stretching a point to say that the states themselves are created wholly by such calculation.

Or, consider Dennis Chong's often acute analysis of rational calculation in the American Civil Rights movement (1991). He makes a convincing case that much behavior on the part of movement activists reflected the calculation of one or another form of rather narrow personal interest. Thus he writes of activists' concern for their reputations within the movement:

> Reputational concerns therefore may counteract the temptation to take advantage of the efforts of others in the provision of collective goods. We refuse one-time grants through free riding in order to retain the esteem, respect, and continued goodwill of those we care about. The selective incentives to participate are the accumulated future benefits that we will reap as a reward for cooperation in the current collective endeavor. (p. 55)

Accounts of this kind can in principle explain certain strategic behaviors among groups of workers engaged in common political tasks. Where they cannot help much is in explaining how a particular cause takes on the moral urgency necessary to attract a movement following in the first place. The same might be said for the entire tradition of studies of collective action in the tradition of Mancur Olson (1965). Theories of rational calculation simply have little that is accurate to say about instances where people willingly incur extraordinary costs on behalf of causes that they never had to embrace in the first place.

Processes of identification with causes of this kind – such as efforts to save the whales or to support the political struggles of people with whom one shares no objective interest – are far-reaching in their import. The interests that emerge in this way are (rather feebly) bracketed in rational-choice writing as "preferences." As Friedman and Hechter have observed, "rational choice theory is mute about what [people's] preferences might be and where they come from" (1988, p. 202). But shifts in such "preferences" are no less fundamental to political life than processes of rational calculation based on stable preference orders. It is simply very difficult to see any grounds for enshrining the particular forces and processes highlighted by rational-choice thinking as the *fundamental* elements of social process – as the elementary "dots and dashes" from which all such processes are constituted.

And yet such shifts – and the effort to promote, direct, or forestall them – are essential to many political processes, and to countless other consequential moments of social life. Any analyst who mistakes this point is unable to account for some of the most familiar political phenomena – notably, the role of rhetoric, exhortation, and kindred forms of public bathos. Politicians do not go about seeking support simply by suggesting to their constituents that they consider their overall utility functions and calculate their behavior accordingly. They also exhort. They may urge their constituents to "show the world that the silent majority is still true to the American way" or "to send the political establishment a message that it can't keep ignoring the rights of people like us." The aim of such appeals is not so much to tap existing preference hierarchies as to revamp such hierarchies. It is absurd to think that such processes of redefinition are any less essential to political life than those consisting of rational calculation.

Objections of this kind, it seems to me, are far more damaging to the claims of the "strong" version rational-choice thinking than objections based on studies like those of Tversky and Kahneman. We are right to acknowledge that efforts at rational calculation do not always succeed and that flaws in human rationality are largely predictable. But in response to such observations, one might observe, with Gudmund Hernes, that rationality

may be a *small* component in the behavior of each individual actor. Yet, if it is a *common* component, it will explain more of the variation in the actions of the collection of actors than will the larger idiosyncratic component in the behavior of each. (1992, pp. 427–428)

A low-key but acute observation. But we must also remember that many forces and considerations besides calculative rationality lend regularity to social process. Nonrational processes are not only "idiosyncratic"; they have their own regularities. But these often require tools of analysis quite different from those provided by rational-choice thinking.

The "blank spots" in rational-choice thinking raise questions about another claim often associated with the theory: that it has unique power to link large-scale social processes with individual dynamics and microsocial realities. The attempt to build such linkages is unmistakably central to the theory. And sometimes the strategy works, producing persuasive accounts of the dependence of large-scale processes and arrangements as results of aggregated individual calculations. But none of this warrants the conclusion that rational-choice thinking differs from "most other approaches in social science" in seeking to "link micro and macro levels of analysis" (Hechter 1987, p. 30).

In fact, many other theoretical worldviews in social science offer accounts of such linkage. They differ from rational choice simply in the nature of the forces or contingencies posited to account for such connections. A case in point is symbolic interaction, a theoretical system which certainly focuses on connections between collective and individual processes as much as does rational choice. The difference, of course, is that for symbolic interactionists these connections are envisaged in terms of such processes as definitions of situations, communication of attitudes, shaping and reshaping of public identities, and so on. It would be hard to deny that such processes need to be recognized for all sorts of analytical purposes in our theoretical work. Yet they are ones for which rational-choice thinking offers no account of its own.

The same can be said for many other theoretical worldviews, from many varieties of Marxism to Foucauldian analysis to network thinking to Parsons's general theory. All of these views envisage some sort of mediating processes between individual and collective realities, or between micro- and macro-level phenomena. It is very hard to see what grounds there could be for claiming that rational-choice thinking, any more than others of these, represents the unique key to such connections.

WHEN RATIONAL CHOICE GOES WRONG

Does the partiality of its analytical focus vitiate the value of rational-choice thinking as a source of theoretical inspiration? Only when enthusiasts of the doctrine insist on mobilizing it to account for phenomena and processes to which it clearly does not apply. Unfortunately, proponents of the strong version insist on doing just this. The effect is to throw misleading analyses after sound ones.

Consider James Coleman's much celebrated *Foundations of Social Theory* (1990). This work holds special interest for present purposes, not just because of the acclaim it has received, but also because of its systematic character. One of Coleman's explicit aims is to show how rational-choice thinking begins at the beginning, starting with the most elementary individual-level processes, and extends to account for complexities of large-scale structures and processes. This determination to defend the strongest version of rational-choice thinking – that is, its claims to generality – leads Coleman to press the possibilities of the doctrine beyond the limits of its applicability.

Consider, for example, his portrayal of the processes that lead parents to inculcate internalized norms in their children:

Parents must pay the costs of internalization, but others will experience some of the future benefits. It is true that parents experience some benefits during the period the child is at home. Since these are only a fraction of the benefits, however, there is an expected underinvestment in internalization from the perspective of the total set of benefits to others that internalization will bring about. . . . This underinvestment should be especially great for internalization of norms which have least to do with a child's actions in the home and are primarily concerned with actions toward others later in life. (1990, p. 297).

Can we afford to take such analyses as *general* accounts of the processes leading parents to encourage internalization of norms in their children? Surely it tells us nothing about some of the most powerful of these processes, those having to do with *identification* between parents and children. Many key socialization processes turn, not on parents' efforts to protect their own interests, but rather on the minimization of the distinction, at least in parents' minds, between their own interests and those of their children. There is something about parenthood that leads many parents to assume as deep an interest in their children's character and behavior as in their own. That is, parents *identify* with the interests and personalities of those they nurture. Sometimes parents' very realization that they will not be present to experience the actions shaped by the internalized directions that they pass on to their children actually seems to sharpen the desire to make the transmission process more effective.

The point is not to deny that people have "selfish" or calculative reasons for impressing rules on their children, or on anyone else whose behavior affects them. I simply mean to note that such interests are far from the *only* ones motivating parental efforts to foster internalization. Analysis based on rational calculation may tell us how hard people will work to inculcate principles of conduct that they seek to establish for any of a variety of reasons; but it cannot tell us anything distinctive about when and how people form bonds of identification. And any account of the transmission of norms and other principles of social action that does not include reference to processes like identification will surely be incomplete. Similar problems arise in other accounts by Coleman of the genesis and perpetuation of norms. Throughout these arguments he is at pains to explain adherence to norms as a result of calculation of individual interest – rather, for example, than portraying norms as shapers of individual interests and calculative processes in their own right.

Do such arguments have any virtue – apart from their ability to preserve the analytical purity of a theory that enshrines rational calculation as its point of departure? It would be easy to show that many norms arise and are perpetuated just as Coleman suggests: through direct or indirect pressure from parties with some sort of demonstrable interest in particular forms of compliance. Some of Coleman's well-chosen examples here include community pressures for trustworthiness among diamond dealers and investment bankers (1990, p. 109). But what about the perpetuation of norms that seem to serve no one's objective interests?

Consider destructive social patterns like the vendetta, where family members are expected to continue never-ending patterns of revenge and counterrevenge long after the original slight has been forgotten by all concerned. In many such cases, those who comply with the norms of vengeance surely would seem to have every selfish interest in seeing the whole destructive system of obligations suspended.

Coleman's rejoinder to this objection, I imagine, might follow the lines of the account he gives of distinctive dress codes observed by religious or status groups. True, failure to observe such norms may not seem to entail *objective* costs, he allows. But,

Each member's obeying the norm strengthens the expression of group solidarity and the differentiation from others. . . . Observance by fellow members aids and supports each member, and failure to observe constitutes a threat to the solidarity of the group. (p. 258)

But such a rationale threatens to make the argument circular. *Why* do people have an "interest" in group solidarity – especially forms of group "solidarity" like the vendetta, which often seem to leave everyone worse off than they would be without such interests? One might argue that the parties concerned, all things considered, really maximize their utility by pursuing such apparently painful and destructive social expectations. But would such an argument really constitute an *explanation* of people's propensity to adhere to norms – or simply a restatement of it? The best that can be said about this twist of Coleman's argument is that it preserves the claims of the theory to generality.

Coleman runs up against difficulties of the same kind when he seeks to account for arrangements like slavery. In accounting for social arrangements of this kind, most social scientists would probably cite institutionalized power differences. But Coleman insists on characterizing slavery as an outcome of rational choice by the enslaved; he writes:

It may appear odd to begin a discussion of authority, a relation in which a superordinate directs or governs the actions of a subordinate, by describing the actions of the actor who becomes the subordinate. Yet this is essential to a conception of authority that is consistent with the theory of this book: Authority must be vested in a superordinate before the superordinate can exercise authority. Authority exists only when the superordinate holds this right. (p. 67)

No one doubts that the actions of slaves in accommodating to their assigned roles may reflect rational calculation. But does it make sense to insist that the *explanation* for slavery – or for that matter an accurate *description* of it – can be predicated on slaves' active granting of rights over themselves?

A heavy price is paid for such insistence, in terms of the accuracy with which the forces at work in such situations are identified. As Charles Tilly characterized this strain of Coleman's thinking,

Coleman's people live in a refreshingly benign world. Their social life includes no exploitation or coercion in the usual sense of these words, since his people take every action – including submission to slavery – voluntarily and to their own advantage. Coleman escapes from the problem of apparently involuntary servitude (at least among the Greeks and Romans; see p. 88), for example, by treating it as better than the death which otherwise threatened the vanquished. He neglects to say that the same people who enslaved also threatened death. Thus he ignores the threat of force that informs every protection racket, including enslavement, not to mention the force that holds the *children* of slaves in involuntary servitude. (1991, p. 1010)

These difficulties are characteristic of the fate that befalls theoretical systems when they succumb to imperialistic ambitions. By insisting that their characteristic analytical tools must generate accounts of phenomena for which they have, in fact, no distinctive account to offer, rational-choice theorists and proponents of many other "general" theories lead us astray. Their efforts to force the full variety of social processes onto the Procrustian bed provided by their favored theory makes distortion inevitable. In the case of rational-choice thinking, the shifts of meaning-systems that reorder human interests are one key category of phenomena that simply lies outside the grasp of the theory. Enduring, structural features of subordination, as in the example above, are another. Once the terms of social interaction are set by such forces and arrangements, rational-choice analysis may tell us much about how people cope with the choices available to them. But to insist on explaining such realities as *results* of rational calculation invites accounts that are not just skewed but actually misleading.

CONCLUSION

Does the elaboration of rational-choice thinking represent "a step ahead?" Does it "move the discipline forward?" In short, do insights like those considered here count as intellectual progress? Or are they simply responses to what one might consider special theoretical tastes – tastes, perhaps, that are both satisfied by theory and whetted by it?

We might consider these questions in terms of the "or-else" clause implicit in rational-choice writings. What do analysts with no particular expressive stake in rational-choice thinking stand to lose, in their own terms, by ignoring the distinctive insights of this doctrine? What sorts of things that any alert analyst *needs to understand* require recourse to rational-choice principles?

It seems undeniable that there are many such things. It is hard to imagine what accounts we could give of such diverse phenomena as runs on banks, or changing family size over historical time, or the working of political repression, without invoking basic rational-choice ideas. Perhaps the principles involved in such examples are so widely accepted that we hardly think of them as being associated with rational choice. Yet they are among the distinctive tenets of the doctrine.

Much more problematic, however, are the more sweeping claims made on behalf of the theory. These are claims reflecting the view that rational-choice analysis somehow taps the most fundamental, most basic levels of social reality. From this conviction proceeds the uninspiring attempt to defend accounts of facts, arrangements, and processes that are qualitatively distinct from those governed by rational choice as some form of *special case* of a reality essentially captured by the theory.

The irony (and the futility) of such attempts ought to be apparent in their intellectual symmetry to the dismissals of rational-choice thinking by defenders of competing theoretical worldviews. By the latter I mean theoretical systems enshrining *other* forces, processes, or dimensions as the *essential* elements of social life. The claim is predictable: *Rational choice misses the point.* The contingencies it identifies are superficial, epiphenomenal – distractions from the most profound social forces or analytical principles. Such attitudes are more than implicit, for example, in the words of Norman Denzin, who criticizes rational-choice thinking from a hermeneutic standpoint:

In . . . moments of existential crisis, consequential action occurs, rationality falls by the wayside, the moral self is exposed, and society – as it is lived from within – is laid bare. (1990, p. 12)

Here Denzin seems to be pointing to moments marked by the emergence of new shared meanings and understandings. It would be hard to deny that such junctures occur with some frequency, or that they can be highly consequential when they do. What is difficult to accept is the notion that these processes are inherently more basic, more fundamental, or more compelling as points of departure than those modeled by rational-choice thinking.

If I am right in my judgment on this point, a nagging question presents itself: Why do talented thinkers go to such lengths to defend one or another "strong" form of the rational-choice theory – or, for that matter, similarly "strong" versions of competing doctrines that give central place to other social forces, facts, or connections?

Surely the reason has to do with the expressive qualities of the doctrines. I am convinced that we look to theories, in the encompassing sense considered here, to encapsulate and evoke what are for us the *salient meanings* of social experience. And insofar as these are our expectations, all judgments of the quality of theoretical ideas are highly context-dependent.

For more delimited judgments the problem is less severe. With a bit of application, social scientists have at least a fighting chance of agreeing on the role of specific contingencies in shaping specific ranges of events, facts, or situations. We might hope to reconcile conflicting judgments on the correlates of school achievement, for example, or the social bases of adherence to various religious faiths. But questions of what theoretical frames serve best for social inquiry *in general* tap much more diffuse and imponderable constraints. As in styles of art, music, drama, or poetry, different analytical visions leave us convinced or unmoved largely because of their fit with our sense of "what matters most" in social life.

Such an argument may seem a strange one to invoke in the case of rational-choice theory – by contrast, say, to sociological feminism or other theoretical worldviews with more obvious links to specific social movements, constituencies, or action concerns. But rational-choice thinking also has its missionary aspect, and its expressive appeal is manifest there. For its most earnest supporters, the doctrine represents an affirmation of the sorts of forces and dynamics that they would *like* to play a central role in human affairs, to the deemphasis of those highlighted by hermeneuticists like Denzin, sociological feminists, network analysts, or proponents of other theories.

Such a view is all but explicit in the words of James Coleman in his editorial introduction to the inaugural issue of the rational-choice journal *Rationality and Society:*

If the future of social organization is to be under the conscious direction of persons, and not guided by the erratic but benign hand of social evolution, there come to be normative and ethical questions. . . .

The general problem can be put quite simply: as increasing fractions of persons' environment – physical, social and biological – come to be under human control rather than the control of nature (or fate, or God) how are decisions to be made that appropriately exercise that control, and what are the criteria for 'appropriate' decisions? Such questions pull ethics and moral philosophy into full participation with the other social sciences in the task of providing guidance for the increasingly extensive human construction of social organization. (1989, p. 8)

Does this passage not amount to a judgment of what aspects of social life ultimately *matter most* – in other words, to a statement not only of how social systems do work but also how we might hope they should work?

4

---

*From Parsons to Alexander: Closure through
theoretical generality*

Upon the death of Talcott Parsons, the *New York Times* carried a lengthy
intellectual obituary by Daniel Bell entitled "Talcott Parsons: Nobody's
Theories Were Bigger" (13 May 1979, sec. 4, p. 6). I have always wondered whether the title was suggested by Bell himself or by someone at the
Times. For it did solve a formidable editorial problem: how to characterize
the distinctive accomplishments of Parsons's work in a way comprehens-
ible to those outside the often hermetic world of theoretical social science.
For those on the inside, the headline raises a question of unmistakable
validity: Is "bigness" of the sort achieved by Parsons's quest for an absolutely *general* theory indeed a desideratum in efforts to understand social
life?

There can be no doubt that it was, in fact, achieved. Central to the
enormous influence of Parsons's thinking in the middle decades of this
century was its claim to embody a view of the social whole. For many
thinkers, his vision accordingly promised a guide to distinguishing what
really mattered in the subject matter – and, not incidentally, for charting
the long-term direction of theoretical enlightenment. At a historical moment when such vision was at a premium, this breadth of reference made
Parsons's thinking seem, to many North American social scientists, the
only theoretical game in town.

Among the most influential claims made for Parsons's system was that it
caught the essential drift of intellectual *progress*. Implying its own distinctive model of closure, this progressive vision succeeded for decades in
defining the terms in which social scientists understood and went about
their analytical work. And, as with other grand theoretical visions, the
appeal of Parsons's system slackened abruptly. By the time of his death in
1979, its grip on the theoretical imagination had greatly dissipated.

Yet since that time many of its key claims have been reasserted by
Jeffrey Alexander, in a clear effort to reconstitute the earlier theoretical
empire. Alexander's work has not approached the breadth of influence of

Parsons's system in its heyday. But the attention accorded to it demonstrates that a constituency remains for a certain vision of theory – a theory whose excellence lies in the sheer comprehensiveness of its conceptual rendering of social life.

For the purposes of this book, the Parsons–Alexander project offers a perfectly apposite case. How, I want to ask, are we to evaluate the appeal of this line of theorizing? Does the quest for bigness or comprehensiveness that it embodies simply represent an expression of irreducible or arbitrary intellectual *taste?* Or does it offer – as its proponents surely would want to insist – reliable analytical tools that no conscientious student of social life could afford to do without? If so, what account can we give of these analytical virtues? What grounds are there for embracing pursuit of these particular forms of theoretical enlightenment as against other possibilities? What, in other words, is the "or-else" clause associated with the quest for total theoretical generality?

PARSONS'S VIEW OF THE WHOLE

Like tribes, political parties, and religious faiths, intellectual movements generate and draw sustenance from foundational myths. The ancient Romans had the epic of the wanderings of Aeneas and his band, culminating in the founding of what became the imperial city. Soviet citizens (until recently) had the heroic narrative of Lenin's decisive leadership of a broadly based popular mobilization, leading to the dictatorship of the proletariat under the Bolsheviks. For jazz lovers, the equivalent might be the account (less historically suspect than the first two) of Jelly Roll Morton's self-conscious "invention" of the form by combining ragtime and the blues.

For the project considered here, the equivalent narrative is that provided in *The Structure of Social Action* (1937). This is, of course, Parsons's account of how his theory grew out of the subtle but profound convergence he identified in the ideas of previous social and political theorists. Beginning with Hobbes, Parsons averred, great thinkers had striven in vain, often without exactly realizing what they were doing, to take account of a basic and crucial fact of social life – people's willingness to accept the constraints on their selfish interests necessary for any enduring and coherent system of social interaction. What all had failed to grasp was the ubiquitous and indispensable role, in every stable social system, of attachment to commonly held ultimate values. By identifying this insight as the solution to the puzzle that his predecessors all had confronted but could not quite solve, Parsons claimed the role of midwife to theoretical progress, moving social science forward to a new, higher level of understanding.

As he put it, toward the end of *The Structure of Social Action:*

A common system of ultimate values precludes the identification of the concrete ends of individual action with the random wants of utilitarianism. The conception is rather that of long, complicated interwoven chains of intrinsic means–end relationships culminating in relatively integrated individual systems of ultimate ends, each of which in turn is to a relative degree integrated in a common system. This common system is related to the subsidiary intermediate sector of the chain in various complex ways formulable for present purposes mainly (1) as supplying the ultimate end of each chain and (2) as forming the source of the moral authority of institutional norms. (1937, p. 465)

This position was the point of departure for Parsons's subsequent theory building. In positing such consensual directions in human strivings, he was convinced, he had cut the Gordian knot that earlier theorists had failed to untangle, with disastrous consequences for their theories.

In *Theories of Civil Violence* (1988, chap. 5), I commented on this line of argument at length. The narrative underlying these assertions, I argued, is highly misleading. Above all, the idea that earlier thinkers had been unable to grasp the role of commonly shared sentiments of ultimate value in weighing against self-interest simply does not withstand examination. Sensitivity to the importance of what could perfectly well be called "common ultimate values" is conspicuous in the works of many thinkers well before the nineteenth century – Montesquieu, for example, or the Scottish moralists. As Camic (1979) and others have shown, recognition of such forces is widespread among the utilitarians. Even Hobbes, often taken as the pure case of insensitivity to such forces, acknowledged their existence. He invokes, for example, ideas like "benevolence" and "desire of good to another" or "to man generally" (*Leviathan,* chap. 6), though such sentiments play little role in his explanations of social phenomena.

The key significance of Parsons's narrative for present purposes is its role in justifying the conceptual scheme to which it gave rise. The shared value-commitments that Parsons identified as his essential discovery formed the basis of his famous system. That system was clearly prefigured in passages like the following from *The Structure of Social Action:*

The elements of structure of a generalized system of action . . . fall into three relatively well defined groups. The first is heredity and environment, seen subjectively as the ultimate means and conditions of action. . . .

The second is the group included in the intermediate intrinsic means–end sector. This group includes the permanently valid precipitate of the utilitarian theories. . . .

The third is the whole group of elements clustering about the ultimate-value system in so far as it is integrated and not reducible to the random ends of utilitarianism. It is, as has been shown, emergent from the positivist tradition and the process of its emergence is that of the breakdown of the positivistic tradition in its transition to the voluntaristic theory of action. (1937, pp. 718–719)

Passages like this adumbrate the model of closure that has animated the work of Parsons and his followers ever since. The key assumption might be expressed as follows: The understanding of social life depends on proper reckoning of the forces governing individual action; and such a reckoning requires an exact catalogue of each qualitatively distinct determinant. The failure of earlier theorists manifested itself precisely in their inability to identify in this way *all* the forces that *mattered* in social process. Only when that task of identification is complete can serious theoretical analysis fruitfully proceed.

Or, as Alexander comments:

Parsons states quite clearly in *Structure* that he wants to develop a theory of analytical elements, that is, a theory which defines elements abstractly rather than in relationship to a historically specific period of time or a specific empirical situation. . . . [He makes no] attempt to explain any particular situation. He leaves open . . . the character of the real world in factually detailed terms. (1987, p. 34)

There is a distinctive logic here. It is like that of the periodic table in chemistry: a painstaking but informative filling-in of hitherto unidentified properties until all the conceptual possibilities are accounted for.

The quest implied here to create a complete, comprehensive, and veridical system of knowledge has all the characteristics of a distinctive model of closure. It generates judgments as to what matters and what does not; it provides rules for analysis of argument or evidence; and it implies a strategy for the mobilization of intellectual efforts. Like all successful theoretical innovations, this one generated a kind of revolutionary fervor among its early converts. Indeed, in the 1950s and 1960s, the recasting of familiar subject matters into distinctively Parsonian conceptual form became a kind of industry. Every branch of social inquiry seemed subject to such reinterpretation: for example, economic life (Parsons and Smelser 1956); collective behavior (Smelser 1962); modernization studies (Bellah 1957); and small groups (Parsons, Bales, and Shils 1953).

This process is a familiar one in the life cycles of theoretical visions. At the height of their powers, models of closure convey an intense sense of meaningful engagement to their proponents, simply by recasting familiar subject matters into the conceptual form given by the new vision. But for present purposes, we cannot afford to take such perceptions at face value. What advantages, we must ask, do such visions afford those not affected by the expressive climates that gave rise to them? Are the special powers of the scheme strictly self-defined, its accomplishments impressive only to the initiated? Or does the theoretical program offer tools of analysis that no reasonable thinker could afford to ignore?

How would proponents of Parsons's system respond to such questions? Parsons's own answers are rare and often ambiguous. At some points in

The Structure of Social Action, for example, he seems to offer relatively modest claims for his vision:

The action frame of reference is certainly one of those in which certain of the facts of human action can be for certain scientific purposes adequately described. It is not the only one of which this is true, but the critical results of the study show that, for certain purposes, which cannot but be considered scientifically legitimate, it is more adequate than any of the alternative frames of references. (1937, p. 756)

This is hardly an overweening assertion. Parsons might simply be telling us that his favorite route to Cape Cod from Cambridge is more scenic, though others may be more direct.

But by the height of his influence, Parsons's claims grew more sweeping. The very fact that his system had been so widely embraced, he held, demonstrated its special powers. It represented a "gradually developing organon of theoretical analysis and empirical interpretation and verification" endowed with the ability to "illuminate a range of empirical problems which were not well understood in terms of the more conventional theoretical positions" (1963, p. 258). To a generation of followers, these claims appeared if anything too modest; for many, his system represented the theoretical frontier, the very embodiment of progress in theoretical understanding.

Today Parsons is generally recalled as the dominant figure in mid-century American sociological theory. But it would be hard to identify any present-day social scientist currently turning out distinctively Parsons-style analyses – that is, studies based on the application of concepts derived from Parsons's oeuvre. Alexander would appear to be the obvious exception to these statements; yet the characteristic language and concepts of Alexander's writing are often quite different from those of Parsons. What remains constant in Alexander's writing are the claims for *comprehensiveness* of theoretical vision.

GENERALITY À LA ALEXANDER

Alexander's bold effort to reconstitute Parsons's enterprise – or at least, his own version of it – represents a theoretical phenomenon in its own right. It is as though he identified, at a moment when theoretical attention had ebbed well away from Parsons, a theoretical niche available for occupancy. In any event, Alexander's first and key work – the vast, four-volume *Theoretical Logic in Sociology* (1982–1983) – received extraordinary attention even *before* its publication, an advance billing characterized by one reviewer as "mega-hype" (Collins 1985, p. 877). Much of this attention seems to have resulted from expectations that Alexander would somehow recapitulate Parsons's role from a few decades earlier.

An unmistakable sign of Alexander's intent was his modeling of *Theoretical Logic* after *The Structure of Social Action*. Above all, Alexander aimed to uphold the narrative underlying Parsons's original claims: the account of Parsons's position as the culmination of a line of progressive theoretical development dating back to the very beginnings of Western social and political thought. And in so casting Parsons's vision as the unique analytical node through which all development must pass, Alexander staked a claim for his own thinking as the continuation of that progressive movement.

But Alexander's heritage from Parsons is selective. In *The Structure of Social Action*, Parsons founded his intellectual system on what he considered his own distinctive solution to "the Hobbesian problem." Central to that solution was the identification of commonly held values as a kind of counterweight to the conflicts of interest that would otherwise make social life unviable. His position, Parsons wrote:

> involves a common reference to the fact of integration of individuals with reference to a common value system, manifested in the legitimacy of institutional norms, in the common ultimate ends of action, in ritual and in various modes of expression. All of the phenomena may be referred back to a single general emergent property of social action which may be called "common-value integration." (1937, p. 768)

Despite the multifaceted changes in his thinking over the years, Parsons continued to affirm the notion of commitment to common values as a kind of ultimate guarantor of continuity and cohesion in social life (e.g., 1961, p. 38).

Alexander specifically rejects this theme in Parsons's message. "Parsons is wrong . . . ," he writes, "to identify normative agreement with social cohesion or consensus" (1987, p. 31). For Alexander, instead, Parsons's overriding claim to greatness lies in the *generality* of his theoretical system. What marks Parsons's vision as superior to those of other theorists is its ability somehow to encompass all the conceptual virtues of his predecessors:

> No general theory since [Parsons's] has matched its potential for analytic precision and its capacity for detailed reference to the empirical world. (1987, p. 89)

> Parsons' intention was to . . . [embrace], in the manner of a truly dialectical transcendence, the positive elements in each school while avoiding their errors. . . . to a significant degree Parsons accomplished this task. (1983b, p. 45)

These are striking claims. How does one get a grip on them? How, for example, are we to recognize and evaluate the "positive elements" that Parsons is said to have grasped, or the "analytic precision" in "detailed reference" to the empirical world? Direct answers in Alexander's writing are scarce. But central to the insights that he develops from Parsons's vision is his own schematization of the conceptual elements of theoretical analysis, as given in the following diagram:

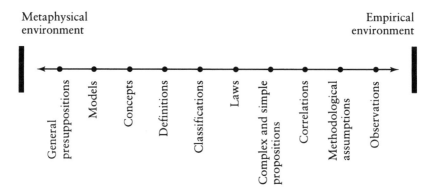

Figure 1. The scientific continuum and its components.

Alexander refers to this scheme as a "continuum." "[S]cientific statements closer to the righthand side," he writes, are empirical, in that "their form is more influenced by the criterion of precisely describing observation," while those at the left are less so (1982a, p. 2). The lefthand elements are, in the term that figures centrally in Alexander's writings, the "presuppositions" underlying the processing of empirical observation.

The exact identity and arrangement of these elements takes on special interest once it is clear just how important *inclusiveness* is to Alexander's claims for his model of closure. Theoretical success, in his vision, lies in the creation of a system of reckoning that has a place, and a name, for everything. "[G]ood theory," he writes, must be "ecumenical and synthetic"; it must "incorporate, through its analytic virtuosity, rational and nonrational elements of action and voluntary and coercive aspects of order at the same time" (1987, p. 281). Theories go bad, he adds a few paragraphs later, when they concentrate on certain analytic elements as against others, claiming that "their particular part was more important than any whole" (1987, p. 282). Parsons's signal virtue, in this view, was his sensitivity to this indispensable requirement of comprehensiveness.

All of this provokes some obvious questions. Above all, how do we know that the elements in Alexander's scheme are *the* elements? What principles govern their designation and arrangement? In what respect, for example, do "models" represented in the diagram above necessarily belong farther to the left than do "classifications?" How are "methodological assumptions" necessarily less specific than "definitions?" And why do "classifications" belong on the conceptual map but not, say, epistemological rules or ultimate value premises? In short, some theory is clearly implied by putting forth any theoretical "map" like the one pictured in the diagram. What is that theory?

Such questions would matter much less, were it not for the emphasis accorded by Alexander to achieving exactly the correct conceptual organization before meaningful analysis can begin. Every effort at theoretical understanding, he suggests, is like a house of cards – doomed to collapse unless each underlying element is in proper order. Unless a theorist's presuppositions, especially those concerning *action* and *order,* are correct, the resulting analyses are bound to be faulty:

> Presuppositions about action and order are the "tracks" along which sociology runs. Whether theorists or not, sociologists make presuppositional decisions and they must live with their consequences. . . .
> Presuppositional choices determine not only theoretical possibilities in a positive sense but also constraints and vulnerabilities. Every presuppositional position closes off certain avenues even while it opens others. (1987, p. 15)

The inspiration for such striking statements seems to lie in the writings of relativist historians or philosophers of science like those discussed in Chapter 2. If no observations are free of the imprint of theory, the argument seems to go, then no investigation can proceed unless and until all theoretical issues are satisfactorily resolved.

On the face of it, the implication that Alexander draws here would seem fantastic – and utterly disruptive for the practice of inquiry. Can it literally be true that analysts who embrace different "models," "concepts," "classifications," or assumptions on "action" and "order" cannot, because of these differences, be expected to agree in their assessments of specific social situations? Do we expect that a pluralist and a Marxist would be unable to agree on the numbers of Democratic and Republican members of Congress because of presuppositional differences? Should we expect such differences to prevent a hermeneuticist and a rational-choice theorist from agreeing on the proportions of births registered to married versus unmarried mothers in a given jurisdiction and period? If such were the case, it is indeed hard to see how theoretical inquiry could be expected to go forward.

It is true that even the most elementary analytical operations imply acceptance of certain principles of a nonempirical kind. These include a priori positions like those underlying the following statement from John Stuart Mill's *A System of Logic:*

What happens once, will, under a sufficient degree of similarity of circumstances, happen again, and not only again, but as often as the same circumstances recur. . . . The universe, so far as it is known to us, is so constituted, that whatever is true in any one case, is true in all cases of a certain description; the only difficulty is, to find what description. (1893, p. 223)

Statements like this are nonempirical, in that their credibility does not depend on any conceivable appeal to observation. And any effort to make sense of empirical inquiry does require acceptance of such assumptions, just as it requires rejection of such notions as entelechies or karma as bases for accounts of the empirical world.

The question is, what role does disagreement over such principles play in actual differences in assessment of specific social processes or situations? Rather little, I believe. Certainly it would be difficult to find common grounds for discussion of research findings with someone who did not subscribe to the position set forth in the above quotation from Mill. But it is difficult to think of a debate in social science in which disagreement on such a point plays a role.

For example, few if any of the theoretical disputes recounted in *Theories of Civil Violence* turned on what Alexander might call "presuppositional" differences. Indeed, most of them seemed to have fairly accessible empirical implications – implications recognizable by proponents even of divergent theoretical perspectives. In some cases, sustained pursuit of those implications in research had enhanced or undermined the credibility of one or another theoretical position, though many historically important theoretical debates yielded no such conclusive results. But the meandering quality of theory on the origins of civil upheaval seems to have much more to do with shifts of theoretical attention or expressive appeal than with the role of conflicting epistemologies or conceptual organization.

None of this is to deny that social scientists bring with them to their analyses distinctive interests, partis pris, personal obsessions, and the like. Such differences are a basic fact of life in our disciplines, as we all recognize. But I can see no reason for characterizing such divergences as matters of "presuppositional" disagreement, as though resolution of clashing assessments were not just difficult but impossible in principle.

Yet this is what Alexander seems to believe. In the opening pages of his review of post–World War II sociological theory, for example, he explains his position with a long example: social scientists' efforts to explain the economic success of Japan in the 1980s. Alexander notes a variety of explanatory factors suggested by various analysts: Japan's policies of economic protectionism; its protected military position; and the strength of Japanese values of social cohesion. Then he comments:

These fundamental differences of scientific opinion cannot, I believe, be resolved simply from a closer look at the facts, although look closely we must. These differences are based upon the general theories scientists hold about what motivates people to act and what kinds of forces hold society together. If we believe that people are naturally competitive and invariably selfish, we will look more toward material factors like government and military policy; if we believe, on the other hand that feelings and morality are vital aspects of the social bond, we are much more likely to be led to such "ideal" factors as values and solidarity. (1987, p. 4)

Here Alexander betrays a fundamental confusion, conflating the influences that incline analysts to one explanation or another with the logical and evidentiary steps needed to assess the adequacy of explanations. There are simply no grounds for categorically characterizing the tropisms that social scientists experience to one or another variety of explanation as resulting from differences in epistemology, conceptual organization, or other "presuppositional" matters.

In the attempt to account for Japan's economic sucesses, the diffuse and far-flung quality of evidence on the subject certainly gives much scope for the hunches and prejudices that investigators bring with them to their work. But this hardly means that conclusions based on evidence are impossible in principle for those who approach the issue with different mindsets. Imagine that it were shown (quite hypothetically) that companies managed by Japanese principles consistently showed higher growth rates than those managed according to other models, regardless of whether the people staffing the organizations were Japanese. Such an observation would clearly weigh heavily in favor of certain theories of Japanese ascendance, and against others. And such a verdict would have to carry force, even for those whose original theoretical expectations had run in quite different directions.

Today, no theoretically minded social scientist would dispute that all sorts of analyses imply acceptance of theoretical principles that could not possibly be justified on empirical grounds. But to conclude from this fact that empirical inquiry to illuminate theoretical questions cannot fruitfully proceed unless and until all parties agree on all such assumptions would be bizarre. To accept such a conclusion would clearly condemn all such inquiry to futility.

Sometimes one can identify instances where theoretically oriented empirical inquiry is blocked by conceptual or epistemological disagreements, as when researchers supposedly investigating "the same" phenomena prove to be embracing quite different definitions of their subject matter. The role of good theoretical criticism here is to identify such disagreements and suggest avenues for their resolution. But the need for such work has to be justified in terms of specific cases, not assumed as an a priori "presupposition."

THE ATTACK ON EMPIRICALLY INFORMED THEORY

In the passage quoted above, Alexander allows that theorists ought to "look closely" at "the facts" (1987, p. 4). One wonders why. Given his view of the role of theory in any understanding of social life, it is difficult to discern what meaningful role empirical inquiry could play. As he insists at another point in the same work:

theoretical reasoning has relative autonomy vis à vis the "real world." Indeed, I have felt compelled to put this last phrase in quotation marks. Because the limits reality places on science are always mediated by prior commitments, it is impossible for us to know, at any particular time, what exactly reality is. (1987, pp. 5–6)

Accompanying this view of theory as a virtually self-sufficient, ratiocinative activity is an assertion that sensitivity to nonempirical issues in theory somehow represents an embattled position. In the opening pages of the first volume of *Theoretical Logic*, Alexander describes his position as "a minority viewpoint, and a steadily shrinking one, among American sociologists today" (1982a, p. 5). In contrast to his own position, he characterizes his opponents as, not only blind to the true importance of "presuppositions," but indeed fixated on strictly empirical questions.

But contra Alexander, many analysts committed to mobilizing empirical inquiry for theory building have written sensitively and at length on nonempirical issues. This is true even of those who embrace natural science models for their work. The most empirically minded investigators, for example, are apt to debate such nonempirical questions as the meaning of causality and the grounds for imputing it (e.g., Costner and Blalock 1972; Gibbs 1972). Similarly, George Homans, accurately identified by Alexander as a wholehearted proponent of natural science models, could hardly be more explicit in his affirmation that "all propositions are accompanied, implicitly or explicitly, by a 'text'" (Homans 1967, p. 10) – which includes the sorts of nonempirical, conceptual elements that make up Alexander's "presuppositions."

The effort to insist that those not sharing Alexander's overwhelming focus on nonempirical aspects of social inquiry are in fact insensitive to their existence leads to all sorts of distortions. Consider his portrayal of Stinchcombe's *Constructing Social Theories* (1968). Stinchcombe, he writes, "disparages any explicitly generalized sociological argument." He "urges that experimental logic should be substituted for argument by conceptual abstraction" (1982a, p. 8).

There is simply no justification for this characterization. Stinchcombe does argue at one point that a kind of experimental logic can be useful in "cases in which we have *explicitly formulated alternative theories*" (1968, p. 24; emphasis in original). But he could hardly be more direct in noting the nonempirical elements of theoretical analysis; "Philosophers of science," Stinchcombe writes, "are generally inclined to admit that there are other concepts ('unobservables') in many or most scientific theories" (p. 38). And a few pages later he goes on to note some examples of what he calls "the elements of theories," ranging from the most abstract (e.g., "general ideas about causality, about what can be accepted as a fact, about what forms of logical inference are valid, and other similar philosophical presuppositions of scientific theories") to "the empirical consequences of theories." Indeed, the scheme Stinchcombe presents in this context (p. 48) bears striking resemblances to Alexander's "continuum" as shown in the diagram above (Figure 1).

One wonders why Alexander presses this theme in characterizing other theorists' positions. His purpose, it would seem, is to uphold the notion that theoretical understanding cannot meaningfully proceed except through preoccupation with the elaborate conceptual system that he espouses. To make this position convincing, it is necessary to portray modes of inquiry that appear to draw worthwhile theoretical conclusions from analysis of empirical material as wrongheaded and futile. This message is the leitmotif of his criticisms of the empirically oriented theoretical analyses of other scholars. Somehow the latter are never quite theoretical *enough*; they always leave some theoretical possibility unstated, some presupposition unpresupposed.

Another case in point is Alexander's discussion of Skocpol's *States and Social Revolution* (1979):

Skocpol (p. 18) proposes to take an "impersonal and nonsubjective viewpoint" on revolutions, which gives causal significance only to 'the institutionally determined situations and relations of groups.' . . . When Skocpol acknowledges at various points, however, that local traditions and rights do play a role (e.g., pp. 62, 138), and that political leadership and ideology must (however briefly) be essayed (pp. 161–73), the theoretical overdetermination of her data becomes apparent. Her structural preoccupations have led her to ignore the entire intellectual and cultural context of revolution. (1987, p. 25)

But Skocpol's celebrated book is not intended as a work of general sociology, nor indeed as general sociology of *all* revolutions (see Skocpol 1979, p. 6). I can find no hint in her work of an assertion that ideas or culture never matter *for any purpose* in social action. Her deemphasis of such considerations has to do with her assessment of the weight that needs to be accorded to them *in answering for some rather specific (though very important) historical questions* – for example, why did three key revolutions happen when and where they did, and with the particular outcomes that they produced? Surely such tasks warrant, indeed demand, a narrowing of analytical focus to specific factors judged causally important for specific empirical outcomes. And, if Skocpol's account is to be considered unsatisfactory in this respect (as it sometimes has been), the objections have been made on the grounds that cultural or ideological forces made more of a difference *in one or more of these outcomes* than she allows – in short, a critique in empirical terms, not on the ground that she has failed to touch every base stipulated by the requirements of general theory.

Or consider Alexander's commentary on a study by Peter Blau, Terry Blum, and Joseph Schwartz (1982) aimed at exploring relations between group size and outgroup relations. The study shows that, in a sample drawn from 125 American metropolitan areas, the size of various minority groups is inversely related to rates of outmarriage – consistently with the authors' theoretical expectations. Alexander finds the study unsatisfactory. He writes:

> out-marriage is a datum that does not, in fact, operationalize "outgroup relations." It is one type of outgroup relation among many others, and as Blau himself acknowledges at one point in his argument, it is a type into which factors other than group size enter. Because of this, the correlation between what is taken to be its indicator and group size cannot verify the general proposition about the relation between group size and outgroup relations. Blau's empirical data, then, are disarticulated from his theory, despite his effort to link them in a theoretically decisive way. (1988, p. 81)

Certainly no single study – perhaps no finite number of empirical investigations – can be expected to *exhaust* the possible manifestations of relations among abstractly conceived variables. One should by no means disregard the possibility that another measure of outgroup relations would have yielded different results from those reported here. But this is hardly to say that the empirical measures adopted in the study discussed here are "disarticulated" from the theory. Frequency of marriage outside one's group is surely one excellent choice as an index of outgroup relations. The findings of Blau et al. increase the credibility of the underlying relationship; studies that establish parallel findings using other indices of the same variables stand to increase it further.

If no finding on these matters should ever be taken as the last word, efforts like those of Blau, Blum, and Schwartz nevertheless hold much theoretical value. Such studies provide bases for dealing with social forces and processes that would otherwise remain mysterious and unaccountable. In the case in point here, for example, action and policy on ethnic relations stand to be informed by the idea that the size of the relevant community is inversely related to the frequency of outgroup relations. No reasonable person seeking, say, to develop programs for encouraging racial integration would want to ignore the implications of the relationship posited by Blau et al., even in the absence of total certainty as to whether it fit every conceivable case.

It is peculiar to imagine that any investigation must yield *definitive* conclusions on relations among theoretical variables, in any and all their instantiations, in order to have theoretical worth. Yet that seems to be the position that Alexander takes. He sounds the same theme in his discussion of Weber's *Protestant Ethic*:

in virtually every broadly gauged theoretical study the sampling of empirical data is open to dispute. . . . Weber's . . . equation of the spirit of capitalism with seventeenth- and eighteenth-century English entrepreneurs has been widely disputed. If the Italian capitalists of the early modern city states are conceived of as manifesting the capitalist spirit (e.g., Trevor-Roper, 1965) then Weber's correlation between capitalists and Puritans is based on a restricted sample and fails to substantiate his theory. (1988, p. 81)

Of course, every empirical investigation of theoretical issues is based on a "restricted sample," in that other instances of the same forces or causal connections could also be studied. But to command theoretical interest, Weber's famous investigation need hardly show that *only* the Puritan worldview analyzed there resulted, or could have resulted, in capitalist or quasi-capitalist activity. *The Protestant Ethic* warrants theoretical interest insofar as it establishes that the specific cultural innovations of the early Calvinists were, in fact, indispensable for capitalism as it occurred in specific western European settings. One may doubt that Weber was right about this. But if Weber's arguments are held to be correct, they establish the *possibility* of certain forms of causality whose role in other settings hold vast interest. Surely such an insight constitutes an authentic theoretical accomplishment.

It simply will not do, then, to equate the *theoretical interest* of particular empirical analyses with the propounding of quasi-Newtonian, ahistorical, universal relationships among abstract variables. Upholding this standard would virtually eliminate the possibility of meaningful empirical inquiry. At some points, Alexander seems to recognize this implication, and to draw back from it. In a discussion of Lieberson's (1980) study of immigration to the United States, for example, he writes off the theoretical significance of the work in terms similar to those he applied to the work of Blau et al. above. But Alexander does enter a qualification: "The measured correlation [between indices of opportunity and cultural heritage], of course, stands on its own as an empirical contribution. Still, the broader theoretical payoff is not there, for the correlation cannot test the theory at which it is aimed" (1988, p. 81).

But what does it mean for any observational analysis to "stand on its own" as an "empirical contribution?" Surely our theoretical interest in any empirical inquiry depends on the insight it yields for our understanding of other situations or analytic problems. The ability to generate such insight, it seems to me, is what we *mean* by the theoretical content of any idea. To take the example from Chapter 1, we do not consider an exhaustive analysis of bottlecap distribution on urban streets as a theoretical "contribution" – or even an "empirical contribution" – unless someone can make a case as to what such patterns tell us about matters of larger interest. The theoretical interest of any finding surely lies in the strength of such a case. Lieberson's study, it seems to me, is rich in such insight. What are we to make of a concept of theoretical success that writes off the value of such understanding?

Is it reasonable for social scientists to expect any empirical investigation to yield definitive, once-and-for-all depictions of the relations between abstractly defined variables? The answer is certainly no. But the question is the wrong one.

Consider a more fruitful question: Can we reasonably expect such inquiry to yield useful insights into social forces and circumstances that impinge upon human interests? Can systematic empirical inquiry meaningfully help us understand, for example, the changing structure of the family, or the role of social control in reinforcing deviant behavior, or the effectiveness of interstate organizations as vehicles for international cooperation, or any of countless other theoretical relationships that engage our analytical and practical interests? If the knowledge we gain from inquiry into such subjects is never exhaustive, may it not nevertheless offer significant advantages in coping with the forces and processes in questions?

THE "OR-ELSE" CLAUSE

The requirements that Alexander applies to others' theoretical work, then, are demanding indeed. To assess them, we must consider Alexander's vision of theoretical *success*. What alternative does he offer to the empirically informed theoretical inquiry that he disparages? What forms of insight do we miss if we ignore his distinctive message? In the terms adopted in this book, what is the "or-else" clause here?

In a number of passages, Alexander portrays the virtues of "fully presuppositional" theory as lying in the ability to "explain" aspects of social life that would otherwise remain unaccounted for. For example, he speaks of the quest for improvement in theory in terms of efforts "to expand the *explanatory power* of any particular theoretical tradition" (1983b, p. 281, emphasis added).

But the notion of explanation invoked here is clearly different from what is normally meant by this term. For Alexander, the power to "explain" seems to mean the ability to *identify* a subject in terms of one's own distinctive conceptual system – to be able to produce a distinctive theoretical term, and a conceptual status, for it. Good theory, he writes in a representative statement, must be

ecumenical and synthetic . . . [it must] incorporate, through its analytic virtuosity, rational and nonrational elements of action and voluntary and coercive aspects of order at the same time. (1987, p. 281)

Again, the logic here is that of matching particular substances found in nature to the elements charted in the periodic table, or of linking specific phenotypic traits to the universal pattern of the human genome.

But, Alexander holds, it will not do for the analyst to apply *just any* term or category to the phenomenon under study. The designation so applied must somehow be suitably entrenched in the logic of the theory. Failure to apply just the right kind of designation, it would seem, amounts to "recourse to residual categories." And only the system founded by Parsons appears to meet this austere test.

I see each of the challenges to Parsons as elaborating one of the possible presuppositional alternatives which are available to sociological theory. . . . Yet no matter how powerfully argued, these alternatives were bound to be only partial theories. The reason is that none of these alternatives takes over Parsons' goals (as distinct from his theory) as their own; none, that is, tries to be synthetic or multidimensional. Only a synthetic position can avoid the resort to residual categories which tears a theory apart. . . . (1987, p. 239)

Of course, no one wants to have his or her theory "torn apart." The question is, what does it mean for this to occur? Is it possible for anyone not sharing Alexander's distinctive theoretical tastes to recognize such an outcome?

If a theorist of Durkheimian persuasion, for example, explained an action by the National Association of Manufacturers as resulting from class interest, would the theorist's worldview thereby be "torn apart?" That is, would such an account perforce be faulty because it does not invoke what we think of as distinctively Durkheimian explanatory principles? Similarly, if a Marxist should invoke religous conviction in accounting for the willingness of early Christians to accept martyrdom under the Roman Empire, has something gone theoretically wrong?

The alternative – vastly more reasonable, one would have thought – would be simply to acknowledge that all sorts of differences on what Alexander would bracket as "presuppositional" matters pose no obstacle to accurate, theoretically fruitful assessments of actual social situations. Social scientists can and do expect to agree in their descriptions and explanations of theoretically important processes, events, or circumstances without embracing precisely the same conceptual or epistemological assumptions.

The standard set down by Alexander for theoretical adequacy, and for explanatory success, is enormously exacting, but it remains unclear why anyone would be attracted to it. Why should we care whether all the "presuppositional" underpinnings that Alexander would identify are in place if the analyses involved are sound and accurate on other counts?

Perhaps the answer would be that other systems of analysis don't really have a place for *everything*, that they don't enable the analyst to recognize every element of social reality as it really is. Alexander often seems to vaunt his own position in just these terms. Thus, at the conclusion of the first volume of his key four-part work, he characterizes his own theoretical accomplishment as follows:

One is left with two sets of fundamental presuppositional dichotomies: social theory can be normative or instrumental in its approach to action, and it can conceptualize the collective arrangement of this action in an internal or external matter. . . . [I]n each case, neither of the two options, taken by itself, is viable. . . . What is the alternative? If neither pole of the dilemma can be taken separately, both must be taken together. . . . I propose that action should be conceived not as either instrumental or normative, but as both. (1982a, p. 123)

To such a striking claim one can only respond with an obvious question: Is it really *news* that both normative and instrumental forces play a role in human action, or that both internal and external dynamics play a role in social order? Contra both Alexander and Parsons, explicit recognition of these forces goes back centuries in our intellectual heritage. Such understanding, for example, is overt in the writings of many of the utilitarian thinkers whose insensitivity to such issues is decried in *The Structure of Social Action.* Consider the words of Adam Smith from *The Theory of Moral Sentiments* (1759):

The man who, not from frivolous fancy, but from proper motives, has performed a generous action, when he looks forward to those whom he has served, feels himself to be the natural object of their love and gratitude, and, by sympathy with them, of the esteem and approbation of all mankind. . . .

It is thus that man, who can subsist only in society, was fitted by nature to that situation for which he was made. All the members of human society stand in need of each others assistance, and are likewise exposed to mutual injuries. Where the necessary assistance is reciprocally afforded from love, from gratitude, from friendship, and esteem, the society flourishes and is happy. All the different members of it are bound together by the agreeable bands of love and affection, and are, as it were, drawn to one common centre of mutual good offices.

But though the necessary assistance should not be afforded from such generous and disinterested motives, though among the different members of the society there should be no mutual love and affection, the society, though less happy and agreeable, will not necessarily be dissolved. Society may subsist, among different men, as among different merchants, from a sense of its utility, without any mutual love or affection; and though no man in it should owe any obligation, or be bound in gratitude to any other, it may still be upheld by a mercenary exchange of good offices according to an agreed valuation. (1976 [1759], pp. 85–86)

To most of us, a passage like this would seem to affirm a key theme of Alexander's "presuppositional" thinking, the notion that both shared normative principles and hardheaded calculation of self-interest play central roles in social action. The question is, what do the pretentious pronouncements of twentieth-century general theory *add* to Smith's insights? Does a thoughtful statement like this reflect recourse to "residual categories" liable to "tear the theory apart?" Is Smith's ability to explain or otherwise understand events, facts, and processes vitiated by his failure to enumerate all the presuppositions required by Alexander? I can see no evidence of such ill effects.

Parsons, in his own accounts of the aims of his theory, generally offered what today would be considered a rather conventional view of its relation to natural science. Certainly he believed that many social scientists of his time had erred in failing to appreciate the need for the sort of finely developed conceptual base for their work that he proposed. But once that system was in place, he asserted, its scientific rigor should bear fruit in the form of successful explanation and prediction. Indeed, as Chapter 2 noted, he and Bales perceived "a very important analogy between the scheme we have developed . . . and classical mechanics" (1953, p. 102).

When he invokes his quest for a theory of expanded "explanatory power," Alexander sometimes seems to hearken back to such aspirations. But in some writings, he departs from this position altogether, declaring a radical distinction between the aims of his sort of theorizing and the aims of empirical inquiry, particularly that oriented to explanation. In contrast to theoretical analysis oriented to "explanation," he insists, his own brand of inquiry is oriented to "discourse."

By discourse, I refer to modes of argument that are more consistently generalized and speculative than normal scientific discussion. The latter are directed in a more disciplined manner to specific pieces of empirical evidence, to inductive and deductive logics, to explanation through covering laws, and to the methods by which these laws can be verified or falsified. Discourse, by contrast, is ratiocinative. It focuses on the process of reasoning rather than the results of immediate experience, and it becomes significant where there is no plain or evident truth. Discourse seeks persuasion through argument rather than prediction. (1988, p. 80)

At several points in this essay, Alexander seems to reaffirm the view that theoretical analysis of the sort he pursues is basically irrelevant to explanation – indeed, to empirical understanding altogether. "Because it is discursive," he writes, for example, "sociology can progress in a narrowly empirical sense without any clear forward movement in more general theoretical terms" (p. 83). To such a remarkable statement, one has to respond, "What justification can be claimed for any sort of theory of social life if it does not afford better, more accurate understandings of empirical material – of events, processes, or forces that bear on human interests?"

Contra Alexander, few if any philosophers of science today would discount the role of nonempirical concepts in theoretical analysis. The idea that empirical "findings" can somehow "build up" without theoretical organization is all but universally held to be absurd. But equally absurd is the notion that theoretical "progress" and the understanding of empirical material are somehow two radically different enterprises. True, we have no hope of making sense of empirical material, without invoking some particular theoretical mind-set. But it ought to be equally obvious that we have little use for theoretical ideas other than as means for understanding the world of social events, arrangements, and processes. No doubt it is feasible, for Alexander or anyone else, to create and pursue a program of theoretical reflection whose elaboration is unconstrained by any form of empirical inquiry. But in the face of such self-referential projects, most working social scientists are bound to ask, "What's in it for us?"

THEORIES OF EVERYTHING

In most of Alexander's writings, it is much easier to grasp what he is against than what he is for. The enduring theme in his commentary on other theorists (except Parsons) is that their systems of analysis are never sufficiently presuppositional or comprehensive. Only gradually does one glimpse the contours of what he considers a suitably general theory. In one statement dealing with this issue directly, he describes the theories he favors as

theories about everything, about "societies" as such, about modernity rather than about any particular modern society, about "interaction" rather than about any particular form or genre of interaction. There are special theories about economic classes, about the middle class, the working class, and the upper class. But a general class theory, for example Marxian theory, combines all these special theories about classes into a single theory about economic development and class relations as such. (1987, p. 3)

What, concretely, would pursuit of this sort of theory entail? No one would dispute that theories differ in the breadth of their reference. But in light of the statements quoted in the previous few pages, Alexander's aspiration to create "theories of everything" seems aimed at something far more debatable than statements of very broad applicability. He seems to seek theories whose success is reckoned strictly in terms of what he calls ratiocination, by their congruence with the sensibilities of the theorist.

The salient principle governing these sensibilities, we have seen, is the quest for generality or comprehensiveness – for a system of reference that has a place for absolutely everything. But does this sort of generality or "bigness" in theoretical development really offer enduring analytic advantage to those not prepared to embrace it as an end in itself? Or does it amount simply to another arbitrary intellectual taste, with no greater prospects of theoretical longevity than others now regarded as little more than theoretical curiosities?

In a famous jibe against certain unimaginitive trends in theory building, Alasdair MacIntyre spun a tale of an investigator who set out to develop a "general theory of holes" (1971, p. 260). This scholar "rejected *ab initio* the – as he saw it – pathetically commonsense view that of the digging of different kinds of holes there are quite different kinds of explanations to be given; why then he would ask do we have the concept of a hole?" MacIntyre's target here was uncritical assertions of theoretical enlightenment on the basis of statistical associations detected in large quantitative data sets. But with a slight twist, his words might apply as well to the quest for total presuppositional generality.

One has to ask whether a theory that aims at characterizing or accounting for the most universal features of social life must not, in the process, sacrifice those qualities that make theory informative in the first place. Would Alexander, for example, counsel pursuit of theoretical questions like the following?

Is the exercise of political power *in general* a source of constraint, or of facilitation, to individual human strivings?

Are religious beliefs and affiliations *in general* sources of stability in social life or sources of change?

Does the growth of industrialism *in general* tend to enhance human welfare or reduce it?

Does education *in general* represent an avenue for rearrangement of social advantage or a means for perpetuating existing stratification patterns?

Posed in such relentlessly general form, such questions can only evoke an exasperated response of "Both!." In fact, they are vacuous, *but only when couched in terms of such total generality*. When the same questions form bases for investigations of specific ranges of empirical material – particular historical periods, specific families of social or political processes, and so on – they become enormously fruitful. We properly find much interest in seeking to distinguish, for example, between periods and settings in American society in which education has served as a mechanism for social mobility versus those where it has served as a brake to the same result. Similarly, theory serves us well when it alerts us to the contrasting stabilizing and destabilizing potentials of religious belief, and points us toward investigation that might reveal when to expect one of these alternatives and when the other. The idea of a bland, one-size-fits-all "theory of everything" in any of these contexts is hardly an attractive alternative to such insights.

So, in his push for totally general theory, Alexander neglects something fundamental – the fact that much of our most valuable knowledge consists of ideal types or models that are, in their nature and purpose, skewed in relation to empirical cases. Their ability to illuminate and organize analyses of specific cases lies precisely in this one-sided, selective character. This is true of theories applied to the most diverse phenomena – ranging from rational-choice models of coalition formation, to functional theories of stratification, to analyses of political movements as the work of Paretian elites, to interpretations of the rise of modern penal institutions as concomitant with new forms of discourse. All such analyses invite us to consider disparities between the pure analytical idea and the richness of specific instances. We do not reject such models because of their partiality, but rather exploit that quality. The paradigms mislead only when their enthusiasts put them forward as general theories, as though those elements of real-world instances that do not fit the ideal type either do not matter or somehow have to be explained away. To reject such models because they are somehow not general enough is to commit the same sort of error in reverse.

CONCLUSION

In the introduction to a recent volume of essays on social trends at the end of the twentieth century, Alexander writes:

> In part because of the strain of continuous warfare, this century has seen the spread of charismatic executive authority on an unprecedented scale. . . . In democratic countries charismatic executive authority has never disappeared. On the contrary, the cult of the personality seems increasingly essential for national integration and effective rational government. (1990, pp. 25–26)

These remarks raise a series of utterly reasonable theoretical questions. Among them are: Has the role of personality cults in national politics indeed grown over the course of this century? Is there reason to believe that such cults are in fact conducive to national unity? Is the trend toward such forms of leadership, if it indeed can be documented, really associated with warfare?

The claim of such questions on our theoretical attention should be obvious, regardless of one's theoretical persuasion. Indeed, their importance should be recognized as much by thoughtful nonspecialists as by professional social scientists. For any answers to such questions – even tentative, provisional answers – are apt to matter in human efforts to *cope* with the processes in question. We have every right to hope, in other words, that knowing more about the connections between charismatic authority and government effectiveness will help us to deal more effectively and realistically with these social forms. If academic research fails to illuminate these questions, the same concerns will have to be taken up by others.

But the kind of inquiry that might yield such insight has little to do with the grand edifice of "presuppositional" theory advocated by Alexander. Here, it would seem, perfection of the conceptual organon of a perfectly general system of theoretical categories represents, not a *means* – for coping, or for anything else – but an end in itself.

The elaboration of this system, the fitting of each element into its place within the conceptual system, can obviously furnish an all-absorbing model of closure for those inclined to pursue it. One can imagine a virtually endless agenda of presuppositional commentary on every aspect of social inquiry. Such commentary would be devoted to demonstrating the failures of most forms of social analysis to invoke the full range of presuppositional possibilities required to fulfill the requirements of the theory. Other efforts might be devoted to specifying additional, previously neglected conceptual elements required to make up a truly comprehensive theoretical system.

The question is, how long should we expect such pursuits to continue? Is there any reason to believe that the distinctive rewards of these forms of insight will prove more enduring than those of other, now extinct theoretical systems? Or will the project considered in this chapter appear in retrospect as another special, and rather peculiar, theoretical taste?

I find it hard to see a role for "general theory" of the sort heralded by Parsons and Alexander in forging a response to what I have termed first-order questions. In its irrelevance to such questions, their worldview seems both overwrought and massively self-absorbed.

5

Network analysis

Network analysis, writes one of its enthusiasts (Knoke 1990), "forms the cutting edge of theory and research" in political studies. "By uncovering these latent deep structures," he continues:

analysts can reveal the subtle ways that power relations shape perceptions, motives, thoughts and actions. Once acquired, the conceptual reorientation required by network thinking about politics cannot be easily relinquished. Social scientists and policymakers alike will come to see the world as a fantastic web of strong and weak connections running from primary groups through organizations, communities, and nations. . . . The new world of political economy is at hand. . . . (1990, p. 232)

These words epitomize the energizing vision of intellectual progress shared by proponents of network thinking. Similar statements could of course be quoted from proponents of countless other theoretical programs. But in the case of network analysis, such claims have recently won particularly wide assent among social scientists. For many, this relatively new theoretical program represents the state of the art, the clearest manifestation of the advance of knowledge in our disciplines.

For the purposes of this book, all of this holds much interest. Network thinking obviously embodies a distinctive model of closure in the sense discussed in Chapter 1. In the last decades of the century, it has attained intellectual sex appeal approaching that of structural functionalism in the 1950s. The question is, does network thinking promise to make a more enduring "contribution" than earlier intense but now less-than-compelling theoretical enthusiasms? Do its special insights promise to furnish to future generations reliable means to enduring analytical ends? Or will its successes, self-evident to so many today, in retrospect appear as a passing theoretical fancy?

One can think of network analysis as a form of knowledge that proceeds by *disaggregation* of complex social wholes into concatenations of discrete connection and nonconnection among elementary social units. These units may be individuals – but they may also be organizations, states, communities, or any number of other social elements. The connections may likewise be defined in many ways: as acquaintance, liking or disliking between persons, trade relations among countries, exchanges of marriage partners between tribes, and so on. Thus, where other analysts might see a neighborhood, a market, or a government institution as a complex, organic, qualitatively unique whole, network thinkers are apt to see something like the following scheme:

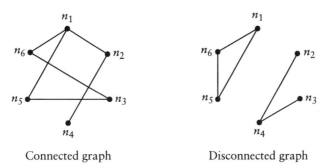

Connected graph   Disconnected graph

Figure 2. A connected graph and a graph with components. From Wasserman and Faust (1994), p. 109.

The patterns of interconnection so identified may be extremely complex in the aggregate. But the individual elements and the linkages between them are specified with austere simplicity.

Much of the appeal of the doctrine seems to derive from this promise of rendering large, complex social structures susceptible to systematic quantitative analysis. Beginning in the 1940s, quantitative methods played an increasing role in the study of labor conflict, public opinion, voting, migration, and many other subjects. Yet the study of large, complex social structures long remained unaffected by the trend. For many thinkers, political power structures, urban communities, international alliances, and the like seemed to require more strictly qualitative, holistic forms of analysis.

To such assumptions, network thinking poses a dramatic challenge. Even the most complex of social wholes, in this view, can be understood in what one might call *molecular* terms – that is, as constituted by specific links (or the absence of links) between elementary social units. By rendering such wholes into collections of discrete elements, and giving exact quantitative expression to the resulting concatenations, network analysis promises to unlock the secrets of the "latent structures" noted in the passage above.

One of the simplest ways to grasp the logic of any analytical principle is to consider its theoretical antithesis. In the case of network thinking, there are a number of contenders for this status. The essential logic of network thinking differs profoundly from that of theories that view social action as shaped by processes of influence disseminated uniformly across large populations. Perhaps the starkest contrast to network models are those derived from *theories of mass action*. This line of thinking had its origins in turn-of-the-century antipopulist reactions against modernity. In this view, modern populations, broken loose from traditional relationships and hierarchies, were pictured as subject to direct stimuli from mass media, demagogic political leaders, or other direct sources of emotion-laden information. Once in the grip of such "mass" influences, in this view, whole populations could have their most basic interests and dispositions to action reshaped simultaneously.

Of interest here are not the antidemocratic obsessions of these theorists, but rather their view of social action itself. For theorists in this tradition, the classic empirical study is Hadley Cantril's *The Invasion from Mars* (1940), an analysis of the response of many credulous radio listeners in 1938 to an imagined portrayal of an interplanetary invasion. The fictional status of this report could easily have been verified, but for hours many listeners in New York and New Jersey accepted it as fact.

The key processes posited by network thinkers differ fundamentally from those of mass influence. In the network view, all action is constrained by microstructures of network connection in which actors are inevitably located. Network thinking does not recognize human populations as "masses." For the network theorist, even apparently undifferentiated populations show, on proper analysis, complex structures of connection and disconnection. Such structures, in turn, shape both the actions of individuals (including their failure to act) and the workings of larger social units in profound and nonintuitive ways. These ever-present but often unnoticed microstructures, for network thinkers, represent something comparable to Durkheim's sui generis level of social reality.

Yet, in another respect, network analysts have drawn quite the opposite theoretical conclusion from many modern followers of Durkheim. Network thinking runs counter to views that explain social behavior as a manifestation of deeply held, universally espoused values, norms, or other internalized principles. Instead, network analysts assume that social behavior depends on the actor's *location* within patterns of social connection and nonconnection. The network mind-set rejects the notion that people will do the same things, or uphold the same principles, regardless of their placement within such systems.

Network analysis

The historical origins of network thinking are more recent than those of many other currently influential theoretical programs. Network thinkers do take some inspiration from the work of Simmel, reading his writings on the dyad and the triad as models of connection and nonconnection in elementary social units. But perhaps the earliest direct intellectual ancestor is the work of Jacob Moreno (1934), founder of "sociometry," the practice of mapping small groups according to their members' reported patterns of liking, disliking, association, or avoidance. The technique was widely applied, both by educationists and by other students of primary groups.

Moreno apart, the most important early chapters in the history of network thinking were works of certain British and European anthropologists. During the 1950s and 1960s, dozens of studies of communities, tribes, and regions analyzed social processes in terms of patterns of dependence, loyalty, and attachment among individuals or families. It appears that this analytical style evolved in part as a reaction against the structural-functionalism prevailing at the time. For the functionalists, social arrangements were "explained" by showing how they contributed to the overall "health" or "efficiency" of the social whole. Such analyses suffered from many difficulties, not least of which was a certain invulnerability to refutation: If prevailing social arrangements are understood to be as they are because of their "contribution," how could one, even in principle, identify a negative case – that is, a social arrangement that remained in place yet *failed* to "contribute?"

Network analysis, by contrast, counts nothing as explained, except insofar as one can identify its causes in specific connections between specific parties. If there is an expressive mystique of network thinking, perhaps it lies in proponents' conviction that their method puts them in touch with concrete, verifiable forces and relationships that actually make social systems tick. This sense of unique access to the "deep structures" of social reality is no doubt enhanced by the nonintuitive quality of network representations. For many, these seem to convey a sense of getting right down to the irreducible molecular or even subatomic level of social reality.

One sees this style of analysis at work in John Barnes's study of a Norwegian fishing community (1954), in J. Clyde Mitchell's accounts of urban life in Africa (1960), or in D. G. Jongmans's study of local politics in Tunisia (1973). In Anton Blok's network study of rural western Sicily, he seeks to explain such processes as the rise and decline of family grouping, changing patterns of law enforcement, and changes in land ownership in terms of specific alliances, obligations, dependencies, and emnities that he documents. In concluding, he writes:

terms such as coalition, social structure, and society may prove useful when we provide them with a meaning which corresponds more closely to what we actually observe. Among other things, this involves the effort to see these social units as formed by individual people linked to one another in numerous ways: the concatenation of the aim-oriented actions of these people results in a fluid pattern of which the course and product are largely unplanned and unforeseen by the very individuals who help bring them about. (1973, p. 163)

These words might be taken as an expression of the essential worldview of network analysis.

Perhaps best known among the early network studies is *Family and Social Network* (1957) by Elizabeth Bott. This work grew out of a survey of the lives of some twenty "ordinary" London families in their early years of child rearing. The survey did not begin as a network analysis. As Bott writes, "We started with no well-defined hypotheses or interpretations and no ready-made methodology and field techniques" (p. 8). Instead, the researchers simply sought to document the microsocial arrangements of families marked by no extreme or troubled qualities of the sort that would have made them foci for studies of social pathology.

Yet in their intensive efforts at description, Bott and her colleagues soon uncovered some provocative network realities. Families differed characteristically, they found, in terms of household division of labor: In some, the customary tasks of husband and wife were quite distinct, while in others both partners did a little of everything. The families where conjugal roles were more segregated generally also tended to exhibit more "traditional" ideas about marriage, attaching less importance to sexual fulfillment, for example. They also tended to be somewhat lower in socioeconomic status, though neither of these associations was perfect.

What struck Bott and her colleagues was the association between role segregation and social networks. The more role-segregated couples reported that they socialized within a circle that was, if not totally "closed," at least composed largely of people who socialized with one another. The families where husband and wife shared each others' tasks, in contrast, reported social contacts that ramified in varying directions, including friends and acquaintances in various and nonintersecting groupings.

Bott explains this association as resulting from the role played by close-knit networks in reinforcing traditional family values (1957, p. 60). This is not the only explanation consistent with the reported evidence; perhaps some unnoted influence had shaped both network pattens *and* family values. But whatever the full details of the reasons for the connection, *Family and Social Network* makes an important point: The position of families within larger social networks may be linked to other basic arrangements of family life, ones that bear no *logical* relationship to network position. Somehow, the microattachments of couples to their social worlds were closely geared to intimate features of their intrafamilial lives.

One might see in this insight the key inspirational theme of the network program. This is the notion that network structures make up an ever-present and potent, but unseen, force in social life. Although it may be unclear what gives these connections their force, as it was in Bott's study, the fact remains that identifying and mapping them yields understanding of causal processes that had previously been hidden.

AMERICAN NETWORK STUDIES

Bott, Mitchell, Barnes, Blok, and other early network analysts did the majority of their work outside the United States. Beginning in the 1960s, work done by Americans came to predominate. Whereas the earlier group were mainly anthropologists and their work mostly qualitative, most American network researchers have been sociologists, and much of their work has been highly quantified.

For many American scholars, it would appear, network thinking took its impetus from the "rediscovery of the primary group," along with concomitant disenchantment with theories of mass action. While mass society theories held great influence in American social science until the 1960s, reaction against them had begun as early as the 1940s.

One manifestation of this reaction – a kind of empirical counterpoint to Cantril's *The Invasion from Mars* – were the early studies of voter behavior carried out by Lazarsfeld and his colleagues (e.g., *The People's Choice* (1968 [1944]). These much noted inquiries made it clear that stimuli propagated through mass media, including both appeals made by candidates and other attempts to sway voters, by no means had a direct and automatic effect on behavior. Rather, voters reported discussing mass messages with their immediate circle, or at least attending to others' remarks on these issues; the views of local opinion leaders and other direct acquaintances acted as a kind of filter or refracting lens to mass stimuli. Thus mass stimuli were hardly *irrelevant* to election behavior; but their force seemed problematic without mediation through what might well be called network microstructures.

A key early network study is the classic investigation by Coleman, Katz, and Menzel (1966) of innovation in medical practice. The authors traced patterns of adoption of a new drug among physicians in several midwestern communities. Network position proved highly predictive of when any given physician would start prescribing the drug. Thus, for example, doctors who were tightly integrated into various networks generally made the switch before their more isolated colleagues.

James Coleman, however, did not continue to produce network research after this one notable study. Since the 1960s, the most influential single figure in American network studies has probably been Harrison White. From his earliest work on kinship, White devoted himself to developing mathematical portrayals of microstructural underpinnings of large-scale social systems. In one of his best-known early studies (1970), for example, White analyzes mobility patterns among Episcopal clergy in America, seeking to identify and analyze patterns of vacancies in the formal structure of church positions – that is, positions in the clerical hierarchy available to be filled by an incumbent. Thus he devotes much attention to determinants of the lengths of such chains, the numbers of positions vacated and filled in the "chain reactions" following the opening and filling of an original vacancy. Note that White defines his subject matter here as the workings of *vacancies,* rather than mobility on the part of individual clerics. "Flow of men alone will not follow any simple, lawful pattern; flow of vacancies may," he writes (p. 244). The statement is emblematic of the determination of network analysts to identify and chart otherwise invisible "deep structures" of social reality.

Partly because of the inaccessibility of his own writing, White has exerted much of his pervasive influence through his many students. The range of subject matters they address is striking, from studies of the social connections leading to securing illegal abortions (Lee 1969) to analyses of occupational mobility (Breiger 1981). The steady stream of sociologists trained by White has significantly changed the face of American sociology since the 1960s.

One of the most noted of the studies originating as a dissertation under White, was Mark Granovetter's *Getting a Job* (1974). Granovetter began with a question that is both theoretically rich and disarmingly direct: What role do personal networks play in peoples' access to jobs? His research strategy was as simple as his question. He interviewed a sample of middle-class men in a Boston suburb about the actual personal events involved in their obtaining the jobs that they currently held. In many cases, he had to overcome respondents' propensity to describe the formal qualifications for the job and the official search procedure followed by the firm. Instead, Granovetter wanted to know *how the jobholder had found out about the vacancy* and, more specifically, *who had put the job seeker in touch with the eventual employer.*

A bit fewer than half of the respondents' jobs, Granovetter found, were obtained through personal networks – that is, from information made available through acquaintances – rather than via mass communications such as newspaper ads or other formal announcements. Often these efficacious network processes yielded jobs in organizations where the candidate had made "cold" inquiries and been told that no jobs were available. Moreover, the jobs acquired through these microstructural processes were generally more desirable (for example, more highly paid) than those allocated through mass processes.

Clearly the network connections at work in Granovetter's sample had distinctive and potent social effects. The ties of acquaintance, often quite circuitous, linking job seeker with eventual employer produced a kind of *information flow* not available through conventional search processes. In many cases, these "inside channels" seemed to provide employers with assurance that the candidate had special qualities that could not be established merely by scrutinizing formal qualifications. Something about the micronetworks in which job seekers were embedded made them better "conductors" of information than the standard "trunk lines" of job information.

Granovetter developed a number of these themes in an article published after completing his dissertation, "The Strength of Weak Ties" (1973). This has become perhaps the best-known single article in the literature of American network studies. As in *Getting a Job,* the key idea is simple but profound: Ties of casual acquaintance in personal networks that are *experienced* as peripheral or secondary may often be more consequential than "strong" ties to family, colleagues, neighbors, and others in the individual's immediate circle; for such "weak" ties are especially likely to connect the individual to information and opportunities that are not generally accessible from his or her normal social orbit. In Bott's terms, loosely knit networks connecting the individual to a variety of social circles may be more efficacious than tightly knit networks, where everyone one knows everyone else.

Comparable in importance to Harrison White as a progenitor of American network studies is Edward Laumann. Laumann and his students have produced an array of ambitious investigations of such diverse phenomena as the formation of legislation and policy in Washington (Laumann and Knoke 1987), political cleavage among elites (Laumann and Marsden 1979), and corporate philanthropy (Galaskiewicz 1985). As in White's work, most of the studies in the Laumann tradition have relied on ambitious mathematical and graphical representations of social networks.

Not all American network studies have aimed at depicting relationships involving formal organization. Many, including some by Laumann and his collaborators (e.g., Laumann and Pappi 1973), describe and analyze structures of acquaintance and affiliation within communities. Notable among these are the works of Wellman (1979) and Fischer (1982), both critical examinations of mass-society visions of modern community life. Is modern life, and especially the cosmopolitan existence of modern cities, characterized by disaffiliation and the absence of social support, as mass-society studies would suggest? As in Granovetter's work, these network analysts followed a disarmingly simple strategy: They interviewed people and inquired about whom they knew, whom they spent various forms of discretionary time with, and whom they turned to for advice, help, or companionship.

Both Wellman and Fischer found a wealth of social contacts in their sample. In Fischer's case, contra the implications of early mass-society writings, urban respondents reported personal networks that were both more extensive and qualitatively more varied than the less urban. Studies like these make it very difficult to accept any categorical notion that modernity brings social isolation.

THE "OR-ELSE" CLAUSE

From the earliest studies by network theorists, it had been clear that this model of closure offered, for those who embraced it, a sweeping and liberating new worldview. For network enthusiasts, like David Knoke in the passage quoted at the beginning of this chapter, familiar institutions and arrangements ceased to appear as organic wholes and reappeared as structures of discrete linkage. Such shifts of perception are a standard concomitant of theoretical change in our disciplines.

But can we recognize more in the rise of network thinking than a simple shift in perceptual set among a group of theoretical enthusiasts? I think we can. Of particular interest here was the trend among researchers from outside the network school to generate network accounts of phenomena of interest to them. Thus, for example, students of social movements reported that patterns of preexisting acquaintance and affiliation had much to do with who got recruited to movement activism – for example, Stark and Bainbridge (1980), McAdam (1986), and Rosenthal et al. (1985).

None of these latter authors seems to have launched his or her investigations with the idea of upholding network thinking; but their investigations of social activism made it apparent that network processes played significant roles in the phenomena they sought to explain. One could argue that those who reported these findings were simply experiencing the expressive contagion of the new theory. But such an interpretation is not particularly plausible. Efforts to explain adherence to social movments, after all, have a long pedigree; one could hardly say that the question itself was generated by the theory.

For the purposes of this book, such developments are straws in the wind. Of central interest here, after all, are the prospects of any theoretical idea to outlast the special flush of expressive triumph associated with its rise. Hence the attention to what I have called the "or-else" clause in theoretical arguments. What does anyone stand to lose, we must ask, in his or her own analytical interest, by ignoring this particular theoretical insight? The fact that network thinking often promises persuasive answers to questions already identified from other theoretical perspectives suggests that one ignores these insights at one's own analytical risk.

Consider Granovetter's study on access to jobs. This work holds special interest precisely because the questions it addresses have been of such sustained concern from so many theoretical perspectives. It is not only that access to employment is a matter of obvious prima facie value relevance. Perhaps even more important in this context is the fact that the familiar processes to which Granovetter gives such an original interpretation are beyond the reach of a major theoretical competitor – namely, economics. He compellingly demonstrates, in other words, that major aspects of job allocation are apt to be governed by network processes qualitatively different from anything described in standard accounts of labor markets and human capital. Whereas economic thinking takes the flow of information about jobs and qualifications for granted, Granovetter shows that certain critical information flows are governed by network position. If this much is granted, it is hard to deny the claim of network thinking to an important place in our store of useful analytical strategies.

Granovetter makes this point explicit in his commentary on status attainment analysis in sociology and its theoretical opposite number in economics, human capital theories. These doctrines model the movement of persons through occupational roles strictly in terms of the individual characteristics of the people involved – for instance, years of education, father's occupation, intelligence scores, and the like. Such models perforce neglect the patterns of social relationships in which job seeking occurs and which, as Granovetter has shown, may have everything to do with the outcomes of such efforts. Although he notes that the path analysis technique central to status-attainment studies "is devoid of theoretical assumptions about social structure," he comments:

it unfortunately lends itself to an atomized conception of individuals, abstracted from their larger socioeconomic context. This bias is so strong that path analysts ascribe to 'luck' any variance that individual variables cannot explain. (1976, p. 126)

But "luck" in such matters, Granovetter notes, need not be considered a theoretical black hole, beyond the reach of further analysis. For there are ample prima facie grounds to suspect that much "luck" of this kind consists of the advantages and disadvantages conferred by network position. If one grants the legitimacy of status-attainment theorists' efforts to account for determinants of social position, then one could scarcely deny the potential relevance of network analysts' contributions to the same questions.

Similar observations hold for studies of community microstructure like those of Fischer and Wellman. The affiliation, or lack of it, prevailing in modern communities has both evident value relevance and a long pedigree in social and political thought. Systematic studies of these issues by network analysts thus command attention whenever social scientists return to these questions – and we have reason to believe such returns will be frequent.

Some qualification is necessary here. In *Getting a Job,* the *precise consequences* of network ties were evident: They made the difference between access to jobs and lack of access. By contrast, studies like Wellman's and Fischer's leave certain questions unanswered concerning the actual social efficacy of the network ties that they document. They demonstrate conclusively that networks of various descriptions *exist* in the communities that they describe. But the methods available to them do not make it possible to compare the *actual force* of such networks with those prevailing in earlier settings. Thus we do not know, for example, to what extent the social constraint imposed by these networks is comparable to what writers like Toennies had in mind, when they wrote of the social solidarities of gemeinschaft. What we do know with certainty, thanks to modern network analysts, is that affiliation is surely not annihilated by modern urban living.

At their best, then, network accounts go a long way toward transcending a hazard that dogs all theoretical programs: the tendency to focus attention on problems whose importance is reckoned only from within the frame of reference of the theory itself. But no theoretical tradition is altogether immune to pressures in this direction. Like all theories, to some degree, network analysis creates its own subject matter in its representation of social systems as concatenations of discrete connections and nonconnections among social units. Inevitably, theoretical insiders find in these distinctive representations a kind of self-evident theoretical importance. In some cases, this perception seems to overwhelm the need to justify that importance in terms of analytical ends that might be shared by outsiders to the theory.

Consider the noted network study of American corporations, *The Power Structure of American Business* by Beth Mintz and Michael Schwartz (1985). Their study seeks to mobilize network thinking to show how banks and other financial institutions exercise power over American business decision making – and, ultimately, American economic life. The authors view corporate boards of directors as units in social networks. Joining these units are links in the form of figures employed by one firm who serve on the boards of others, or who serve simultaneously on boards of two firms – a common pattern, and one readily amenable to quantification. With great thoroughness, Mintz and Schwartz document the composition of hundreds of corporate boards and chart their network linkages.

Mintz and Schwartz rest their claims for the significance of the resulting portrait of American business squarely on an appeal to the theoretical authority of network thinking:

> The single most important theorem of network analysis . . . is that we can discover the content of the relations among social actors by analyzing the shape of their structural relationships. (1985, p. xii)

The authors interpret the network structure adduced from their data as demonstrating what they characterize as *bank hegemony*. Their analyses reveal, as they put it, "that the network of interlocks is largely a structural trace of capital flows, and that it reflects and consolidates financial hegemony" (p. 151). As in Granovetter's study of job allocation, they appear to see the individual serving as the intercorporate "link," as a conduit for *information flow*:

> The exchange of directors between banks and major industrial firms is . . . simultaneously an expression of, and a condition for, efficient planning and execution by bank decision makers. (p. 220)

But, unlike Granovetter, Mintz and Schwartz show little systematic evidence that information flow is either the reason for or the key effect of board membership.

Mintz and Schwartz buttress their argument with elaborate network representations of their corporate data, diagrams of such things as "peaks" and "hubs" formed by linkages among corporate boards. A number of their findings are quite intriguing – for example, the fact that banks and certain other financial institutions are in general more extensively "connected" through shared directors than other firms. For the authors, as one might imagine, this finding adds fuel to the theoretical fire of "bank hegemony."

The trouble with all this is simply the lack of proof of the actual social force of the network ties in question, apart from the theory that the authors invoke. What reason has the reader to believe that the "connectedness" of banks constitutes evidence of their dominance? Such centrality in network position could just as well be interpreted as evidence of the banks' necessity to ingratiate themselves with, and inform themselves about, firms whose business they need. And indeed, other observers (e.g., Edward Herman 1981) note that banks must often compete with one another for scarce business with those over whom, in the view of Mintz and Schwartz, they exercise "hegemony."

Mintz and Schwartz supplement their network analysis with accounts drawn from the press, all to the same ultimate point as their statements quoted above. But their analysis does not really afford the possibility of refutation in its own terms. Thus they discover that certain of the largest American industrial corporations seem relatively free of network ties. But, they conclude: "This isolation should not, however, be confused with independence from all outside influence, especially from the hegemonic leadership of financial institutions" (p. 222). Here as elsewhere, what would appear to be inconsistent findings are simply explained away.

Throughout *The Power Structure of American Business,* the authors ascribe to the network patterns they so painstakingly chart a significance that is apt to seem unwarranted to outsiders to the theory. From the evidence actually presented in the book, it would be more reasonable to conclude that the network "connections" they identify have *no single* interpretation, that the forces leading to such a connection in one case may have rather little to do with those underlying such connections elsewhere. The authors might have clarified some of these ambiguities by a relatively simple step: contacting some of the many living figures with direct inside acquaintance with corporate boards and interviewing them about what transpires in these settings. But the results of such an inquiry would have shared none of the theoretical mystique of network diagrams.

Another instance of drift toward absorption in what I have called "second-order" theoretical questions is evident in *The Organizational State* (1987) by Laumann and Knoke. Like the work by Mintz and Schwartz, this is in many ways an impressive piece of research, especially in its rigorous detailing of the network patterns that the authors identify. The networks they portray are complex patterns of mutual assistance and opposition, information exchange, and mutual engagement in specific policy issues (usually proposed legislation) among the 333 energy and health-policy organizations. As in *The Power Structure of American Business,* however, these authors often seem to base claims for the meaningfulness of the networks that they document largely on the authority of network theory itself.

A simile often invoked by Laumann and Knoke is the *crystalline structure* of the relationships they chart. For example:

> Returning to the analogy of breaking a crystal, we know that given the structure of the crystal, how it splits depends on the strength and precise incidence of the chisel blow. Similarly, much of the strategic action of event participants, including even the question of who decides to participate and on what side, concerns the negotiation of how the issue will be framed so that it selectively energizes the interests and actions of certain domain members in behalf of particular outcomes and discourages others from entering the deliberations. (p. 322)

Laumann and Knoke devote much effort to presenting statistical and pictorial representations of this "crystalline structure." Much of this portrayal takes the form of graphs representing similarity and dissimilarity among organizations in terms of distance and direction on a kind of sociological "map." And indeed, these painstakingly developed visual models do generally show that organizations linked by the exchange of information or assistance prove to be on the same sides of policy controversies.

The authors' efforts leave no doubt that network techniques can be used to represent the sort of complex reality under study; it is equally clear that the representations so developed depict propensities to act in the policy process. But it often remains unclear how any of their analyses alter our existing theoretical understanding of policy-making, or of social systems more generally. Often the payoffs of their investigations, once stated, seem flat and unremarkable:

our argument is that a set of issues possesses differing levels of commonality with respect to each other that are based on conceptual, institutional and/or sociopolitical similarities and differences. To understand the unfolding issue development of a policy domain, one must be able to characterize the structure of commonality among such a set of issues. (p. 111)

Or,

With respect to event linkages, we suggest [the following] . . . proposition . . . : events with similar characteristics tend to attract the same set of actors. (p. 293)

The Organizational State offers many statements like these. One does not doubt their truth, but rather their claims on our attention. One cannot help feeling that the authors have produced the most sophisticated of analytical weaponry, then used it to shoot theoretical small game.

At issue here is the justification, and the rewards, for invoking network analysis. In works like those of Granovetter, Fischer, and Wellman, I have argued, those rewards can readily be reckoned from outside the frame of reference of the network Weltanschauung. For *The Organizational State*, such a case is harder to make. Insofar as one defines network structures as ipso facto important, Laumann and Knoke's work represents a substantial contribution. But if one asks, as a theoretical outsider, why one needs to invoke the analytical tools that they develop and employ, the answer is less clear-cut. From this perspective, interest in the "crystalline structures" depicted in *The Organizational State* appears more as a special taste, induced by the theory that produces the network representation in the first place.

But such limitations are by no means inherent to the theory. The most impressive studies succeed in showing that network thinking does much more than merely furnish a coherent and comforting model of closure for those who embrace it. More compellingly, they make it clear that this form of analysis illuminates social constraints and forces whose interest, even to outsiders to the theory, would be hard to mistake.

Part II

Consider Mark Mizruchi's *The Structure of Corporate Political Action* (1992). Inspired in part by the Mintz and Schwartz work, this is also a study of network relations and political action among American corporations. Yet Mizruchi's work transcends a number of the earlier work's self-referential arguments, providing well-documented answers to certain questions left unanswered there.

Mizruchi frames his work in terms of the long-standing debates over pluralism in American politics. Is power in the United States more aptly described as multicentric and dispersed or as concentrated and monolithic? With regard to the role of big business, the key question becomes one of how concentrated and concerted business is as a force in political life. Do American corporations act as a cohesive, class-conscious community of interest, Mizruchi asks, or is their impact on political process dispersed and self-canceling?

Mizruchi analyzes data from a sample of fifty-seven large U.S. manufacturing firms in the early 1980s, detailing both their linkages to other companies and their political activities. Much as in the Mintz and Schwartz study, network relations among the companies are a key variable. "Direct interlocks" are defined as instances where a figure from one company sits on another company's board of directors. "Indirect interlocks" occur where one of a number of large banks and insurance companies "have direct interlocks with both manufacturing firms in the dyad" (1992, p. 108).

The special accomplishment of Mizruchi's study is his analysis of the relations beween network position and actual corporate political behavior. With considerable care and ingenuity, he develops measures for such variables as similarity in corporate contributions to political campaigns and causes, and corporate testimony before congressional committees. Network relationships between firms often prove to be more successful predictors of political action than such variables as common ownership of stock or location in same industrial sector (p. 139). Among the strongest predictors of similarity in contributions to political action committees (PACs), for example, were indirect interlocks among pairs of companies. Thus, companies who supported similar political interests were highly likely to share directors via banks and insurance companies.

These findings include some intriguing and unexplained insights into interlocks. In the analyses of contribution to PACs, for example, it was *in*direct linkages that predicted similar political behavior; the effect of direct interlocks was much less and not statistically significant. By contrast, in analyses of agreement in congressional testimony, the two forms of connection played a similar role, and a potent one (p. 169). Mizruchi speculates about the explanation for such patterns, but evidence from his study does not provide conclusions on these matters.

The Structure of Corporate Political Action is also perforce inconclusive on the question with which Mizruchi originally framed his study: the dispersed versus concentrated character of corporate influence over American political life. He shows that major corporations are often allied in their overt political designs, occasionally at odds, and often just playing in quite different political arenas. These analyses simply do not have any unique or salient implication for the role of business as a whole in American political life. The study demonstrates hardly anything like class-wide solidarity, for example. Yet it leaves no doubt that companies do cooperate on the political front, even in the absence of obvious short-term interest. Where such coordination does occur, some form of network relation is often associated with it.

The more striking accomplishment of Mizruchi's work is his demonstration of the potency of network thinking as an analytical strategy. He demonstrates that network affiliations represent a predictor in their own right of important outcomes – independent of an array of other determinants of a more familiar sort. The *reasons* for the significance of these ties, it should be noted, remain to be explained. Where indirect interlocks (via banks and insurance companies) prove to be strong predictors, for example, what accounts for the association? Does it represent evidence of "hegemony" by financial interests, as Mintz and Schwartz seem to believe? Or does it suggest that some prior interest or constraint moves these firms *both* to accept directors from the same institution *and* to contribute to the same PACs – to take just one possibility? And why the difference between the role of direct and indirect interlocks in these cases versus other forms of political action, such as congressional testimony, where the two forms played a much more similar predictive role? Such questions cannot be answered from the sorts of data that Mizruchi has assembled. But the conclusions he does reach matter a great deal.

Mizruchi's is just one of a number of studies demonstrating that network relations *matter* in shaping outcomes of much interest – interest defined as much from the standpoint of outsiders to network thinking as from within. Another strong case here is Ronald Burt's work on structural equivalence. Like other network thinkers, he focuses on "structural action" – defined as "behaviors performed in the pursuit of structural interests" (1982, p. 332) – as an alternative to action taken on the basis of internalized normative commitments. In a long series of studies, he has shown how actors occupying similar positions in network structures are likely to show similar patterns of action. The reasons for this, he holds, have to do with the ways in which *contingencies* of action (in the sense of this term often used by rational-choice thinkers) are shaped by network position.

Thus, in a reanalysis of data from the classic study by Coleman, Katz, and Menzel of drug adoption by physicians, Burt (1987) entertains two models for the process underlying such adoption – what he terms models of *cohesion* versus ones of *structural equivalence*. Burt accepts the earlier authors' finding that network position predicts timing of acceptance of the new drug among physicians in a single community. His question is, what is the precise mechanism that causes adopters in similar network positions to resemble one another in their adoption behavior? Is such similarity a function of solidarity among people in similar positions, such that actors follow the example of their immediate peers and hence end up doing things at about the same time? Or is the mechanism one in which actors in similar positions (who may not even know one another) respond to similar cues at similar points?

By careful analysis of the exact timing of innovation, Burt shows that structural equivalence offers the better account. It appears that the physicians in the population were responding to (perhaps unintended) cues as to when figures like themselves should find it appropriate to act. In other works, Burt develops similar structural-equivalence arguments about the behavior of corporations (Galaskiewicz and Burt 1991), the use of sociological methodologies (1982, chap. 6), and a variety of other forms of action.

Considerably more remains to be understood about exactly how such effects occur. Are the actors in effect imitating the actions of others in the same position as themselves, as competitors often do in business and other settings? If so, how can those in similar structural positions (but not united by ties of acquaintance) be expected to know about one another's actions? Or are the structurally equivalent actors simply responding to similar sorts of options with similar resources for action? Or is there some still different account to be given, or perhaps a variety of different accounts for different instances of structural equivalence?

However these questions may be answered, the point made by Burt and students of other forms of network equivalence commands attention. These studies, like Mizruchi's and many others, establish not just that complex social systems can be represented in network terms, but also, and more importantly, that relationships defined strictly in these terms relate (often in nonintuitive ways) to other social states of evident analytical interest.

CLAIMS TO GENERALITY: NETWORK NOMINALISM AND NETWORK REALISM

The term "social structure" exercises an evidently irresistible attraction for theorists. It has been appropriated by analysts of virtually every theoretical persuasion to describe what they perceive as the most basic, the most fundamental social forces or relationships – the "bedrock" level of social reality. But what theorists *mean* when they speak of social structure varies almost as widely as social theory itself.

Thus, in the work of Parsons "social structure" refers to the systems of ultimate values presumed to underlie and sustain any viable system of social interaction. Peter Blau, of rather different theoretical persuasions, means by social structure "the distribution of people among different social positions" (1978, p. 27). For most Marxists, social structure is apt to mean some aspect of class structure. For followers of Lévi-Strauss, by contrast, the essential structures of social life are cultural mind-sets that set the terms for all social action. And of course, network thinkers are hardly immune to these temptations; they often refer to their work as "structural analysis."

David Knoke (1990, pp. 16–17) catalogs various of these "structuralisms." Their sheer variety reminds us that the language of theoretical analysis is endlessly tendentious. Of course, if what is at stake is simply an arbitrary choice of terms, no harm is done. But in many cases, the mind-set that gives rise to the terminology also leads to an insistence on defining *other* social forces, patterns, or levels of analysis as secondary, derivative, or epiphenomenal. Consider the words of an ethnomethodologist upholding her own view of what constitutes the ultimate social "structure":

> By bracketing a priori assumptions about social phenomena, relationships, and even outcomes, the investigator can go and look at the world and observe what is happening in a rigorously empirical manner. . . . Through the microscope, one can see glimpses of the fine structure. (Boden 1990, p. 191)

The inclination to consider one's chosen form of "social structure" as *the* bedrock level of social reality represents an occupational hazard of theoretical social science.

To their credit, network analysts seem less prone to such self-absorption than proponents of other theories. Occasionally, however, one does encounter manifestos that portray network structures as *the ultimate* social reality – and, at least by implication, bracket other forces and processes as illusory or epiphenomenal. For example,

> presently existing, largely categorical descriptions of social structure have no solid theoretical grounding; furthermore, network concepts may provide the only way to construct a theory of social structure. . . .

The authors accordingly suggest that

> the stuff of social action is, in fact, waiting to be discovered in the network of interstices that exist outside the normative constructs and the attribute breakdowns of our everyday categories. (White, Boorman, and Breiger 1976, pp. 732–733)

Taken to the extreme, such views would imply what might be called *network realism* – the notion that networks constitute a priori the essential social reality.

In most cases, fortunately, analysts in this tradition seem more inclined to embrace what might be called network nominalism. That is, they assume that the nature and significance of network relations can only be judged in relation to the particular analytical tasks at hand, and that the very notion of "network structure" takes on value only through imaginitive application.

There are good grounds for adopting such low-key assumptions. One is that the *content* of relations laid bare by network analyses is hardly uniform from case to case. Indeed, many notable studies in the network genre never fully identify what it is about network connections that create observed associations.

In the case of Bott's study of London families, for example, the authors posit that close association with kin created patterns of influence that reinforced traditional values. This interpretation is plausible but hardly conclusive; in fact, the evidence collected by Bott and her associates simply does not suffice to demonstrate *why* networks have the important associations documented in the research. Similar questions arise about many other informative network analyses – for example, those discussed above by Mizruchi. Here, too, the study makes it clear that network position is highly associated with certain forms of political action of evident analytical interest. But it is by no means clear how or why these associations work as they do. Why, for example, do *indirect* interlocks predict similarity of contributions to political action committees so much more strongly than direct interlocks? What is the precise content or mechanism of interlock influence at work in cases like these? Available evidence simply does not afford answers here, though such questions are hardly unanswerable in principle.

In other network studies, the mechanisms giving force to network connections are far less obscure. In the case of Granovetter's study of job mobility, it is clear that networks of acquaintance mattered because they afforded transmission of rare and highly pertinent information about vacancies and qualifications. Yet there is no reason to believe – and much to doubt – that all network processes gain their force from this sort of mechanism. In other studies (e.g., Blok 1973), what makes networks important is their role as systems of organization of obligations, antagonisms, or alliance. My point is simply that there is no one "content" to network relations; the essential logic of the approach is to identify patterns of connection and nonconnection, not to specify a single form of causality operating within those connections.

To put matters a little differently, the relationships understood to constitute networks may be defined in the most various ways. Among individuals, these might include patterns of liking or disliking, acquaintance, sexual contact, communication, alliance and antagonism, and so on. Among larger social units, the possible defining bases for network construction are at least as various: economic exchange, joint action, the exchange of personnel (as in studies of corporate boards), for example. The art (and perhaps also the science) of network analysis clearly lies in identifying the particular sort of tie in the particular sort of system that matters for outcomes of analytical interest. At its best, network analysis does much more than simply demonstrate that networks (in the form of crystalline structures or corporate interlocks or any other) are *there,* that the social world can be represented in terms of such relationships. The doctrine wins its greatest intellectual victories by showing that these connections *matter* in far-reaching ways to outcomes of widely shared interest. But attaining such informative results demands the verve necessary to grasp *what kind* of network ties are apt to matter in *which circumstances.*

All of this is simply to say that network structures are "made, not born" – made, that is, by the ingenuity of the analyst in defining precisely *what form* of network relations matter in a particular context, and to what effect. Thus network thinkers will do best, not by assuming the existence of some unique deep structure that *must* be present and *must* represent the master principle for analysis of any subject matter. Instead, they should ask, "Of all the possible networks in terms of which this subject matter might be represented, which are most likely to have a bearing on states or outcomes of wide analytical interest?"

CONCLUSION

Enthusiasts of network analysis, like those of other theoretical programs, often approach their work with a certain missionary zeal. This is hardly unusual. Every successful new theory appears to its adherents to fulfill precisely the suddenly recognized needs that alternative mind-sets leave unfulfilled. But for present purposes, the essential question is what elements of the theory, if any, promise to *last?* Which show the best prospects to provide widely needed tools of analysis once the enthusiasm that attends the rise of every new theoretical program subsides?

Perhaps the best way to begin answering such a question is to consider the limits of the theory. What sorts of social facts, situations, or processes are *unlikely* to be illuminated by network analysis? What kinds of insight should we *not* expect this approach to provide?

One such domain, I would suggest, consists of processes of mass influence, those modeled by theories sometimes considered the theoretical antithesis of network thinking. These are processes in which socially salient information from a central source reshapes the action potentials of broad publics by direct, unmediated transmission. Examples are instances where news of a single dramatic event brings about parallel changes in the consciousness of large populations more or less at once. I am convinced that such events and processes do occur and that, in their pure form, they manifest dynamics different from those modeled by network theory.

This is not to suggest that network thinking has no role to play in understanding the absorption of widely diffused stimuli by large populations. The theory obviously focuses on mediation of such information flows through specific social relationships – by discussion with "opinion leaders," for example. But it would be disastrous to imagine that these are the only forms of transmission worthy of attention.

One can easily imagine dramatic disseminations of public information via "mass" media having direct effects on social behavior, often quite sweeping ones. Examples include the assassination or resignation of a president, terrorist acts of mass destruction, or the trials of those charged with notorious crimes. Sometimes the effects of these events can be sweeping enough to override and even rearrange established social structures – including network structures. A case in point might be the new networks of affiliation created when members of "mass" publics reach out to others with whom they have had no preexisting ties. One thinks of grass-roots groups that occasionally form through telephone "networks" constituted for the first time when people contact someone who has taken a well-publicized stand on some controversial issue.

Or consider the social and political realignments in America that ensued in the immediate aftermath of the assassination of Dr. Martin Luther King, Jr., in April of 1968. Just before that event, proponents of a key civil rights bill were facing stubborn resistance from conservatives in the Congress. Then came the assassination, followed by days of rioting by black inner-city dwellers, leaving at least forty-six dead and vast property damage. Among the immediate results was speedy passage of the legislation whose prospects in Congress had previously been highly uncertain, along with other establishment gestures toward black Americans.

To understand these processes, one must look to theoretical ideas like Park's notions of "the public" or Durkheim's concept of *conscience collective*, rather than, say, to network maps of the "crystalline structures" of political decision making under more settled conditions. The point is not that such structures never matter for any analytic purpose. It is that their precise efficacy is subject to reshaping, sometimes drastic, by forces that are strictly speaking *holistic* – felt with similar, direct impact throughout large social aggregates.

I do not suggest that network thinkers categorically deny the existence of mass dynamics like those posited above. But it is important to acknowledge that such dynamics constitute an important body of forces and processes that are qualitatively quite distinct from those modeled by network thinking.

For all sorts of analytic purposes, disaggregation is a useful strategy. Network thinking exploits one version of this strategy. Another version, with its own distinctive analytical successes, is rational-choice theory. But for either of these views to serve, a certain stability is required in the identities and action potentials of the fundamental units of analysis. It must be assumed, in other words, that the premises of rational calculation or that the force and configuration of network ties are enduring enough so that the principles identified as crucial at one moment continue to govern action at later points.

Often such assumptions are eminently reasonable. In Granovetter's study of job access, all the population studied were (quite properly) considered to have been motivated job seekers. What formed the basis for Granovetter's striking explanation of job access, of course, was variability in access to certain relationships and, hence, information flows. But imagine an instance where job seekers were to be swept up in a mass conversion to a charismatic religious faith, and for this reason would foreswear any participation in such worldly processes as job markets. Where the basic action-dispositions of individual units (whether natural persons or organizations) change so abruptly and sweepingly, network thinking (or rational-choice analysis) may not provide much guidance as to what will happen next.

Such dramatic mass transformations of social consciousness are obviously rare – which is by no means to say that they are theoretically unimportant. But at a more pedestrian level, alteration of unit properties through public redefinition of social situations is ubiquitous. If political issues were decided *solely* by the activation of relatively enduring network connections – or for that matter, by rational calculation – political life would not be marked by the pervasive rhetorical clangor, hype, and demonstrativeness that are so familiar. The holistic, dramaturgical processes are more consequential in certain kinds of political contexts than others – more in electoral campaigns, for example, than in backroom caucuses. But no analyst can afford to ignore them altogether, and disaggregative methods are not always the most fruitful means for unlocking them.

Or consider the analysis of another complex social process: the actions of a military unit under combat. A number of sociological investigations – notably, *The American Soldier* (Stouffer et al. 1949, p. 110) – have shown how something very like network forces sustain soldiers under pressure. Indeed, according to that account, some combatants might more accurately have been described as fighting to uphold the solidarity of their unit rather than to support the (perhaps rather vaguely recognized) higher purposes of the war effort. And insofar as this is true, network analysis might well be indispensable to gauging the strength and responsiveness of a unit under fire.

But it is equally true that every effective military force must for some purposes be governed by principles more like those of mass action than those of network affiliation. When a commander issues an order to attack – or indeed, any other command requiring quick action under pressure – all those subject to the command are expected to respond at once, without regard to the specific relationships to others involved, or lack of them. No military unit would long survive if its response to such a command resembled that of the physicians studied by Coleman et al. (1966) to the availability of a new drug – that is, with varying degrees of promptitude, according to the closeness of their integration in informal networks.

It should be clear that the point of these examples is by no means to "debunk" network thinking, in the sense of minimizing its strengths in the domains of its clear applicability. My concern is simply to deflect any version of what I have called "network realism" – that is, the conviction that network structures and forces could somehow be taken as the only, or ultimate, manifestation of social reality. Not all consequential social states and processes are susceptible to network accounts. Even if the network structure of an army unit and a church bureaucracy are isomorphic with one another, one should hardly expect identical performances from the two. Let us hope that network thinkers, in the flush of their theoretical success, do not lose sight of such distinctions.

With these qualifications, the prospects of certain network ideas to represent a lasting "contribution" appear strong. For the purposes of this work, the key insights of the theory appear to meet two crucial tests: First, they point to forces, relationships, and dependencies that promise to prevail not just in transitory contexts, but in a wide variety of past, present, and future settings. Second, the forces and processes so illuminated are ones likely to continue to engage analytic interest for considerable time to come. Subjects like the allocation of people to jobs, or the extent and form of social relationships within communities, or the mechanisms of diffusion of innovation appear to me unlikely to be matters of indifference to future thinkers – regardless of inevitable changes in the social, political, and cultural contexts of analytical work. And network thinking has every prospect of continuing to provide tools for understanding such things that are not available from other theoretical sources.

What *form*, then, will the theoretical inheritance from today's network analysts to future generations be likely to take? For some observers, the optimal intellectual payoff might appear as a series of reliable quantitative formulas, easily applicable to any social setting and offering reliable prediction of future outcomes in the most diverse contexts. The mental image guiding such expectations might be the fundamental certainties given in Newton's laws of conservation of energy, or in formulas on relations between temperature, pressure, and volume of gasses.

But I do not think it reasonable to expect this sort of outcome. The essential insights of network thinking, I have argued, represent a source of promising hypotheses or informed hunches, along with a kit of sophisticated strategies and methods for pursuing these possibilities. What they do not offer are invariant formulas. Network analysis will always succeed or fail according to the individual imagination of the analyst in applying network ideas to new subject matters. Both the units of analysis in such efforts and the definition of what constitutes linkage will most likely always require imaginative intepretation by an analyst who remains close to his or her subject matter.

It seems likely, for example, that structural equivalence (and other forms of network equivalence) will retain their analytical utility well into the future. But I do not think that we shall ever see a useful "general theory of structural equivalence" that can be applied without considerable adaptation to local contexts. The same can be said for the role of personal acquaintance in labor markets, or board membership among corporations, or many other social settings. The exact role and importance of network relations for understanding such subjects, it seems to me, will always be dependent on a host of contextual factors.

Thus I believe we should regard network thinking as a kind of theoretical hunting license, or perhaps as a series of promising strategies for tracking big theoretical game, rather than a source of certainties. Perhaps this is the most that we should expect of any theory.

6

Feminist analysis in social science

JAMES RULE AND LESLIE IRVINE

Many social scientists of other theoretical persuasions, one suspects, find it difficult to recognize in feminist analysis a "theory" in the same sense as their own. Much work done in the feminist tradition is bound to strike outsiders more as the expression of a political mood or the affirmation of a set of embattled values than as a distinct analytical position.

But for present purposes, the similarities between feminist thinking and other approaches are more important than the differences. And many of the differences appear, on closer consideration, to be simply ones of degree. True, feminist social science differs from other theoretical programs considered here in its obvious links with a major social movement. In this respect feminist thinking more closely resembles certain Marxist and populist views than it does strictly academic theories. But even the most abstract and purely academic theories clearly show elective affinities to distinctive value positions on matters of social and political practice – vide the documented inclinations of neoclassical economists toward calculative, individualistic approaches to social relations noted in Chapter 3.

As with other theoretical programs, feminist social science has come as a powerful, energizing, formative intellectual experience to those who embrace it. Feminist analysis promises, for its enthusiasts, to provide exactly what is most seriously lacking in other forms of understanding. It promises to offer more far-reaching, more veridical alternatives to "standard" social science. All of this adds up to a vision of intellectual progress.

True, many feminist social scientists would probably disclaim any association of their work with "scientific" models of intellectual cumulation. "I . . . don't put much credence in positivist, cumulative, 'objective science' notions of 'progress,'" wrote one noted feminist sociologist, commenting on plans for this book (Barrie Thorne, personal communication). And indeed, skepticism of "standard" science as a model of theoretical inquiry is widespread among feminist analysts – though hardly universal.

Yet all feminist social scientists would surely want to affirm that their approach yields improved understanding of the social world. For many of them, it would not be too much to say that the distinctive insights of feminism mark the most dramatic advance in social analysis in recent history – in short, as much "a step ahead" as the advances claimed for other theoretical programs. The force of such perceptions, and the numbers of thinkers moved by them, make feminist analysis a natural focus for the concerns of this book.

FEMINISM: THEORY AND SOCIAL MOVEMENT

It hardly takes a specialist to note that feminist social science has been borne to prominence by the same cultural and social forces that have shaped the fortunes of the movement more generally. And for many (if not all) of its proponents, the value of feminist theory is inextricably bound up with the pursuit of movement goals. "Feminist research must be part of a process by which women's oppression is not only described but challenged," goes one typical statement (Gorelick 1991, p. 462).

Clearly the view of feminist inquiry as a tool for the advancement of the social movement has played a key role in shaping the doctrine. At stake in the movement are both symbolic and material interests. In terms of the latter, the success of feminist activism has led to the staffing of courses, the making of appointments, and the creation of academic programs – in short, the full set of arrangements that mark institutional success within the academy.

The objectives of the movement are no less apparent in symbolic terms. Feminism is after all, among other things, a status movement. Feminist thinking, both inside the academy and out, aims to uphold the public worth and honor of certain forms of experience, certain roles, or certain forms of social action over and against others. Just as classic Marxism effectively extols the provider of labor, as Veblen upheld the role of the engineer, and as rational-choice thinking implicitly endorses the social contribution of the entrepreneur, so feminist thinking serves to uphold a certain vision of the role and contributions of women.

Thus the expressive valences, the symbolic and material payoffs of feminist analysis, are more conspicuous than those of many other theoretical programs in social science. The question is, what relation do these bear to the strictly analytic content of the program?

We emphasize these concerns at the outset, because of the dual status of feminism as a form of mobilization and as a form of analysis. As we shall argue in concluding this chapter, the feminist movement of the late twentieth century will inevitably pass through a life cycle like those of other social movements. Our key concern, for feminist social science as for other theoretical programs, lies with the long-term intellectual "contribution" of the doctrine. What ideas distinctive to feminist analysis – what strategies of inquiry, findings, principles of analysis – are apt to hold the attention of social scientists as intellectual and social contexts change?

How would feminist social scientists characterize their essential theoretical inspiration? If one were to cite a single, empirically relevant idea, it would no doubt be the following: that women's roles, experiences, and views have been systematically neglected in earlier theoretical programs; that such exclusion is a concomitant of pervasive gender inequality and a source of grave gaps in understanding; and that the role of feminist analysis is to correct these distortions and reform the male-dominated intellectual apparatus that gave rise to them.

The neglect at stake here is seen as much more subtle and far-reaching than a simple refusal to study and write about women. It is more a pervasive and systematic failure to acknowledge or focus on the reality and importance of women's roles, experiences, and viewpoints. Such failures in the analyses of social scientists are simply concomitant of much broader distortions pervasive in culture.

Consider a feature article that appeared in The *New York Times* (31 January 1993, 13LI, p. 2), entitled "On the Farm, Stress Grows like a Weed." The story detailed the punishing and anxiety-provoking routines of a farm couple, emphasizing the long hours, hard work, and chronic uncertainties of their way of life. "It's enough to send a farmer's wife to a stress-manager's workshop," commented the writer, Diane Ketcham. A reader later commented that, given that the article demonstrated the similarities both of the demands on the couple and of their exertions, it would surely have made more sense to describe the woman as one of two farmers rather than as "a farmer's wife."

Such "invisibility" of women's actual social roles has exact parallels in social science. In 1963, for example, a team from the Middle East Technical University (Ankara) conducted a survey of labor activity in a Turkish village in the province of Bursa (METSU 1963). Finding no productive labor during the month of February, the researchers characterized this as the "slack" season. Later, however, an ethnographer visited the same village and made a quite different observation (Magnarella 1979). Though men indeed spent most of the month in the coffeehouses, women's labor was hardly "slack." In addition to the cooking, cleaning, weaving, washing, spinning, and other household work done year around, the women also devoted special time during the winter months to certain handcraft activities. As a feminist analyst commented on the two studies, "The most 'invisible' form of labor is that which is exclusively female" (Isvan-Hayat 1986, p. 4).

The consequences and implications of such systematic distortion, feminists agree, are far-reaching and often far from obvious. One such consequence is that the experience of being a woman is fundamentally different from that of being a man. The assumption here is that "one is not born a woman but, rather, becomes one." Feminist thinkers note that the very concept of "woman," as well as women's roles, life chances, self-perceptions, and the like, all originate in specific social processes that can be unraveled with the proper analysis. As with Marxism and other theories linked to the interests of specific social groupings, the task is to countervail against these systematic deformations of social life by making them apparent.

By contrast, one can also identify what might be termed the diametrically opposite assumption: the notion that differences between the sexes in experience, behavior, or social position are somehow fixed – determined by genetic heritage, physical capabilities, or other inborn endowments. When these forces are held to be immutable, as in the inevitability of patriarchy argument made by Wilson (1975, 1978), Tiger (1969), Fox (1971), and Goldberg (1974), this view has served to portray gender inequality as part of the "natural" social order.

Thus the origin of a major element of the agenda of feminist analysis: the effort to identify and account for the processes by which differences between the sexes have arisen and are perpetuated, and how they have come to result in inequalities of advantage. This topic has been a prolific source of debate as different theoretical strains within feminism have identified different explanations for gender inequality. For some analysts, for example, the key cause lies in male control of the systems of production and reproduction (Firestone 1970; Mitchell 1971; Rubin 1975; Harding 1981; Hartmann 1976, 1981). Others see deformations of language or discourse as the key mechanisms perpetuating patriarchy (Fishman 1983; Irigaray 1977; Wittig 1981; Scott 1988; Tannen 1990). Each of these positions, of course, has its own distinctive implications for the social action necessary to bring about true equality between the sexes. Debates among their proponents have often been highly charged.

THE INTELLECTUAL EVOLUTION

Feminist social science traces its theoretical inspiration directly from some classic statements of twentieth-century feminism. These include Virginia Woolf's *A Room of One's Own*, Simone de Beauvoir's *The Second Sex*, and Betty Friedan's *The Feminine Mystique*. None of these are works of theoretical social science in the sense of central interest here. Yet they share in embracing, implicitly or explicitly, the three premises noted above.

Our central interest in this chapter lies with the repercussions of such ideas in the systematic study of social life. By this we mean the agenda for empirical social inquiry, the assumptions and principles organizing such inquiry, and the vision of analytical success associated with these elements: in short, both the research agenda inspired by feminist social science and the principles, rationales, and organizing assumptions that give research its sense and direction.

One of the earliest feminist works in social science, strictly speaking, was Mirra Komorovsky's *Women in the Modern World* (1953), an indictment of the limitations imposed by women's roles. Another early landmark was Alice Rossi's "Equality between the Sexes" (1964). This is a critique of functionalist defenses of the restriction of women to separate spheres of social life; ahead of her time, she called for innovations in education, housing, and child care to facilitate equality between the sexes. Both these authors wrote at a time when there was not yet a women's movement to address.

Another notable example of early feminist scholarship, coming just as the movement was taking form, was Cynthia Fuchs Epstein's *Woman's Place* (1970). Subtitled *Options and Limits in Professional Careers,* this influential work detailed the social forces weighing against women's pursuit of distinction and accomplishment in professional careers. Soon Epstein's book was joined by an series of analyses of women's position in corporations (Kanter 1977), science (Reskin 1978), the family (Skolnick 1979), and a variety of other settings. In anthropology, Sally Linton (1971) attacked the validity of evolutionary theories that ignore or diminish women's contributions to early human groups. By the end of the 1970s, the position seemed widely accepted in American social science that gender inequality was the product of distinctive social processes, and that the analysis of these processes represented a legitimate task for social scientists.

Most of these early studies relied on methods and intellectual strategies that were standard in social science at the time. Kanter's studies of the corporation, for example, drew on field research and participant observation techniques familiar to all students of organizations; Reskin's studies of scientific productivity relied on familiar techniques of quantitative analysis. Observing this pattern, one might imagine that feminist analysis fits relatively gracefully within existing structures of inquiry, pursuing a broader range of concerns yet relying on standard research modes of the disciplines. Such approaches have more recently been dubbed "feminist empiricism" (Harding 1986).

As years passed and feminism became established within the academy, many feminist social scientists grew critical of standard research methods and strategies. The notion that the familiar analytic structures of social inquiry might escape virtually unscathed from the revolutionary claims of feminism became altogether suspect. In what quickly became a catch-phrase, the less revolutionary vision of feminist empiricism was described as urging the discipline to "add women and stir" (D. Smith 1974).

By the 1980s, such supplementing of standard social science fare no longer sufficed for many. Whereas in the 1970s, the study of women had itself counted as a bold departure, by the 1980s, the feminist community was questioning epistemological assumptions in general and those under-lying knowledge about women in particular. Many held that the familiar intellectual structures of social science represented barriers to the explora-tion of women's interests. What these thinkers sought was a fundamen-tally new mode of inquiry, one that would apply the insights of feminist thought to *all* social science, thus transforming all forms of social inquiry.

To this end, many feminist analysts turned to variants of the relativist epistemologies noted in Chapter 2 – including constructivist, postmodern and "postempirical" approaches. Some took discourse analysis a la Foucault as a key inspiration (Scott 1988; Fisher and Davis 1993); others embraced Marxist-influenced cultural studies (McRobbie 1978, McRob-bie and McCabe 1981; Press 1991) and participatory or "interactive" research methods (Kleiber and Light 1978; Oakley 1981).

But this revolt against established paths of thought poses problems of its own. Feminist social scientists have hardly spoken with one voice on matters of epistemology and conceptual organization. The various insur-gent positions share a mistrust of standard intellectual strategies and epis-temologies; but what they propose to substitute are themselves a mutually heterogeneous and not necessarily compatible array of intellectual programs.

These alternative positions share with feminist analysis more generally a determination to seek knowledge somehow distinctive to the interests or position of women. Presumably this knowledge would support feminists' claims in a larger public forum. Yet the quest for such a view in itself entails logical difficulties, at least where empirical inquiry is concerned. For the very logic of constructivist and postmodernist analyses tends to preclude any expectation that their conclusions should be persuasive to those not spontaneously attracted to them. If no analysis or intepretation of any situation has a "privileged" claim to truth value, why should anyone who is unmoved by the views of feminists (or theorists of any other persuasion) concern himself or herself with those views?

These concerns take on special import for the purposes of this book. The key aim here, after all, is to identify ideas that promise analytical utility for students of social life in times to come – thinkers from intellec-tual and existential contexts quite different from those that have fostered the rise of this particular theory at this particular historical moment.

Many a present-day social scientist would identify at least a few valuable ideas deriving from Marx, for example, without considering himself or herself "a Marxist." But identification of such intellectual debts inevitably raises questions about the necessary relation between the doctrine and the ideas supposedly derived from it. Is the *distinctive logic* of Marxism, for example, really essential to the idea in question? Or is the idea simply one that happens to be espoused by those identified – by whatever process – as "Marxists."

Thus, in the case of feminism, one must ask what quality or qualities distinguish ideas as characteristically feminist. It will not do simply to accord that designation to all ideas espoused by those designated as feminists – how, after all, could one know whether that designation was made accurately or inaccurately? Presumably, feminist analysis must be distinguished by some characteristic principle, such as an affinity to what might be identified as strictly feminist viewpoints or interests. In the absence of such a link, "feminist thinking" runs the risk of appearing as a heterogeneous list of notions flying under a flag of intellectual convenience.

Then there are questions about the relationship between feminist analysis and its implications for the pursuit of what are proclaimed as feminist interests in the public forum. If the *premise* of the inquiry is taken as pervasive and systematic injustice toward women, what persuasive power can results of such investigations have for those who do not accept that premise? Such questions have preoccupied some feminists. Allison Kelly, for example, expresses dissatisfaction with the notion of "feminist research," precisely because the term

> implies that the results are known in advance. This is clearly unacceptable. . . . The fundamental indeterminacy of outcome of research means that feminist research cannot be defined as research which supports feminist beliefs. There is a place for polemic and committed literature, but that is not research. (1978, pp. 225–226)

But Kelly's position would clearly appear insufficiently feminist to many. For these analysts, distinctively feminist logic must enter into the very constitution of the research process (see, for example, Cook and Fonow 1986). And essential to that constitution, it is often held, is the requirement that analysis articulate distinctively feminist experiences – either those of the researchers or others. Consider the words of Liz Stanley and Sue Wise:

> Radical feminism argues that there must be a relationship between theory and practice which not only sees these as inextricably interwoven, but which sees experience and practice as a basis of theory, and theory as the means of changing practice. We argue that a similar relationship should exist between theory, experience and research. We feel that it is inevitable that the researcher's own experiences

and consciousnesss will be involved in the research process as much as they are in life, and we shall argue that all research must be concerned with the experiences and consciousness of the researcher as an integral part of the research process. . . .

We . . . [seek to] make 'the researcher' and her consciousness the central focus of the research experience. . . . we see 'objectivity', as this term is presently constructed within the social sciences, as a sexist notion which feminists should leave behind. (1983, pp. 48–49)

A position like this certainly ensures that the results of inquiry will accord with the need to uphold women's interests. If research must accord with experience, then research undertaken by those whose experience is ordered by a feminist mind-set can hardly avoid yielding a feminist message.

But such a solution raises problems of its own. For one thing, it offers no way of resolving disputes among researchers whose experience draws them toward conflicting analyses. Perhaps more seriously, the Stanley and Wise formulation provides no hint of how theory might *add* to experience – how it might organize, condense, or revise the givens of life as it is perceived by the liver. Surely even the most diverse thinkers would agree that some measure of interpretation and analysis is essential to any program for the elaboration of knowledge. Without efforts of this kind, the study of social life (or anything else) is indistinguishable from simple *transcription.*

THE CLAIMS TO GENERALITY

Not all social scientists designating themselves as feminists would make such sweeping theoretical claims for their work as those stated by Stanley and Wise. A more low-key approach would be to conceive of feminist inquiry more as a particular subject matter or focus of concern than as a distinctive world view. Seen in this way, feminist social science would be like rural sociology or – perhaps more in keeping with its cross-disciplinary character – development studies.

But at the time of this writing, many feminist social scientists would probably want to make stronger claims than this for their work. They would want to see their project more as a comprehensive way of understanding, embodying distinctive principles of analysis. They would want to insist, for example, that the rest of social science doesn't just *fail to pay attention to an important subject matter,* but that it *applies inherently faulty modes of understanding.* Only by applying distinctively feminist principles of analysis to any and all material, it might be said, can the deficiencies of standard social science be corrected.

Following Stimpson (1983), one might call this the "maximalist" version of feminist analysis. It amounts to a vision of feminism as a *general method* of social inquiry. In the words of one writer, feminists "are not interested in having their work be *part* of a broader relativism, one of many multiple realities. Their goal is to *replace* patriarchal models with feminist ones" (Nielsen 1990, p. 18; see also Harding 1986, p. 27).

The split between "maximalist" and "minimalist" positions forms part of a larger tension among feminist social scientists. This is the long-lasting antinomy between views of women as "essentially" different versus "essentially" similar to men. Some proponents of the former view, in the words of Cynthia Epstein:

believe the differences [between the sexes] are biologically determined; others believe that they are a product of social conditioning (typically set early in life) or lodged in the differing psyches of the sexes by the psychoanalytic processes that create identity; still others believe the causes of the differences are a mixture of both factors. These scholars typically believe that differences are deeply rooted and result in different approaches to the world, in some cases creating a distinctive "culture" of women. . . .

The other model . . . insists that the two sexes are essentially similar and that the differences linked to sexual functions are not related to psychological traits or social roles. This perspective suggests that most gender differences are not as deeply rooted or immutable as has been believed . . . [but are] kept in place by the way each sex is positioned in the social structure. This perspective is critical of the notion of a separate women's culture and of the idea that women's psyches or values are different from men's. (1988, p. 25)

Obviously this latter position (which Epstein embraces) requires much less far-reaching retooling of standard theoretical equipment. Minimalist proponents – like those engaged in development studies – would plausibly preach a refocusing of analytical attention toward the social processes of concern to them. They might, no less plausibly, argue that these processes are more far-reaching in their bearing on other analytical issues than is commonly believed. Thus we are not surprised to hear students of development maintaining that the fate of the world's poorer regions matters more to the future of highly developed regions than is ordinarily acknowledged – just as feminist social scientists are apt to insist that inattention to women and gender have distorted conventional social science understanding. But in neither case would it be necessary to identify a special analytical principle or "way of knowing" to distinguish the program in question from standard social science.

By contrast, proponents of the "maximalist" position, those intending to replace "patriarchal models with feminist ones," have a more complicated account to give. They must specify what exactly is to be replaced, and what to replace it with. How do proponents of "maximalist" views characterize the essential deficiencies of other approaches? And what are the special virtues of their modes of understanding – most particularly, for those who begin with no special stake in them?

Or, in terms more specific to this book, what is the "or-else" clause here? If the intent is indeed to invalidate and replace alternate approaches, the maximalists need to provide convincing arguments identifying things that others *need to know* but can only be understood through the maximalist lens. Otherwise, their "contribution" runs the risk of appearing simply as a response to a special intellectual taste – something one might or might not find appealing, but does not admit of reasoned justification.

Complicating these requirements is the fact that feminists typically conceive of their work as being pursued on behalf of a particular constituency – women. Here feminist analysis resembles various forms of Marxism and other doctrines that seek enlightenment on behalf of all, based on analysis from the standpoint of a particular social group (see Rule 1978, chap. 2). Proponents of all such theoretical programs face some weighty logical demands. First, they need to establish how the particular forms of insight that they yield will serve the true or ultimate interest of their natural constituency – workers or women, in these two cases. And, once this is established, they need to show that the interests thus served in turn redound to some yet broader, *general* interests – ones that might be shared by any reasonable analyst.

Imagine that claims similar to those of the maximalist position were made for development studies. Suppose, in other words, that those who study the social and economic prospects of poor countries were to proclaim a distinctive method of analysis predicated on the special interests and viewpoint of the citizens of these countries. Application of this method or approach, it might be asserted, would generate knowledge that would both uphold the dignity of residents of developing countries and lead to social changes benefiting their material interests. And ultimately, application of this special form of analysis would speak to the interests of the broadest intellectual community. That is, it would reveal things that any reasonable thinker would want to understand, whether or not he or she began with an interest in development.

The example should simply make it clear how complex the logical demands of such positions are; as far as we know, students of socioeconomic development have advanced no such claims. But some theoretical programs – most notably, Marxism – have developed a rationale for resolving such issues. In the Marxist classics, recall, the proletariat plays much the same role that women play in the logic of some versions of feminist thought – that is, as the "bearers of historical rationality." Marx and Engels thus aimed to elaborate a distinctively proletarian form of analysis, oriented to the special interests and perspective of workers. Yet by promoting this special (and, they believed, more veridical) approach, they intended to serve the broader interests of creating a more rational world for all. As *The Communist Manifesto* states:

If the proletariat during its contest with the bourgeoisie is compelled, by the force of circumstances, to organize itself as a class, if, by means of revolution it makes itself the ruling class and, as such, sweeps away by force the old conditions of production, then it will, along with these conditions, have swept away the conditions for the existence of class antagonism and of classes generally, and will thereby have abolished its own supremacy. (1959, p. 29)

Feminist thinking has not gone so far as Marxism in developing such a rationale. Those embracing the maximalist postion are apt to hold that their approach is both morally and analytically superior to alternative programs. But what distinguishes feminist principles of inquiry, and how such principles could be made persuasive to those not initially attracted to them, are often not closely worked out.

True, the feminist literature contains many discussions of feminist epistemology and methods; but these typically do not provide much help in resolving the logical issues noted above. Consider the summary by Cook and Fonow of five "principles of feminist methodology" from "scholars . . . in the field of sociology" (1986, p. 5):

1. The necessity of continuously and reflexively attending to the significance of gender and gender asymmetry as a basic feature of all social life, including the conduct of research;
2. the centrality of consciousness-raising as a specific methodological tool and as a general orientation or "way of seeing";
3. the need to challenge the norm of objectivity that assumes that the subject and object of research can be separated from one another and that personal and/or grounded experiences are unscientific;
4. concern for the ethical implications of feminist research and recognition of the exploitation of women as objects of knowledge;
5. emphasis on the empowerment of women and transformation of patriarchal social institutions through research.

This list is undoubtedly an accurate characterization of views and practices of many present-day social scientists who would designate themselves as feminist. What it lacks is conceptual unity. It is simply hard to see what logical relation the various points have to one another, or how the pursuit of these points would necessarily redound to any specific conception of the interests of women, or of humanity more generally. What makes concern for the "ethical implications" of research a distinctively feminist characteristic, for example? Why is distrust of the "norm of objectivity" a specifically feminist complaint? Doesn't one note much the same concerns from other theoretical quarters?

Other discussions of feminist methods or epistemologies have also steered clear of providing any one distinctive principle or conceptual rule to characterize feminist thought. As in the Cook and Fonow statement, commentators typically identify as feminist those approaches adopted by writers generally agreed to be feminists (see, for example, Reinharz 1992).

Often the resulting heterogeneity is defended as a positive thing. For example,

one of the major lessons of critiques of traditional social science has been that when one approach becomes hegemonic, this reinforces domination and limits knowledge. (Cancian 1992, p. 629)

or,

Once we admit the existence of feminist stand*points* there can be no a priori reason for placing these in any kind of hierarchy; each has *epistemological* validity because each has *ontological* validity. (Stanley and Wise 1990, p. 28)

or,

Abandoning the Enlightenment quest for one unitary theory to explain the oppression of women, we can best acknowledge the diversity of women's experiences by embracing theoretical diversity. . . . Our task then as feminists is to carefully examine the strengths and weaknesses of each theory, to expose the presuppositions and prejudices of one theory through the lens of an alternative theory, which is in turn offered up for critical examination. . . . (Tuana 1993, p. 282)

Thus many authors share the conviction that feminist analyses should draw from a variety of methodological or epistemological sources. The value of each should be assessed, as Tuana notes, in terms of its "strengths and weaknesses" in comparison to other sources of theoretical insight.

The obvious question here is "How are we to reckon strength or weakness?" What counts, in other words, as analytical "success?" No model of closure can do without a response to such a question, and any such response amounts to a theoretical statement in its own right. Lacking one, proponents may appear to assert simply that "successful inquiry consists of those ideas that we happen to like." And such a position becomes vulnerable to a discomfiting question: "Why should we regard *these particular* concerns, rather than others, as distinctively feminist?"

Again, these questions take on special significance in the context of any effort to identify potentially enduring "contributions" associated with feminist social science. As with Marxism or other diverse theoretical inspirations, one wants to know whether ideas bracketed as "feminist" really share any defining or distinctive qualities. If not, then the fact that the ideas in question endure may warrant no conclusions about the theoretical program as a whole.

Marxists have worked out one kind of response to these requirements. They do not conceive of the interests of the proletariat as isomorphic with the interests of particular workers at particular moments. Instead, they put forward a conception of workers' "true" interests – for example, the destruction of capitalism – as contrasted to such illusory interests as the pursuit of higher wages under capitalism. And they claim to show how specifically Marxist sorts of understandings conduce to the realization of these interests and, beyond this, more general human interests.

With a bit of imagination, one might interpret principles like those listed by Cook and Fonow to offer such a rationale. Successful, authentic feminist analysis, one might say, is any form of thought that upholds the interests of women – that conduces to their "empowerment," to use the term adopted by these authors.

It is not clear that any feminist author has actually taken such a highly simplified position. We hope not, because it is extremely vague. What exactly does "empowerment" entail? Would ideas somehow tending to concentrate *all* power – political, economic, judicial, military, and so on – in the hands of women meet the criterion? Probably no feminist analyst would give the concept that interpretation. Most no doubt have some other vision of women's "empowerment" involving specific understandings of what constitutes "a good society" and good female–male relationships within such a society. For that matter, many feminist thinkers probably have some notion of how the sorts of learning that they seek to disseminate can be expected to lead to the realization of such relations. But published, coherently thought-through versions of such ideas are scarce. The scarcity of such statements makes it difficult to draw conclusions about what constitutes distinctively feminist thinking on these matters.

These issues do not seem to have greatly preoccupied feminist social scientists. Perhaps the reason has to do with the moral fervor generated by feminism as a social movement. The afflictions imposed on women's interests may seem so obvious, and the need to combat them so compelling, as to leave no ambiguity as to which ideas count as support to the cause, and which do not.

But our task here is to judge the staying power of distinctively feminist ideas, to weigh their prospects for continued usefulness once current political and cultural contexts have changed. And a close look at the notion of an analytical program dedicated to the pursuit of women's distinctive interests raises questions in this connection. From almost any standpoint, such interests are themselves *socially constructed* – and hence subject to dispute among contemporaries and to revision over time. Expression of such interests has ranged from the attempts at suppression of saloons (in late-nineteenth-century America) to efforts to secure the right of women to enter and and patronize certain similar establishments (in the late twentieth century). Indeed, considerable debate prevails within the feminist movement at the time of this writing on what should be understood as women's interests in a number of disputed realms – pornography, for example, or special labor legislation for women.

Thus it seems to us that any vision of the distinctive aim or method of feminist thinking must do more than uphold "women's interests" or "women's empowerment" in whatever form particular women may interpret such things at particular moments. Needed instead is a conceptually precise specification of the distinctive content of feminist analysis, coupled with identification of what precisely would be lost, should distinctively feminist insights be ignored. In short, an "or-else" clause.

RELATEDNESS AS A FEMINIST PRINCIPLE

Some feminist thinkers have struggled to identify such an approach. One of the most sophisticated attempts is that of Evelyn Fox Keller. She makes her case in the context of an appeal to end the exclusion of women from science:

> The most immediate issue for a feminist perspective on the natural sciences is the deeply rooted popular mythology that casts objectivity, reason, and mind as male, and subjectivity, feeling, and nature as female. In this division of emotional and intellectual labor, women have been the guarantors and protectors of the personal, the emotional, the particular, whereas science – the province par excellence of the impersonal, the rational, and the general – has been the preserve of men. (1985, pp. 6–7)

But Keller credits this "popular mythology" as largely true – not, to be sure, as the inevitable order of things, but as an account of the way modern science has actually been practiced. Like many feminist analysts, she ascribes great import to what she regards as the association between the practice of modern science and a characteristically male penchant for control and exploitation:

> For the founding fathers of modern science, the reliance on the language of gender was explicit: They sought a philosophy that deserved to be called "masculine," that could be distinguished from its ineffective predecessors by its "virile" power, its capacity to bind Nature to man's service and make her his slave (Bacon). (1985, p. 7)

Thus the "normal" practice of science is seen as guided by an underlying interest in control, manipulation, or exploitation of the natural world – interests pictured as somehow deriving from masculine viewpoints or concerns. Keller devotes much attention to demonstrating this linkage in the minds of key scientists – Francis Bacon, especially – by presenting passages from their diaries and other writings. This theme has the widest resonance among feminist writers – for instance, Harding (1986, 1987, and 1991) and Merchant (1980).

What Keller sees as the masculine obsessions of modern science actually lead, she argues, to distortion and error in the scientific quest. For examples of an alternative way of doing science, she turns to the work of Barbara McClintock, the geneticist and Nobel laureate. McClintock's work epitomizes the virtues of science uncontaminated by conventional assumptions:

> To McClintock, science has a different goal: not prediction per se, but understanding; not the power to manipulate, but empowerment – the kind of power that results from an understanding of the world around us, that simultaneously reflects and affirms our connection to that world. (p. 166)

The success of McClintock's work, Keller is convinced, reflects a distinctive way of knowing. As Keller puts it:

> I am suggesting that we might learn . . . to be wary of imposing causal relations on all systems that seem by their very nature to be more complexly interactive. As scientists, our mission is to understand and explain natural phenomena, but the words *understand* and *explain* have many different meanings. In our zealous desire for familiar models of explanation, we risk not noticing the discrepancies between our own predispositions and the range of possibilities inherent in natural phenomena. (1985, p. 157)

Keller's words have been inspirational for those seeking to identify a distinctive method for feminist analysis. One might paraphrase her view of this perspective as follows: "Keep your eye on the whole, interactive system; don't imagine that any one element can be identified as preeminent in its effects. The role of each part depends on the state of the whole." For many, such a formulation epitomizes a typically feminist understanding of the *relatedness* of the natural and social world.

Perhaps, then, *relatedness* is the key, the principle of analysis that distinguishes feminist thinking in all domains from the bad, old thought-ways of standard science. Many feminist thinkers have embraced such a position, and one can readily see how it suits the requirements noted above. The question is, does the notion of relatedness admit of conceptually distinct specification? Can one show that its application yields analytically distinctive results?

Much of the interest in some form of "relatedness" principle as a basis for distinctively feminist insight derives from Carol Gilligan's celebrated *In a Different Voice* (1982). By any account, this must be one of the most noted works in the feminist literature. The point of departure for Gilligan's work is her critique of psychologists' standard thinking on moral development. Because of the underrepresentation of women in studies on this subject, she argues, psychologists have failed to credit the existence of certain styles of moral reasoning. The neglected moral sensibilities, identified by Gilligan both in women and in some men, involve what she terms "an ethic of care and response" (1986, p. 326).

Many readers have understood Gilligan's work as pointing to a special form of reasoning, one employed more readily by women than by men. Feminist writers have accorded a positive valuation to this special vision. As the authors of *Women's Ways of Knowing* state:

Gilligan has traced the development of a morality organized around notions of responsibility and care. This conception of morality contrasts sharply with the morality of rights . . . , which is based on the study of evolution of moral reasoning in boys and men. People operating within a rights morality – more commonly men – evoke the metaphor of "blind justice" and rely on abstract laws and universal principles to adjudicate disputes. . . . Those operating within a morality of responsibility and care – primarily women – reject the strategy of blindness and impartiality. Instead, they argue for an understanding of the context for moral choice, claiming that the needs of individuals cannot always be deduced from general rules. . . . (Belenky, Field, Clinchy, Goldberger, and Tarule 1986, p. 8)

Or consider Nancy Hartsock's statement:

The articulation of a feminist standpoint based on women's relational self-definition and activity exposes the world men have constructed and the self-understanding which manifests these relations as partial and perverse. . . . The experience of continuity and relation – with others, with the natural world, of mind with body – provides an ontological base for developing a nonproblematic social synthesis, a social synthesis which need not operate through the denial of the body, the attack on nature, or the death struggle between the self and other, a social synthesis which does not depend on any of the forms taken by abstract masculinity. (Hartsock, in Harding 1987, pp. 174–175)

For these and many other authors, some form of "relatedness" offers a perfect expression of the characteristic approach of feminist analysis. It has seemed to provide a "kinder, gentler" form of understanding than that supposedly offered by traditional, male-dominated science – and one that could be applied in virtually any form of analysis, including both social and natural science. As the political theorist Seyla Benhabib wrote, commenting on Gilligan's thesis:

Women's moral judgment is more contextual, more immersed in the details of relationships and narratives. It shows greater propensity to take the standpoint of the "particular other," and women appear more adept at revealing feelings of empathy and sympathy required by this. Once these cognitive characteristics are seen not as deficiencies, but as essential components of adult moral reasoning at the postconventional stage, then women's apparent moral confusion of judgment becomes a sign of their strength. (1987, p. 78)

There can be little doubt that "relatedness" – as distinct from judgment based on some sort of noncontextual principle – ought properly to play a role in moral decision making. The question is, should anyone consider these two ways of dealing with human relationships as constituting an either-or choice? Wouldn't any reasonable person prefer to foster arrangements that accommodate potentially conflicting interests wherever that option is open while still insisting on the need for some overarching principle for deciding cases where compromise is impossible? Indeed, it seems to us that any real-world actor incapable of adopting both such approaches – and, for that matter, of distinguishng when each should apply – would be a highly inadequate social personality.

One might make a similar observation about Keller's claim to detect a distinctively feminist sensitivity to "relatedness" in the researches of Barbara McClintock. Isn't the injunction to be wary of imposing "causal relations on all systems that seem by their very nature to be more complexly interactive" simply good advice for any and all inquiry? Haven't such insights long served both male and female researchers, figures from both the establishment and the fringes of scholarly inquiry?

In other words, what responsible natural scientist, of any orientation or persuasion, would deny *in principle* that many systems of interest in scientific investigation are multicausal, interactive, or contextual? A number of disciplines, like statistical mechanics or econometrics or population ecology, would seem to take such assumptions as their points of departure. Surely, by the same token, no astronomer would dare to claim to have identified the unique cause of one planet's movement in the gravitation force of another single heavenly body. Or, similarly, in social science, wouldn't any analyst be remiss in overlooking the holistic, interactive qualities of a stock market, a family, or a troop of primates?

It is easy to believe that scientists' efforts often fail in their own terms when investigators insist on looking for unique causes in what are better modeled as highly interactive systems. But it is difficult to imagine any formal doctrine of traditional science that would condone such failings. And, like fixation on unique causality, contextuality can surely be taken to fruitless (and demonstrably erroneous) extremes. To imagine that genetic phenomena are influenced, say, by the purity of the investigator's karma, for example, is probably not a useful axiom for a working biologist.

The mark of brilliance in scientific analysis is having the wit to entertain connections that others have missed, and which prove, on empirical investigation, to make a real difference in the outcome in question. But it is very difficult to state any rule for successful scientific analysis *in general*. What would such a rule be? "Consider all the possibilities before jumping to conclusions?" "Don't impose assumptions of systematicity/unique causality when the outcome you're attempting to account for really turns on unique causality/systematicity?" Such advice is not so much inaccurate as vacuous.

Thus we see serious difficulty with notions of relatedness as a distinctively feminist principle of analysis. There can be no doubt that contextual, systemic forms of reasoning have to play a role in any approach to understanding the world, whether "scientific" or otherwise. But it is hard to specify how such principles relate specifically to women's experience or interests.

No one can miss the strictly expressive appeal of ideas like relatedness as an emblem of feminist analysis. To its enthusiasts, this idea has seemed to combine the special qualities of compassion and inclusion claimed for feminist thinking with the promise of insights unavailable to analysts of other persuasions.

One might make much the same observation about the charges leveled by many feminists against "traditional" science. Here, too, the energizing message has been that distinctively feminist thinking transcends the moral and political failures of established forms of thought. For example:

the epistemologies, metaphysics, ethics, and politics of the dominant forms of science are androcentric and mutually supportive; . . . despite the deeply ingrained Western cultural belief in science's intrinsic progressiveness, science today serves primarily regressive social tendencies; . . . the social structure of science, many of its applications and technologies, its modes of defining research problems and designing experiments, its ways of constructing and conferring meanings are not only sexist but also racist, classist and culturally coercive. (Harding 1986, p. 9)

But Harding goes on to acknowledge (p. 10) that she does not reject *all* scientific thinking – just the part that is "androcentric." By this she seems to have in mind those aspects of science oriented toward control or domination.

And indeed, it is hard to see how her indictment could possibly apply to broad domains of "standard" science. A major theme in her complaint is that science is organized and used for purposes of domination or manipulation. Yet entire realms of scientific investigation seem unsuited ever to play such role, however these diffuse notions are understood. Much science – medical and epidemiological research, for example – is evidently oriented to extending life and alleviating suffering. And much scientific investigation has always dealt with subject matters inherently beyond the reach of human intervention – the extinction of dinosaurs, for example, or the transformation of Latin into vernacular languages, or the origins of the universe. Why these are less important aspects of science than the "racist, classist and culturally coercive" ones that Harding deplores is not clear.

Not unless one considers their strictly expressive dimension. That is what these two themes – the notion of "relatedness" as a special, distinctively feminist principle of analysis and the notion of "standard" science as a categorically masculine, manipulative activity – have in common. Both unmistakably uphold the notion of a special and indispensable

161

(if not actually superior) form of understanding specifically associated with a feminist standpoint. And both ideas purport to dissociate feminist thinking from the ugly, destructive, insensitive aspects of "standard" thought-ways. As such, they appear to have enjoyed enormous currency, without anyone's subjecting them to much critical attention.

But expressive contexts change; ideas enormously attractive to given constituencies at specific times often lose their broad appeal with unexpected abruptness. If analytical ideas are to pretend to any enduring claim on the theoretical imagination, they surely need to embody insights whose utility outlasts the cultural climates of their origins. And judgments on this point require that we attend constantly to the gap separating the expressive content of theoretical ideas and their pragmatic value as bases for coping with social life.

That these two dimensions may, and often do, diverge is a key premise of this work. Ideas that are all but irresistible in the sheer contemplation may nevertheless prove disastrous as bases for dealing with the social facts, forces, and processes that constrain human experience. But seeking understanding of this latter kind requires that we constantly confront theoretical ideas that look attractive with evidence that could, in principle, undermine their credibility. Feminist theorizing has not always generated efforts of this sort.

Consider another much noted work, Nancy Chodorow's *The Reproduction of Mothering* (1978). Beginning almost immediately with its publication, this book commanded vast attention from virtually all feminist analysts of the family.

Chodorow's book is strictly an exercise in theory. It is an extended effort to trace certain implications of psychoanalytic theories of development – notably, those of Melanie Klein's object-relations school – for the modal personalities of men and women. What are the implications for personality structures, Chodorow asks, of the fact that both boys and girls receive much more of their nurturing and upbringing from their mothers than from their fathers? Invoking a byzantine chain of reasoning, Chodorow concludes that certain assymetries in male and female personality are attributable to the nearly exclusive control over mothering by women. As Nancy Hartsock characterizes the argument,

> The more complex female relational world is reinforced by the process of socialization. Girls learn from watching their mothers; boys must learn roles from rules which structure the life of an absent male figure. Girls can identify with a concrete example present in daily life; boys must identify with an abstract set of maxims only occasionally concretely present in the form of the father. Thus, not only do girls learn roles with more interpersonal and relational skills, but the process of role learning itself is embodied in the concrete relation with the mother. The male, in contrast, must identify with an abstract, cultural stereotype and learn abstract

behaviors not attached to a well-known person. Masculinity is idealized by boys whereas femininity is concrete for girls. (Hartsock 1987, p. 168)

Thus emerges a doctrine with endless expressive possibilities. Chodorow's book not only upholds the status and character of women as a group; it also has the virtue of justifying the sharing of parental responsibilities, an idea with a burgeoning constituency among feminist activists. For ideas of such extraordinary expressive appeal, the inherent charm in their contemplation often seems to dampen any inclinations to entertain potentially discordant evidence.

This is what seems to have occurred with Chodorow's work. There has been a vast amount of commentary on it, by no means altogether supportive. But most of the discussion has been in strictly theoretical terms. We can find virtually no research aimed at exploring what we take to be one of the key empirical implications of *The Reproduction of Mothering*: the notion that the experience of being reared primarily by a female produces distinctive personality constellations that persist into adulthood.

There would appear to be a particularly apt opening for exploring this question. One would want to look at a sample of childen, especially males, reared by fathers. Although these represent a small proportion of the total population, in absolute terms they are numerous and accessible to study. On the strength of Chodorow's doctrine, one would expect to find a distinctively different modal personality among these males. Failure to do so would tend to undermine the credibility of Chodorow's theory. It is striking that, despite all the commentary on Chodorow's book, no one seems to have found it worthwhile to pursue this possibility.

Empirical demonstration of such differences – or of their absence – would bear rich implications for all sorts of "coping" interests. For example, knowledge that nurturing by both male and female care givers is conducive to a fuller range of personality strengths would yield useful policy directions for foster care and adoption organizations. Indeed, truly reliable guidance in this respect would go a long way toward justifying the exceedingly long-winded theoretical exertions that lead up to the empirical insight. In this light, it seems regrettable that the intellectual public has treated Chodorow's work more as an expressive "consumption item" than as an effort to fashion analytical tools for coping.

THE "OR-ELSE" CLAUSE

Does Chodorow's work represent a theoretical success story, then? The question is, what kind of success is at issue? This is a question that has to be posed about feminist social science more generally.

The language used in some feminist writings suggests that expressive rewards are the main concern. Consider the influential article by Judith

Stacey and Barrie Thorne, "The Missing Feminist Revolution in Sociology" (1985). Stacey and Thorne decry the absence of what one might call a consensus feminist theory in their own discipline of sociology, and they set down their notions of what such a feminist sociology would accomplish. They give much emphasis to the need for a "paradigm shift":

> The process of paradigm shifting, by which we mean changes in the orienting assumptions and conceptual frameworks which are basic to a discipline, involves two separate dimensions: (1) The transformation of existing conceptual frameworks; and (2) acceptance of those transformations by others in the field. (p. 302)

Here it sounds as though the success that the authors seek for feminist analysis consists in a shift of attention, a reordering of moral significance – in short, changes of a strictly expressive sort. Passages like the following reinforce this impression:

> Feminist scholars begin by placing women at the center, as subjects of inquiry and as active agents in the gathering of knowledge. This strategy makes women's experiences visible, reveals the sexist biases and tacitly male assumptions of traditional knowledge. (p. 303)

Yet other statements in the article leave open the possibilty that the virtues they seek in feminist analysis might hold interest even for theoretical outsiders.

> Feminists have done extensive and extremely valuable work in uncovering and filling gaps in sociological knowledge. This work has demonstrated systematic flaws in traditional sociological theory and method. (p. 302)

What do Stacey and Thorne mean when they speak of "flaws" in traditional sociological analysis? Do they mean flaws like those identified in the Irrationalists' theories, where ideas of great expressive appeal may simply prove inaccurate in the picture they yield of social processes? Or do "flaws" refer simply to a failure to focus attention on the "right" sorts of issues or subject matter – from the standpoint of feminist sensibilities? In other words, a critique on rhetorical or expressive grounds.

One might pinpoint what is at stake here by asking, "How would we know, if feminist analysis *failed* – if it somehow did not produce the kinds of results that its proponents hoped for?" Would such failure manifest itself in an inability to note and deal with aspects of social reality whose existence had to be acknowledged by any and all observers? Or would it consist in failure to uphold values, interests, or concerns shared by the community of theoretical believers? In the first case, let us note, failure would have that status from the standpoint of any analyst. In the second, failure would count as such only from the standpoint of those who share the interests and values inspiring the particular theoretical community.

We have noted the diversity of views on these questions among feminist social scientists. For many theorists, what we have termed the expressive payoffs of feminist thinking – however the essence of the doctrine is understood – appear to be the only rewards that matter. But for others, like Evelyn Fox Keller, there is another kind of "or-else" clause. Keller insists that the value of insights like those yielded by Barbara McClintock's researches are not just matters of taste, but rather things that no conscientious scientist would want to miss. To the extent that this or any theoretical school yields such insights, it involves something more than simply a shift of attention or evaluative emphasis. It offers tools whose usefulness is apt to outlive the expressive climates of their origins.

CONCLUSION

The dissatisfactions of writers like Stacey and Thorne notwithstanding, feminist thinking has had a far-reaching impact on intellectual life in social science. Indeed, it is hard to think of any theoretical program that has represented more of a "growth industry" in the last decades of this century. And certain salient ideas of feminist social science have gained wide acceptance well outside the community of theoretical "insiders" – notably, the idea that social arrangements and understandings associated with gender are socially constructed, and hence subject to revision. Equally widely accepted, we would judge, is the notion that the processes by which ideas of maleness and femaleness are generated, and the social arrangements associated with these ideas, are legitimate subjects for inquiry.

For many members of an entire scholarly generation, feminism has clearly been a conveyor of a highly *meaningful* vehicle for understanding social life. For its enthusiasts, feminism has appeared to provide exactly those insights most grievously lacking in alternative approaches. Indeed, as we have shown, feminist social science to many of its proponents appears as much more than a distinctive subject matter or focus of interest. Instead, it represents a distinctive way of understanding, a competitor to other forms of analysis, potentially applicable to any and all subject matters.

Enthusiasts of many other programs would no doubt express the same sorts of perceptions of their chosen theoretical visions. The question is, should we expect the distinctive accomplishments of this theory to outlast the immediate context of its initial flourishing? Do the special analytical virtues of feminist thinking, one might ask, provide answers to questions that can be expected to arise in a wide variety of social and intellectual contexts? Or does the theory constitute – as is undoubtedly true of many theories – a source of answers to questions that make sense only from within the rather special world of the theory itself? Such questions can only be answered, we have noted, in light of some judgment of what constitutes the distinctive analytical insights of feminist thinking.

Consider two extreme scenarios. In one of these, feminist studies might undergo a trajectory something like that of ethnomethodology or Balesian small-group studies. On this assumption, feminist thinking would come to be regarded as a kind of historical curiosity – or, at most, a rather special theoretical taste peripheral to newly defined "core concerns" or "mainstream inquiry" in the rest of social science. At the other extreme, one might envisage a future rather like that urged in the essay by Stacey and Thorne. In this scenario, feminist programs would sweep the disciplines, "placing women at the center" of all analysis. Other theoretical programs, from status attainment studies to game theory to Marxist structuralism, would be cast into oblivion – unless these specialties could somehow be adapted to dramatize the role of women. In the extreme case, one would suppose that no form of social inquiry would command any interest without such dramatization.

Note that the notion of "placing women at the center" bears striking parallels to the appeals made for countless other theoretical programs. These are claims to have identified *the* key conceptual order, causal principle, human concern, or historical narrative supposed to provide the "starting point" for all social inquiry. The history of our disciplines is the record of successive waves of interest in and sympathy for such claims. Yet the notable fact is that none of these has come close to accomplishing what all, to their most enthusiastic supporters, promised to do: provide unique and indispensable means for attaining the full range of analytic ends that draw people to the study of social life in the first place.

Thus it is difficult to imagine that efforts at "putting women at the center" could long prevail as a *comprehensive* program for the organization of social inquiry. Taken literally, such a program would require that distinctively feminist interests or investigative styles, however understood, shape all forms of social inquiry. This does not seem to us a plausible prospect. There are simply too many other theoretical issues having little directly to do with gender that intrude themselves on our attention. People simply *need to know* about a range of what Chapter 1 termed first-order questions – questions about the causes of stratification, for example, the conditions of economic growth, or the forces shaping international conflict and peace. Although gender issues may play a role in any or all of these matters, it would be peculiar to ignore the rest of their content. The fact that stratification, economic growth, and international conflict compel attention as enduring human concerns suggests that these issues may never remain in theoretical eclipse for long.

To such observations some theoretical enthusiasts might still reply that, whatever the *subject matter* of social science inquiry, distinctively feminist *forms of analysis* must come to pervade social science. Clearly such an injunction, if heeded, would ensure the claim of feminist thinking to a central place in our disciplines. But we have sought to show how difficult it is to identify any such principle as uniquely or distinctively associated with feminism. The principles espoused most convincingly in this connection sound to us like principles of sound thinking that one could find applied in many familiar forms of social and political inquiry.

But if total and permanent rewriting of social scientists' theoretical map in feminist terms is an implausible prospect, the idea that feminist thinking might go the way of Balesian small-group studies seems even less likely. In the short to medium run, the position of feminist thinking in academic social science in the the English-speaking world seems assured. For many members of a generation of scholars, feminism has provided the context in which one's most basic approach to social inquiry was formed. It is hard to believe that members of this cohort will ever be indifferent to the ideas that played this formative role. And for as long as women's roles remain subjects of public controversy and struggle, the demand for intellectual commentary in these conflicts will continue.

But what about the longer term? What ideas from feminist thinking are most likely to remain useful to analysts even beyond the lifetimes of those living today? Thus far, the fortunes of the doctrine have remained closely linked to those of the movement associated with it. But that movement can be expected to follow a life cycle like those of other relatively successful movements, as some key aims are achieved and others deferred or redefined. At some point, the ideas associated with the movement must seek a place in the thinking of those whose mind-sets will be shaped by expressive climates very different from those of today.

Proponents of the most charismatic vision of feminist analysis, of course, would set no store by this reasoning. In this view, feminist analysis represents a distinctive and generic method of inquiry. Once its true powers are appreciated, the most committed enthusiasts might claim, no reasonable thinker would show any interest in the blinkered tradition of male-dominated thinking.

But we find such a view hard to credit in light of the precedent of other theoretical movements, including those considered in this book. Like every emergent theoretical worldview, feminism has flourished in some measure by projecting criteria of success that only it can fulfill. Under the spell of the theory, people have been willing to devote attention to intellectual performances that will surely mystify thinkers from later theoretical contexts. In the terms invoked in Chapter 1, feminist social science has fostered its share of obsessions with second-order questions, lines of speculation unlikely to make a difference to anyone other than those gripped by enthusiasm for the theory as an end in itself. A particularly good candidate for such status, it would appear, is *The Reproduction of Mothering*. How its labyrinthine explorations of the logic of object-relations theory will matter to anyone, once the expressive mystique of the theory has subsided, is difficult to imagine. Unless, that is, the connection between nurturing and personality formation posited by Chodorow can be empirically established and hence potentially mobilized as a basis for coping.

Other insights, however, appear as strong candidates to endure. It should be very difficult, for example, for future analysts to resurrect the idea that males and females have the sorts of special aptitudes (and ineptitudes) for specific occupations that were once taken for granted. It should be nearly as hard to deny (in the case of gender, as for race and ethnicity) that long-entrenched hierarchies of gender privilege can be broken down quickly, without unraveling the very bases of social cohesion – this, contra the position of William Graham Sumner and a long tradition of thinkers who stressed the conservative drag of mores on social change.

But the most important lessons to be derived from the rise of feminist social science, we judge, are more diffuse than this. They have to do with that leitmotif of feminist criticism, theoretical perspective. Feminist critiques have made it difficult to miss the point that traditional analytical practices of social science, like those of mainstream culture, have simply obscured the distinctive roles and interests of women. Often this exclusion has been built into the very conceptual organization of analysis, as in the treatments of women's work noted at the begining of this chapter. Yet the nature of the conceptual system responsible for the exclusion long made it impossible to note what was being missed.

We believe that these observations offer lessons for our understanding of theory that go beyond gender. Theory is not simply a collection of propositions about the workings of the social world, though no worthwhile theory can ultimately fail to yield such propositions. Theory, in the comprehensive sense intended in this book, must be seen as a series of responses to analytical *needs* – ways of answering questions that people can be expected to ask, and keep asking. This means that distinguishing between successful and unsuccessful theory requires some hard judgments about the relationship between the answers offered by any theoretical program and the questions likely to be posed. And this, in turn, requires some assessment of the breadth of the interests enshrined in the perspective animating the theory.

As the preceding discussion suggests, we do not believe that one can point to any single, qualitatively distinct principle of analysis peculiar to the feminist perspective. Indeed, we suspect that, as history unfolds and the social context of theory changes, the notion of a unitary body of feminist thought will itself lose currency. What will endure from the feminist challenge of recent decades, we hope, is an appreciation that every theoretical system implies some particular perspective or interest, and that the universality of such perspectives must never be taken for granted.

PART III

In the study of ideas, as at the movies, the best seats are not always closest to the action. In the preceding chapters, I have sought to develop a measure of useful distance from the theoretical visions considered there.

The result has perhaps conveyed the feeling mentioned in Chapter 2 – that of experiencing an optical illusion. Up close, each model of closure, each theoretical program generates a powerful sense of accomplishment and intellectual direction. Each seems, at least to its proponents, to meet the most pressing of intellectual needs, to chart precisely the most crucial aspects of the subject matter – to "move the field forward," to increase our overall grasp of *what really matters* in social life. In short, to represent an unmistakable instance of intellectual *progress*.

From greater distance, such impressions are less powerful, more qualified. What appear as dramatic accomplishments to enthusiasts of the moment are apt to seem banal, pedestrian, or even embarrassing from the vantage point of other times and constituencies. The theoretical progress so painstakingly traced by working out the implications of the theory may appear, from such a view, as obsession with points of obscure or dubious import. The empirical researches inspired by such theoretical programs may well seem like nothing more than elaborate efforts to document and analyze facts that no one needed to know in the first place.

By now it is clear that such "built-in obsolescence" is endemic in social science. Yet I hardly see such transience as the last word in our theoretical prospects. Here and there, one or another theoretical tradition generates insights apt to serve the analytical needs of thinkers who approach the study of social life from quite different existential and theoretical perspectives. The strictly *expressive* appeals of theoretical ideas rarely if ever endure, I hold. But some insights may legitimately claim relatively enduring *pragmatic* value – usefulness as tools for coping with the demands of social life. In the preceding chapters, I have sought to identify ideas of various theoretical origins that show promise of such lasting value. This section pursues these issues in detail.

Chapter 7 probes the logic of what I call expressive criteria for theoretical understanding. Here I seek to identify some of the vast variety of social forces and circumstances that endow theoretical ideas with expressive appeal. And I seek to demonstrate the anomalies and problems that arise if such considerations are taken as the only criteria of theoretical success.

Chapter 8 considers the role of theoretical ideas as bases for coping. Here I argue for the enduring usefulness of certain theoretical ideas, and for the possibility of organizing our work so as to maximize the chances of developing such insights.

Chapter 9 summarizes these arguments and considers their implications for the place of social science in its larger social context.

7

Theory as expression

Whatever one's formal views on the matter, it is hard to overlook the force of the *experience* of progress in our work. Without some overriding sense of intellectual direction how is anyone to justify any program of inquiry? The wide-ranging theoretical exertions described in the preceding chapters, for example, surely would not have taken place had it not been for a sense among theoretical enthusiasts that they were "moving the field ahead."

Moreover, our self-presentation to the outside world routinely involves implied or explicit claims for our work as a progressive or cumulative enterprise. The Institute for Advanced Study at Princeton, where these words are being written, describes itself as dedicated to the pursuit of "basic knowledge" – implying unmistakably that some forms of understanding are prior to, and necessary for, others. Similarly, in praising an author, genre of study, or investigation, we aver that the work "advances discussion" or "breaks new ground" – presumably in a direction that all concerned could identify as "ahead." Conferences are convened, volumes edited, and symposia organized to implement the growth of understanding, or to extend the "frontiers" of knowledge. Books, articles, and doctoral dissertations are judged in terms of whether they constitute "contributions" to knowledge – as though it were transparent what constitutes the established sum of understanding and what meaningfully adds to it.

Evidently, the case is quite the opposite. Profound confusion and deep ambivalence prevail among working social scientists as to what legitimately constitutes a "step ahead" in theoretical understanding – along with sharp and endemic contest as to what ideas, programs, or works warrant the prized distinction of "moving the field forward" at any particular point.

Close scrutiny of how such progressive developments are actually experienced and ratified by scholarly publics makes it apparent that what I have termed "expressive" principles often play a crucial role. What counts as "a step ahead" is reckoned in terms of the ability of ideas to capture the inner experience of their "producers" and "consumers." In the pure case, such expressive standards impose no requirement whatsoever in terms of the fit of any representation with constraints imposed by a world outside the consciousness of the thinker. As in poetry, fiction, or drama, the test of success is strictly internal and aesthetic. We judge a sonnet, after all, not in terms of whether the sentiments of the poet are indeed as represented in the poem. Instead, we ask whether the work has succeeded in capturing a particular set of experiences or perceptions according to a particular set of aesthetic conventions.

In judging such works, one quite properly distinguishes among more and less competent realizations of the requirements of a particular aesthetic form – better or worse Elizabethan sonnets, Kansas City jazz, Noh plays, or the like. But one would hardly look for progress in such strictly expressive endeavors, as though T. S. Eliot had been seeking to improve on the representations of the world created by Ronsard or Chaucer. If the notion of progress makes any sense at all in this realm, it would have to be reckoned in terms of the working-out of formal possibilities of different aesthetic conventions – as in the unfolding of the immanent logic of classic Greek tragedy, or abstract expressionism, or modernist architecture.

Views picturing theoretical social science in terms closely akin to these have gained much ground in the last decades of the twentieth century. This chapter explores some of their key implications.

I seek to show how essentially expressive visions of theoretical development have arisen as alternatives to other views – notably, classic natural-science accounts of intellectual progress. I want to convey some idea of the vast array of expressive attractions offered by theory and how these appeals are subject to transformation over time. And, ultimately, I argue that visions of theory in social science appealing *solely* to expressive criteria are deeply problematic.

MODEL I: THEORY AS OBJECTIVE MAPPING

Once, these questions seemed much simpler. In one traditional view, the growth of understanding of social life, like that of the natural world, amounted to something very like the mapping of newly discovered terrain. The features of social life that demanded discovery – variously conceived as laws, principles, or facts – were believed to exist in objective form, awaiting the attentions of analysts acute enough to uncover them. The problem was simply to record each feature accurately.

This notion of the growth of knowledge as a form of "objective mapping" takes as its basis certain natural-science models of social inquiry like those developed by Carl Hempel, Ernest Nagel, and George Homans. I present it here as an ideal type, a model perhaps more extreme than would be articulated by any real analyst. But these authors, like others, did share the notion that theory grows by recording the realities of a world that exists "out there," independent of the human imagination. Thus the theorist's work is a matter of "filling in the unknown spaces" with reliable knowledge, adding incrementally so that blank spaces gradually give way to reliably documented, stable features.

Less metaphorically, this view takes it for granted not only that the law-like relationships constituting theoretical knowledge are real, but also that their relative importance is readily apparent. As in the genome-mapping projects that have lately entranced molecular biologists, the existence and significance of each unit is unambiguous. Principles, laws, or generalizations that govern wider slices of reality are self-evidently more important than statements that characterize smaller intellectual spaces. Imagination and creativity may well play a role in forming hypotheses as to what contours to look for. But the validity of the result is measured by its "fit" with an external reality, and the importance of each analytical insight is measured by the amount of analytical "space" that it covers.

Note the direct and reassuring implications of this doctrine for intellectual progress. As more "features" of the landscape of reality are discovered, verified, and documented, one can reasonably claim that knowledge has increased. At the same time, the notion of theoretical growth as a process of objective mapping also offers some heartening implications for relationships between theory and practice. For a reliable, objective map has a kind of prima facie usefulness. No one would want to travel the territory in question without it, and the more bits of the territory in question are mapped, the better off we are. A good, reliable map, one might say, is an all-purpose *means* for virtually any *end* involving travel within the territory in question.

I have sought to make the mapping model sound almost unexceptionable. Who, after all, could doubt that the elaboration of theoretical understanding is at least *something* like making maps of social life? But in fact the analogy does not take us very far, at least in terms of the concerns of this book.

The problem has to do with an assumption of some kind of natural "grid" giving the relative importance of "features" on the "map" of social life. Real-life cartographers do find it feasible to agree on two-dimensional coordinates, against which features of terrain are depicted. But we have no such criterion in the study of social life. That is, we have no simple or unambiguous way of classifying the relative importance of findings, concepts, social processes, causal principles, or the like.

No proponent of the models on which I base this ideal type has offered a persuasive solution to this problem. George Homans did as well as any, when he wrote:

we can look on theory as a game. The winner is the man who can deduce the *largest variety of empirical findings* from the smallest number of general propositions, with the help of a variety of given conditions. . . . A science whose practitioners have been good at playing it has achieved a great economy of thought. No longer does it face just one damn finding after another. It has acquired an organization, a structure. (1967, p. 27; emphasis added)

Homans is of course describing his own chosen model of closure, the rationale he developed for his own later work, and one that has exercised great influence over certain other investigators. But as a way of reckoning the extent or importance of theoretical knowledge, it leaves crucial questions unanswered. For if the importance of propositions is to be measured by the *variety* of findings that they can explain, how do we reckon variety? If Newton's theory of gravitation explains the action of the tides, does it grow more compelling each time the tide comes in and out? Or, in social science, is a theory that explains the distribution of bottlecaps on urban streets – to take the example from Chapter 1 – equal in importance to one that explains the high concentration of women in low-paying jobs? Most social scientists would deny this, I think, on the grounds that the value-relevance of the two *explananda* are hardly comparable.

I do not mean that social scientists have no ideas about the relative importance of different facts, findings, and principles. On the contrary, we have such ideas in abundance, but no universally persuasive way of resolving them. Any criterion to determine the relative import of different elements of theoretical knowledge *itself assumes a particular theory* – and such theories are almost always contested. Thus a basic fact of life in our disciplines is endemic controversy over the changing significance ascribed to different properties of what we rather ambiguously speak of as "the same" subject matter. Such controversy bedevils efforts to assess progress in theoretical understanding.

My *Theories of Civil Violence* afforded many examples. Perhaps the most dramatic was described in Chapter 1 of this book: the dramatic decline in the 1960s and 1970s of "collective behavior" theories of militant phenomena in favor of theories based on assumptions of individual or collective rationality. This theoretical shift, I argued, derived part of its energy from identification of authentic weaknesses in the earlier theories. But to some extent it also involved a simple *shift of attention* from certain aspects of the subject matter to others. Under the new theories, the more continuous, rational, and strategic aspects of militant phenomena came to matter more than the innovative, emotional, or improvisatory aspects. The question for present purposes is, is there any overarching standard for determining the relative importance of these different aspects of the subject matter?

Similar stories can be told of countless subject matters and subfields in our disciplines, including topics treated by feminism, rational-choice analysis, and many other theoretical visions. The shifting ascendancy of one kind of theoretical account over the other turns on which aspects of the subject matter bulk largest to analysts addressing it at the moment in question.

Note carefully: None of this is to deny that judgments of *accuracy* are possible in theoretically inspired representations of social life. As I argued in the precursor to this book, nearly all theories of civil violence imply, on close consideration, some forms of empirical evidence that would enhance their credibility, and others that would undermine it. But to establish this much helps us rather little to decide what *forms* of accuracy (or inaccuracy) should matter most in assessing the overall importance or success of the theory in question.

Judgments on these matters may strike the reader as abstract and speculative; but there should be no mistaking their centrality in our intellectual lives. Assessments of the relative import of alternate principles, findings, and intellectual strategies are the stuff of everyday theoretical life in our disciplines – and, concomitantly, the basis for judgments of what constitutes "progressive" developments. The outcomes of such judgments have profound effects on our intellectual "maps" of what we know and what we don't.

Consider a study by Robert Keohane (1986) on "neorealism" in theories of international relations, a respectful critique of the works of Kenneth Waltz. This doctrine, whose origins go back as far as Thucydides, holds that peace or turmoil in international affairs are to be explained by asymmetries of power among nations, rather than, say, by the ideological or other character of the regimes themselves.

Keohane finds serious deficiencies in Waltz's position. For example, he holds that "Waltz's theory of the balance of power is inconsistent with his assumption that states seek to 'maximize power'" (1986, p. 18). Nevertheless, Keohane's overall assessment of Waltz's work is high:

> Waltz's contribution to the study of world politics is conceptual. He helps us think more clearly about the role of systemic theory, the explanatory power of structural models, and how to account deductively for the recurrent formation of balances of power. He shows that the international system shapes state behavior as well as vice versa. These are major contributions. (pp. 174–175)

Thus, notwithstanding his skepticism about some basic assertions made by Waltz, Keohane rates the latter's work as "a major contribution" – a progressive development, presumably, or an overall *improvement* in the state of theoretical understanding.

My point is not that there is anything anomalous about Keohane's words, but that the judgments he makes here are so ubiquitous in our disciplines. What Keohane does is draw distinctions among different kinds of facts, observations, principles, and the like, and assert that the distinctive successes of Waltz's thinking ought to outweigh the weaknesses. He thus imposes his own "grid," one might say, over the subject matter, exercising his own judgments about which insights ought to count most heavily.

We recognize judgments of this kind when we hear that an author, theory, or publication "raises issues that have been too long neglected," or "casts light on some of the most important problems," or "breaks important new ground." These predictable clichés of scholarly communication carry the claim that a particular theme, subject matter, interest, or the like is notably *deserving* of attention in contrast to alternate, possibly contending possibilities. They are the very sorts of claims, let us note, that attended the redefinition in the 1960s of "what matters most" in theories of civil upheaval.

And note the implications of such judgments for the perception of direction or progress in the study of social life. When a new way of understanding is successfully portrayed as "casting light on problems that have been unjustly neglected" or the like, the stage is set for claims that the new way of looking at things represents a net theoretical *advance*. Thus the predictable tenor of theoretical rhetoric – the claims, for example, that a particular way of seeing things "breaks new ground," "sheds new light," "opens new horizons," and so on – always with the implication that the departures involved generate just the kind of knowledge most urgently needed.

Can anyone doubt the pivotal role of such judgments in our disciplines? Yet acknowledging this much raises intriguing and perplexing questions for any understanding of intellectual progress. For it could hardly be clearer that the forces shaping definitions of what constitutes significant or worthwhile insight are highly contextual and constantly subject to reinterpretation.

This fact poses severe problems for proponents of "neutral mapping models" – for example, those who, like Homans, see the growth of knowledge in terms of the propounding of law-like relationships embracing ever greater "varieties" of social phenomena. The problem is not that the sort of "growth" they have in mind cannot be documented. It is simply that *those particular forms* of growth which appear of the essence to them may simply hold no interest for other analysts. And how can it be meaningful to assert that knowledge "grows" if the sorts of "growth" in question simply lose their interest for later thinkers?

MODEL 2: THEORY AS EXPRESSION

Views of social inquiry as a process of objective "mapping" have lost support over the last generation. I hardly deny that many researchers in a variety of disciplines exert themselves to apply what they see as the equivalent of natural-science methods with an eye to achieving precise, objective renditions of their subject matter. But, since Homans, fewer and fewer social scientists have been willing to characterize the essential logic of their work as a quest for Newtonian, law-like relationships.

It seems to me that the difficulties of such a view are intractable. This is not because the measurement systems or the standards of analysis employed in social science need necessarily lack precision. The problem is that of determining the relative importance of facts, findings, and regularities ascertained by such methods. There is simply no unique "grid" available to provide a firm and objective measure of the relative import of empirical findings or theoretical ideas. Instead, any version of such a grid, most present-day commentators would agree, must take some account of the relevance of the materials being "mapped" for the values or interests of the analyst.

Nowadays, the pendulum has swung sharply away from the "neutral mapping" extreme. Instead of ability to map features of the social world that exist "out there," independently of human consciousness, theoretical success is more apt to be reckoned in terms strictly internal to the analyst. In its extreme form, this alternate view pictures theoretical success solely as the ability to capture the *experiential reality* of the analyst. Thus, if theory is expected to "fit" anything, that something is the sensibilities of the thinker.

Here, as before, I am describing an ideal type more sharply drawn than anything one would expect to encounter in the real world. But the basic themes are widespread and unmistakable, and some instances approach the extreme. Consider the words of two feminist sociologists:

"Be true to the phenomenon" is an axiom often stated within the naturalistic approach. It suggests that we should attempt to present reality as it is experienced and lived by the people that we carry out research on. But the only way that it is really possible to do this is for those people themselves to present their own accounts of their own experiences. The best alternative is that researchers should present analytical accounts of how and why we think we know what we do about research situations and the people in them. The only way we can avoid overriding other people's understandings as "deficient" in some way is not to attempt to present these within research. Instead we should be much more concerned with presenting *ourselves* and *our* understandings of what is going on. . . . (Stanley and Wise 1983, p. 168)

And, a few pages later, in responding to anticipated criticisms that their view is more akin to "novels and poetry" than to social science, they add:

"Truth" is a social construct, in the same way that "objectivity" is; and both are constructed out of experiences which are, for all practical purposes, the same as "lies" and "subjectivity." And so we see all research as "fiction" in the sense that it views and so constructs "reality" through the eyes of one person. . . . If this kind of research can open people's eyes, can influence and change them, to the extent that literature has done, then it will do better than any other social science research that has appeared to date. (p. 174)

Note the explicitness of the claim. What counts as theoretical "success" is the ability to capture or dramatize the experience of the analyst – presumably in such a way as to resonate with the sensibilities of the reader. In this case, of course, the authors have a specific sort of theoretical consumer in mind: women, and perhaps others sensitive to their distinctive needs, experiences, and interests. But one can easily imagine similar tests being applied to theoretical representations of other slices of human experience. Note that the authors seem indifferent to concerns like Homans's for a formal reckoning of the scope of analytical ideas, either in terms of the "variety" of phenomena that they describe or by any other standard. What matters, apparently, is the combination of the importance of the experience to writer and reader and the adequacy and force of its expression.

When congruence with inner sensibilities or "truth to experience" becomes the guiding criterion for theoretical success, the study of social life does indeed come to resemble art, fiction, drama, or other works of pure imagination. Under such assumptions, one would reasonably expect an endless multiplicity of valid representations of "the same" slice of social reality, reflecting different experiences and different aesthetic conventions.

Again, few social scientists are apt to invoke such a position in its pure form. But it is very common to partake of it in some degree – vide Robert Keohane's evaluation of Waltz's theories of international conflict. The virtues of those theories, Keohane thinks, have particularly to do with their ability to capture just *what matters most* in the material. Thus, the success of the work has at least partly to do with its fit with the sensibilities of the analyst concerning the relevance and importance of various aspects of the subject.

To be sure, Keohane (and Waltz) seem to take it for granted that they are describing a subject matter that exists independently of their thoughts and sentiments about it. Accordingly, one imagines, both assume that theoretical statements about that reality may be *wrong* on objective grounds and that generating such inaccurate statements vitiates the credibility of the theory. Yet Keohane clearly attributes a significant role to what one might characterize as the *meaningful* status of Waltz's work, in according it the high evaluation that he does.

The question at issue here is, what forms of accuracy matter most in judging the worth or success of theoretical analysis? What distinguishes any way of interpreting the world as an "improvement" over existing understandings? How do we know an authentic "contribution" or "advance" when we encounter it? Perhaps few would go so far as Stanley and Wise in embracing truth to inner experience as the sole or central criterion here. But in various degrees, I hold, most present-day social scientists invoke criteria of *meaningfulness* as central to their valuations of one or another form of theoretical work. And for some analysts, the fact that a particular theoretical picture seems to capture what *matters most* about the subject matter, from the standpoint of the analyst's own sensibilities, outweighs other tests of analytical success – including empirical accuracy.

Consider *The Hidden Injuries of Class*, by Richard Sennett and Jonathan Cobb (1973). This work drew considerable interest in the 1970s, evidently capturing a key expressive mood of that period. Based on long, intimate interviews conducted by the authors with working-class Bostonians, its aim was to convey the damage inflicted by social inequality in America on the self-concept of members of the stable working class. A major subtheme of the work is the authors' efforts to reconcile their own relatively privileged social position with their sympathy for the social underdogs whose lives and thoughts are depicted in their book. The expressive payoff of their inquiries is aptly summarized on the last page of the book; characterizing their subjects' retreat from the bruising realities of their lives, they write:

What fled to an interior life was their loving, because love was violated when they were working for rewards from someone else. Could it be that, in abolishing a hierarchy of reward, a society might bring these feelings back into the productive forms of men's lives? (1973, p. 262)

Thus the authors leave no doubt about the rhetorical effect that they seek for their work. Yet, for our purposes, one would also say that they have a *theory* – that is, a representation of the social world the acceptance of which they in effect commend to their readers.

But what about analysts inclined to dispute the representations of Sennett and Cobb – those, for example, who posit that blue-collar workers experience no more inner conflict or psychic wear-and-tear concerning their working lives than do members of the middle class? Does the empirical material presented in the book *constrain* the authors' original theoretical inspiration, or is it strictly a vehicle for conveying that inspiration? Here Sennett and Cobb are candid. "We have taken certain liberties," they write:

In a few instances, we have put words in people's mouths, words they were struggling for, we felt, but couldn't find. Twice we have combined elements from several life histories into one. . . . It is for clarity and art that we have done so. . . .

... Art creates a different truth from the recitation and interpretation of facts. (pp. 42–43)

And, a bit later:

We have tried as far as we could to see through the eyes of the workers talking. Sometimes, however, we have also tried to explain experiences they had but which we felt they did not fully understand. . . . (p. 45)

No doubt many social scientists have "put words in people's mouths" that they did not hear, though not all would be so direct as these authors in acknowledging it.

Sennett and Cobb are right to note the tension between the requirements of "art" and other competing demands that might be applied to analytical work, including empirical accuracy. And clearly the choices one makes in these connections make profound differences, both in the kinds of representations that result and in the standards we adopt for theoretical "success." On the one hand, we have a view of theory as a guide to a reality that exerts its constraints over our experience, whether we are aware of those constraints or not. On the other hand, we have theory as an expression of perceptions, sensibilities, and understandings that reside in the consciousness of the analyst and that of his or her audience, regardless of their accuracy as guides to any external world.

It is precisely the tension between these two demands that is highlighted by the constructivist study of science discussed in Chapter 2. The epistemology and style of analysis invoked by these writers is not just a way of thinking about science, but an approach to knowledge in general. And the hallmark of this approach is to debunk *any* notion that a reality beyond the consciousness of the analyst might be expected to constrain theoretical representation of that reality.

Thus the characteristic efforts of the constructivists to show how the supposedly "hard" attestations of scientific inquiry are in fact "constructed" – that is, produced by conscious and unconscious efforts at persuasion, including self-persuasion, by working scientists. The question then becomes, not how researchers succeed in uncovering facts, so much as how facts are created and ratified as their creators promote agreement from all concerned that their authenticity is beyond reproach. Recall the statement from Latour and Woolgar, quoted in Chapter 2:

In a fundamental sense, our own account is no more than *fiction*. But this does not make it inferior to the activity of laboratory members: they too were busy constructing accounts to be launched in the agonistic field, and loaded with various sources of credibility in such a way that once convinced, others would incorporate them as givens, or as matters of fact, in their own constructions of reality. . . . (Latour and Woolgar 1986, pp. 257–258)

What would Latour and Woolgar have to say about the validity of representations like those put forward by Stanley and Wise, or by Sennett and

Cobb? Do their ideas deserve to take their place in the canon of authoritative knowledge? From the constructivist standpoint, any representation would have to be counted as good as any other in this respect – if only people can be moved to accept it. So long as it attracts consumers, the product is a success. As with other works of pure imagination, the resonance of the formulation with the experience of the analyst, or the "consumer" of the analysis, is the ultimate criterion of success.

What do such views imply about the possibilities for progress in social inquiry? I am unaware of any direct statements on these matters from the constructivists. But, to be consistent, they should characterize progress in social science in much the same terms as in the natural sciences. Progress, they might hold, is an account that participants in scientific communication create for themselves. The notion may be useful for all sorts of purposes – not least of which may be appeals for funding, appointments, and other resources. But progress, like scientific knowledge more generally, is *constructed*. And what is constructed at one juncture can readily be deconstructed at the next.

For consistent constructivists, it makes no sense to distinguish between good and poor grounds for theoretical statements. If the community embraces an idea, that fact attests to its success. And what defines the boundaries of this community? Presumably whatever principles its members may construct.

The constructivists' position represents something close to a totally expressive rationale for theory. I suspect that few working social scientists would be willing to endorse their doctrine in its full form – to the extent, for example, of rejecting the very possibility that an external world might constrain our understandings of that world. Yet some expressive principles have gained considerable currency – for example, the notion that some form of "truth to one's inner experience" ought, for some purposes, to outweigh the importance of empirical accuracy in theoretical analysis. And most social scientists, like Keohane, would probably endorse the view that the value-relevance or meaningful status of phenomena ought to have *something* to do with importance ascribed to theoretical ideas.

All of these views pose problems for any attempt to define and chart progress in theoretical understanding.

THEORY AS END: THEORY AS MEANS

It is of course true that analytical worldviews cannot simply be bracketed as "right" or "wrong," as one might do for strategies for finding needles in haystacks. Such a view would picture social science inquiry strictly as a means to ends that all could agree upon. By contrast, an opposing position would be to conceive of theoretical work as oriented to ends defined only by theory itself. Such a consummatory view of theory would place no importance on the usefulness of theoretical ideas for any form of guidance in dealing with exigencies of social facts, forces, or arrangements.

All of this may strike some readers as hopelessly abstract. Abstract it is, but scarcely hopeless. And the issues involved are utterly pertinent to our day-to-day analytical work. For representations of the social world that may be held successful in one set of terms may be quite disastrous from the other. To put matters crudely, ideas that provide useful guidance for coping may fail as vehicles for the expression of our most deeply felt sensibilities and meanings. And representations that may bring the greatest meaningful satisfaction in their contemplation may be useless as guides for dealing with the world they depict.

Consider a simplified example: the creation of a character portrait of one's worst enemy. Such an effort amounts to a kind of theoretical exercise, yielding a model of the person's makeup bearing implications for how she or he might be expected to act in future situations.

I suspect that nearly everyone has engaged in such model-building efforts, and where the target is indeed an antagonist, the criteria of success are apt to be strictly expressive. One constructs a devastating account of the subject's moral failures, showing the dark side of every apparent virtue and weaving together seemingly innocent shortcomings into a meaningfully integrated, comprehensive totality of mean-spiritedness, hypocrisy, and superficiality. The ability to create such portraits so that "consumers" find them moving and convincing is of course a key skill of the novelist or dramatist. And in fiction, as in everyday life, the expressive elegance and aesthetic unity of such a portrait may make the characterization indelibly convincing, both to the creator and to others exposed to it.

But the success of such representations in comforting the thinker, or in mobilizing others to share the creator's view, have to be distinguished from their trustworthiness as bases for practical action. If the figure so devastatingly represented as the embodiment of treachery and selfishness in fact proves to act expansively and decently, one kind of analytical requirement has been violated. Representations that bring satisfaction in the contemplation – even if they are laden with meaning and elegant in execution – may nevertheless be completely misleading as guides for dealing with the social forces that inspire them.

The same issues arise constantly in social science proper. Consider the case of Elton Mayo and his "human relations school of management," a notable example of a once respected theoretical vision now in eclipse. The theory, and Mayo, rose to prominence at the Harvard Business School in the 1930s and 1940s. Appalled at what he saw as the insensitive practices of management in his day, he held that conflicts in organizations, such as those between labor and management, were the result of *misunderstanding*. Accordingly, the best way of resolving conflict and getting people to work more harmoniously with one another was to get them together, and encourage them to talk out their differences, and thereby resolve their alleged misunderstandings.

For years, Mayo's doctrine was a theoretical success story. In the consensus-hungry climates of the forties and fifties, it conveyed to many people concerned with organizations exactly what they wanted to hear.

The only trouble with all this, as nearly all subsequent students of organizations have seen the matter, is that Mayo's doctrine is gravely misleading for anyone needing to cope with real cases of organizational conflict. Many disputes – both inside organizations and out – arise from authentic conflicts of interest that do not necessarily stand to be reduced by the parties' knowing more about one another's positions. Indeed, it appears that communication between antagonistic parties is often extremely counterproductive as a strategy in getting people to work together. Often, if people learn what their antagonists *really* think about them and the situations in hand, conflict is apt to grow so destructive as to be virtually irresolvable.

In strictly expressive terms, Mayo's doctrine could hardly have been a more meaningful manifestation of the spirit of its times. Yet on closer scrutiny it appears to be of dubious value as a source of guidance for coping with the rude constraints of organizational forces and processes. Similar observations can be made for countless other theoretical themes and doctrines – ranging from the self-comforting views of militant political activity as a symptom of social disorganization put forward by mass society theorists, to the insistences of pro-Moscow Marxists in the 1980s that the Soviet Union was poised to overtake capitalism. These representations, and the theoretical worldviews generating them, clearly offered every satisfaction in the contemplation. Where they failed was in providing guidance to the working of social processes that, we must assume, impinge upon us whether we choose to contemplate them or not.

Note carefully: My point here is *not* that all theoretical doctrines that we find comforting or satisfying to contemplate are ipso facto misleading. Sometimes, after all, our worst enemies prove to be every bit as treacherous as our uncharitable theories about them suggest. Still less do I advocate any attempt to exorcise ideas having strong aesthetic or emotional resonance from our theories – as though such a thing were even possible. What I do insist is that we cannot afford to ignore the distinction between these two quite different notions of theoretical success.

In most scholarly communication, this Janus-faced character of theoretical work seems to go unremarked. We often assume that the pictures of the social world presented by our theories, if "true" for one purpose, are valid for all. And the patterns of "consumption" of theoretical work are such that discrepancies between these two aspects of theory may pass unnoticed almost indefinitely. Many, perhaps most, representations of social life are unlikely ever to become bases for the sorts of practical interventions that would reveal discrepancies between their expressive appeals and their trustworthiness as bases for coping. Instead, most theoretical representations live and die, one might say, strictly as "consumption items" – as reflections aimed at giving satisfaction in the contemplation.

This fact is perhaps most easily recognized in journalistic renditions of tidbits of quasi-social-scientific insight – for example, in vivid thumbnail surveys of sexual behavior, or accounts of personality determinants of success in the workplace, or other topics with which nearly everyone can identify. The most casual attention to television talk shows or popular writings on current affairs often makes it clear that the immediate satisfaction of the consumer is the overriding organizing principle. Like the readers of horoscopes and the contents of fortune cookies, the consumers of such representations of the social world probably do not care very much whether the accounts represent a reliable guide to constraints imposed by the social world. Comparing one's own sex life or workplace experiences with the representations conveyed in a lively but haphazard survey at least makes life more *interesting,* if only for a few moments.

It may seem bizarre to link theoretical social science with the lowbrow diversions just mentioned. But who can deny that many waves of theoretical enthusiasm rise and fall among one or another intellectual community simply because of their appeal as intellectual "consumption items"? In *Theories of Civil Violence,* I sought to show a number of junctures where models of the origins of civil strife came and went very much on the strength of such considerations. Indeed, such sequences were much more conspicuous than those in which evidentiary considerations had played a major role in theoretical change. Like journalistic accounts of the Loch Ness monster or the Abominable Snowman, certain theoretical ideas in our disciplines are simply too seductive to be ignored – regardless of the guidance (or lack of it) they offer for dealing with the world that inspires them.

"Just because it didn't happen, doesn't mean it's not true." So wrote a noted novelist, in a perfect evocation of the expressive logic of his craft. In works of the imagination, the fact that a text does not offer practical guidance for dealing with specific events, people, or social arrangements is irrelevant to the success of the work. That success turns instead on the ability of the novelist to make his or her rendition of experience meaningful to that of the reader and to cast these renditions into elegant, satisfying, understandable aesthetic forms. These are consummatory virtues, the virtues of art pursued for its own sake. The question is, are virtues of this kind the only ones that the theories of social scientists ought to maximize?

THE ORIGINS OF EXPRESSIVE REWARDS

What gives theoretical ideas expressive appeal? What circumstances, relationships, social positions, or the like tend to make such ideas attractive as "consumption items"? Any complete response to this question is far beyond my powers here. The best I can do is to note some of the extreme diversity of such appeals.

Clearly, many theoretical visions draw adherents through the sheer aesthetic elegance of their concepts and formulations. Recall Donald McCloskey's statement on economic theory:

In the flight of rockets the layman can see the marvel of physics, and in the applause of audiences the marvel of music. No one understands the marvel of economics who has not studied it with care. (1985, p. xix)

Here McCloskey comes close to affirming something left veiled by enthusiasts of other theoretical visions: that the worldview he favors defines and validates the terms of its own success, and – by implication – that those outside the circle of theoretical initiation are unable to pass judgment on such success. Economic theory, and the representations of the world that it yields, are not means to ends that just any of us might entertain; they are ends in themselves.

Elsewhere, theoretical systems seem to derive their appeal simply from their role as status markers for the theorists who embrace them, casting the latter as a theoretical elite in relation to exponents of less worthy visions. The neoclassical economic theories touted by McCloskey clearly exercise this sort of appeal for many enthusiasts, but the case is by no means unique. Consider, for example, Jeffrey Alexander's claims for the virtues of his style of general theory:

the temptation to depart from such stringent and elevated standards is great. To maintain a synthetic aim is consistently to resist any presuppositional bias, to maintain an objective, multidimensional orientation rarely achieved in the history of sociological thought. (1983b, p. 151)

In other contexts, it appears that certain theoretical positions hold special expressive appeal for thinkers of specific personality types. Theoretical visions are supposed to tell us something about the world of social forces, facts, and processes. But they also tell us something about the people who embrace them. They make statements, more often implicitly than explicitly, about all sorts of highly charged value issues. In so doing, they convey messages about the social identities and self-concepts of those

187

who embrace them – messages both to outside "consumers" of these ideas and, perhaps more importantly, to the theorists themselves.

Surely every working social scientist has noted such influences. It would be hard to deny, for example, that we expect adherents of different theoretical positions to be different sorts of people – in personality and political conviction as well as in analytical style. On learning that someone we meet styles himself a feminist, we entertain rather different expectations of him from those we would of someone who presents herself as a sociobiologist or a rational-choice theorist. The research on the effects of training in economics on the personalities of students reported in Chapter 3 (Frank, Gilovich, and Regan 1993) suggests that these expectations may be well founded.

Elsewhere, theoretical ideas draw their appeal from their role in status contention or defense of shared material interests in the broader social context. One of Weber's great insights was that no privileged group is ever satisfied with a worldview that pictures its own privilege as resulting from simple accident or opportunism. Much the same observation must hold, mutatis mutandis, for the worldviews of insurgent groups seeking more generous allocations of status or material preferment. In all such cases, *ideas* that make satisfactory sense of one's most cherished interests are necessary. Social science theories are not the only ideas that serve these purposes, but they offer the same sorts of consummatory satisfactions as do more blatant affirmations of group honor or other interests.

Consider a theoretical enthusiasm discussed at length in *Theories of Civil Violence* (1988, chap. 2): the "vogue of Pareto" among conservative and centrist intellectuals in the 1930s. Faced with the collapse of parliamentary systems in the face of militant social movements of the right and left, intellectuals sought a theory that could make meaningful sense of the situation. For some, Marxism was an obvious answer, but its implications for established interests were disturbing. Pareto's dense, long-winded works seemed to offer an equally "deep" interpretation of the origins of militant movements, without necessarily casting conservative interests in a negative light. Largely because of such expressive appeal, it appears, Pareto became for a time what one commentator called "a Marx for the middle classes."

Like many other theoretical worldviews, Pareto's provided, often without overtly purporting to, *moral definitions or redefinitions* of human experience. In the case in point, it seemed to accord moral recognition as much to determined defenders of established regimes as to successful revolutionaries. As bases for either insurgent ideologies or those of established regimes, such mind-sets obviously exercise enormous expressive appeals for specific constituencies.

Similarly, some versions of rational-choice thinking and neoclassical economic thought make it impossible to attribute any meaningful status to the notion of exploitation. If a theory casts all action as the outcome of free choice by all parties, the notion that anyone could be systematically wronged by any system of exchange simply makes no sense. By contrast, the official Marxism–Leninism that until recently dominated public discourse in much of the world made it impossible to conceive of any relationship between capitalist and employee as *anything other than* exploitation. The expressive appeals of such idea-systems to thinkers in specific social positions hardly require interpretation.

Or, consider the intense expressive appeals of feminist analysis in academic social science in recent decades. Clearly these theoretical efforts to "put women at the center" of analytical attention have succeeded largely by tapping a deep vein of "pent-up demand." Apparently on careful assessment of the relations between theory and interest, academic feminists have effectively institutionalized the claims of their constituencies. They have developed a theoretical position self-consciously aimed at promoting the interests of their movement, with the insistence that this way of looking at the world take a prominent place among other varieties of theoretical work. These efforts have generated courses, journals, literatures, and university programs – in short, the full panoply of material and symbolic arrangements that serves to establish and institutionalize theoretical success in university life.

Theory, among all forms of intellectual endeavor, seems to play an especially potent role as a vehicle for consolidating group identity – and hence as a means for advancing status claims and other collective interests. It is hard to miss the difference between a group of claimants with a list of demands and the same group whose interests are organized and encapsulated in a coherent doctrine. The latter, after all, provides complex justifications and rationales for action; more, it makes the aims of adherents appear as more than simple expressions of ad hoc or self-serving wishes. Theories that can accomplish this are bound to hold special appeal for their "natural constituencies."

Indeed, in the status contests and material struggles that so pervasively shape our intellectual life, theory often confers advantages of the sort described by Thorstein Veblen. Like other embodiments of group honor – seals, ancient mottos, and similar totems of group identity – theory can serve to support claims of abstract and high-minded justification for shared interests. Moreover, it creates opportunities for what Veblen identified as exercises in conspicuous consumption or conspicuous waste. Like Sanskrit ritual in Hindu culture, foot binding in traditional China, or the learning of Latin and Greek among the British upper classes, "theorizing" may play the role of a demanding and expensive activity publicly touted as indispensable to the honor of the group.

THE SHIFTING APPEALS OF THEORY

The dual role of theoretical representation – as a vehicle for expression of inner sensibilities versus as a guide to constraints imposed by an exterior world – raises far-reaching problems for any effort to understand theoretical change. For we have no reason to assume that the appeals that bring any particular theoretical vision into currency in the first place will be the same as those that underlie support for it later on. On the contrary, theoretical ideas that initially attract attention because of their claims to yield guidance for practical action may later come to justify themselves in consummatory terms – as ends in their own right.

Consider the distinction between magic and religion. Magic is a kind of technology, a means for manipulating the world. Thus the efficacy of magical practices may be directly assessed in terms of how well they serve the interests of those who invoke them. By contrast, religion is a set of beliefs and practices that specify what our interests *should* be, and which guide us in pursuing the "proper" interests.

True, religious practice often involves magical elements, as when the faithful pray for solution of practical problems. But, for the devout, failure to have one's prayers answered can always be explained away – for example, on the ground that one's requests do not suit the inscrutable will of the Deity. Thus, if magical practices don't work – if they don't solve the problems that cause us to take recourse to them – we are justified in simply rejecting them. But if religious faith fails to make us rich, or to bring spiritual peace, or to settle conflicts with our loved ones, true believers will likely insist that we are asking the wrong things of it. In this case, we are expected to adjust ourselves to the demands of the faith, rather than expect it to resolve questions that we bring to it from the outside.

Serious Christian believers sometimes pose the following question: If we are all to be resurrected bodily after the second coming of Christ, along with our loved ones, with which of my former spouses will I be reunited? Such questions can take on a certain urgency, depending on the feelings of the faithful about the partners in question. To such dilemmas, one standard response of church doctrine is: Do not worry about such things; these concerns will not matter in the New Age. In short, those interests that the faith does not satisfy, the faithful must redefine as unworthy of concern. If magic is a means for solving problems that people define for themselves, religion is a series of solutions to problems that it defines for itself – and a series of exhortations to embrace those problems rather than others.

Parallels to theoretical social science should not be missed. Both religious worldviews and theories of social life must address the fact that the concerns, interests, and needs people bring with them to the system are not necessarily ones that the system is capable of solving in their own terms. Hence the necessity to redefine, for outsiders to the system, what should constitute a valid or reasonable expectation. In their efforts of self-perpetuation, proponents of both kinds of systems are apt to alter, over time, what they promise to deliver. Instead of promising answers to concerns that just anyone might experience, for example, successful systems may insist on defining what constitutes a reasonable concern in the first place.

Something very similar happens constantly with strictly aesthetic conventions. When a new aesthetic comes to the fore in music, art, or drama, it is apt to strike "consumers" as jarring or demanding; yet the minority of innovations that succeed eventually come to dictate standards for future appreciation. In the jazz world, when innovators in the 1940s abandoned swing for bebop, many longtime jazz lovers were revolted. They found the music unlistenable-to, a rude disappointment for what they considered normal aesthetic yearnings. Yet within a few decades the new music had become the norm to jazz listeners, to the extent that swing and other earlier styles sounded old-fashioned.

In the study of social life, claims made on behalf of an insurgent theory hungry for attention may be quite different from those made for the same theory when it can dictate expectations for theoretical success. Consider psychoanalysis – surely one of the major theoretical success stories of twentieth-century social science. Freud began the inquiries that gave rise to his system through pursuit of an explicitly *practical* problem: the treatment of certain particularly resistant forms of psychosomatic disease among middle-class, mainly Jewish women. These studies, of course, marked the beginnings of Freud's theories of the unconscious.

By all accounts, Freud was an intensely ambitious man. Having propounded a highly original theory of hysteria, he was quick to apply his ideas to a stunningly wide variety of new phenomena – from the causes of forgetting and slips of the tongue, to the etiology of dreams, to the formation of different personality types, and, ultimately, the origins of civilization and the bases of ethical judgment. In short, his psychodynamic theories made the ticklish transition from a rationale for medical treatment to a comprehensive theoretical worldview.

By the middle of the century, psychoanalytic ideas were becoming a common reference in all branches of humanistic culture throughout the Western democracies. The doctrine flourished especially on the strength of its claims of access to the "real" meanings of all sorts of familiar phenomena – especially in the once secret domains of sexuality. By the 1950s and 1960s, in many circles of academic social scientists, one could hardly expect to be taken seriously without claiming some acquaintance with psychoanalytic thinking. In the terms developed here, one would say that the once obscure doctrine was coming to set the terms of theoretical expectations that other theories were expected to meet.

During this period, many social scientists joined psychoanalytic institutes and underwent psychoanalysis. Citations to the psychoanalytic literature became de rigueur, even in writing about subjects where the connections would have seemed far from obvious. The force of psychoanalytic thinking in the theories of Parsons and Bales, as discussed in Chapter 2, was simply one instance of this strikingly pervasive influence.

Note a key advantage of psychoanalysis in extending its theoretical sway. As a theoretical system, it was enormously productive of *meanings*. Like horoscopes, but with far more impressive claims to scientific authority, psychoanalytic interpretations of personal events, political phenomena, group process, literary work, art, and a vast variety of other matters of human concern, were always provocative. Exponents of the doctrine claimed to identify the *true* reasons for all sorts of phenomena in the steamy realms of inner feelings, impulses, and processes. These were areas that people somehow felt *must* be important, but where other forms of analysis seemingly could not venture. And skeptics could always be elegantly debunked as unwilling or unable to confront the potent but threatening truths that psychoanalysis alone was held qualified to convey.

By the 1970s, however, the cachet of psychoanalysis was distinctly on the wane. Part of the reason, one suspects, was the inevitable decline of the scarcity value of the theory; because of the theory's very success, psychoanalysis was losing its ability to differentiate the cognoscenti from the rest.

At the same time, empirical research had begun to catch up with some of the doctrine's substantive claims. Perhaps particularly because of the considerable cost to patients (and increasingly, to third-party payers) of undergoing psychoanalysis, researchers were beginning to question the efficacy of psychoanalytic treatment versus other treatments of psychological complaints. One striking result of these studies was to cast doubt on the notion that psychoanalytic treatment offers any special advantages over other forms of counseling in terms of alleviation of symptoms (see MacMillan 1991, chap. 14). The special social and theoretical cachet of Freud's classic treatment notwithstanding, it seemed no more effective than many less pretentious (and expensive) approaches.

These findings hold special interest here. For they bear on the original claims of psychoanalysis as a method for treating mental or emotional difficulties – that is, as a means of solving problems that virtually anyone could define as problematic. Yet, of course, by the time these claims came in for systematic investigation, the doctrine had already attained the status of a compelling worldview in its own right – a theoretical "aesthetic" that to some degree set the terms of inquiry rather than responding to expectations that theoretical "outsiders" brought to the theory.

I remember a comment made in the 1960s by an eminent psychologist on the competition between psychoanalysis and conditioning therapies for treatment of neurotic symptoms. Psychoanalysis enjoys a distinct advantage, he argued, simply because it is more *interesting*. People like to *talk* about their own psychoanalyses and those of others. By contrast, behavior therapies generate no distinctive *interpretations* of life experience. Indeed, the brief, straightforward (but often effective) treatments seem to leave little to talk about.

At first I thought this observation was simply witty and entertaining. Now it seems to me profound. In effect, the commentator was distinguishing between the expressive or consummatory value of psychoanalysis, on the one hand, and its pragmatic value as a form of treatment. The extreme vogue that the doctrine enjoyed seems to have had much more to do with the former than with the latter.

Psychoanalysis has been in decline since roughly the 1970s. No longer commanding much scarcity value in university circles, it has ceased to represent a principle of demarcation between the intellectually sophisticated and others. Its special prolific qualities of indeterminacy, richness in the generation of meanings, and subtlety have been all but equaled by more recent – and accordingly, scarcer – sources such as Habermas, Foucault, or Derrida. By the time these words are read, this list is apt to be obsolete in turn.

I hardly mean to suggest that nothing endures from the insights of Freud and his followers. On the contrary, a number of psychoanalytic ideas seem to represent enduringly valuable tools for coping with fundamental perplexities of human relations. Thanks to psychoanalysis, it is hard to discount the role of unconscious mental processes or dismiss the possibility that childhood psychosexual conflicts, including ones lost to conscious memory, may cause apparently unrelated symptoms later in life. In fact, these insights have entered so thoroughly into our common lore that we may forget the role psychoanalysis played in making them apparent. But to endorse the practical benefits of such insights, one need hardly embrace the entire ornate extravaganza of psychoanalytic theory, most of which, I suspect, will appear in historical retrospect to have been a passing taste.

In a wide-ranging commentary on the life cycles of theoretical worldviews, Neil Smelser makes an observation that is highly apposite here. He notes the tendency of purportedly general theories in social science to "theoretical degeneration" (1992, p. 35). They may begin with sweeping claims to describe and explain all aspects of social behavior. But in the face of criticism from the outside and on further reflection from within, they devolve over time toward "circular reasoning, tautology, and lack of falsifiability . . . [and a resulting] capacity to explain everything and nothing" (p. 36).

Smelser applies this description specifically to psychoanalysis; Freud's original doctrine, he observes, had "a certain theoretical determinacy."

> But as psychoanalytical tradition evolved, the numbers of drives and strivings multiplied . . . as did the number and types of defenses. . . . It also came to be appreciated . . . that defenses can have the significance of drives and drives can become defensive in character. . . . Finally, the concept of the unconscious has been something of a theoretical respository where the analyst can find and elaborate motivational tendencies and strategies that are not otherwise explicable. The result of these kinds of theoretical loosening is that *any and every* item of behavior can be explained by reference to *some* combination of elements in the loosely organized repertoire found in the psychoanalytic perspective. As a result, the perspective has lost both explanatory power and theoretical determinacy. (1992, pp. 400–401)

In short, it became more and more difficult to imagine any form of empirical observation that might conceivably count as evidence against the theory.

I believe that Smelser is right in this observation – both as it applies to psychoanalysis and as an account of a more general life-cycle process in theoretical systems. And I believe that the process he is describing amounts to a shift in the essential claims of theories, from those justified in terms of coping to those of an essentially expressive nature. What has happened in the case of psychoanalysis, I believe, is that, as that worldview has become less credible as a means to other ends (i.e., to the treatment of neuroses), it has come to present itself as an end in itself.

Anyone who has personal experience with psychoanalysis – even simply through acquaintance with patients or practitioners – quickly understands that it is something much more far-reaching than just a method of solving preexistent "problems" as experienced by the patient. For those seriously involved in it, psychoanalysis redefines areas of life as problematic that had not previously been experienced as such and specifies new understandings of what constitutes satisfactory or unsatisfactory resolutions to such problems. Its most notable successes, for the initiated, can thus only be appreciated "from inside," after deep acquaintance with the system. Like the "marvel of economics" touted by Donald McCloskey, its marvelous qualities are accessible only to those properly initiated into the doctrine.

Such a life cycle of theoretical claims, I suspect, is widespread among theoretical worldviews in our disciplines. Originally presenting themselves as tools for solving problems that virtually anyone can recognize, they eventually defend themselves against empirically based criticism by defining themselves as ends in themselves. Thus they lay their claims to theoretical attention to their "suggestiveness," "richness," or "elegance." These claims are easily defended – so long as people are willing to attest that they experience the views in question in these terms. If I report that I find psychoanalysis – or structural functionalism, or rational-choice theory – highly "suggestive" as a means of making sense of the social world, who can dispute my reports of my own experience?

STRUGGLES FOR THEORETICAL SUPREMACY

Theories do not come and go gracefully on our intellectual stage. The thumbnail account above of the rise and decline of Freud's system omitted the wheeling and dealing, personal manipulation, threats, and cajolery involved in promoting that worldview or resisting such promotions. Given that theories bear such conspicuous relations to down-to-earth social interests – from status to employment to political power – it would be surprising if their proponents accepted success or failure quietly and with good grace.

Instead, proponents of theories engage in constant efforts at persuasion. The aim, conscious or not, is to achieve what always occurs when a particular artistic form gains general currency – that is, a sense that the way of seeing provided by the theory puts one in touch with the most basic levels of reality, with what really matters in the material. This is not easily achieved. Almost all theoretical activity in social science involves obsessions with abstractions or aims that are bound to puzzle theoretical outsiders. Why should anyone *care* about representing a community as a series of network ties, for example, or about classifying countries according to their position in something called a world system?

Efforts to make such seemingly arbitrary interests seem natural and indeed indispensable take many forms. One of the most common is simply the insistence – preferably with suitable rhetorical flourish – that the focus of one's favored theory indeed constitutes *the most basic, most elementary* dimension of social life. Thus, the standard ideas of the theory are held to represent *core concepts, fundamental social relationships* – in short, *the bedrock reality* of the subject matter. No point in theoretical discussion is defended more vigorously than the "natural" status of such theoretical conventions. Such defenses amount to assertions that one's own cherished worldview offers the unique means for grasping what any reasonable analyst would want to understand.

Theoretical proselytizers often do not present well-worked-out rationales as to why their way of seeing things solves puzzles recognizable from any theoretical perspective. Instead, they exhort would-be "consumers" to *redefine* what constitutes worthwhile or authentic theoretical understanding. Note the words of a proponent of ethnomethodology insisting that her specialty is "here to stay" (Boden 1990, p. 185); she writes:

[C]oncern with the *details* of action also . . . [requires] firm bracketing of all conventional sociological theorizing and an insistence on what Garfinkel and Sacks . . . termed "ethnomethodological indifference." Far from abandoning systematic method, ethnomethodological indifference is actually central to scientific enquiry. By bracketing a priori assumptions about social phenomena, relationships, and even outcomes, the investigator can go and look at the world and observe what is happening in a rigorously empirical manner. . . . Through the microscope, one can see glimpses of the fine structure of the social universe. (1990, p. 191)

I quote this passage not because of anything unusual about it, but because its appeals are so predictable, regardless of the theoretical persuasion on behalf of which they are made. The author insists that the distinctive way of seeing things that she espouses is uniquely capable of revealing what *really matters* about the subject matter. By stripping away the distortions seen through other theoretical viewpoints, she asserts, one gets right down to the most basic, the most fundamental layers of social reality – those that occupy the distinctive focus of her theoretical apparatus.

These statements really amount to an exhortation to redefine the domains or dimensions of social reality highlighted by ethnomethodology as the most worthy of analytical attention. There is no systematic case made as to what standard of judgment is to be used to uphold such claims. What one does find in Boden's essay are efforts at what one might call theoretical seduction. Try it, she tells us; imagine for a moment how the world would look as interpreted through our theoretical lens. Statements to much the same effect could be cited on behalf of the most diverse theoretical visions.

Boden's efforts at intellectual enticement are typical of one rhetorical strategy for portraying seemingly arbitrary theoretical preoccupations as natural or indispensable. Another tack is to invoke a *narrative* of intellectual progress in which one's own theoretical position represents the logical and inevitable development of earlier theoretical understandings. We work with these concepts, we focus on these issues, the story goes, because they are the precipitate of the successful intellectual struggles of our forebears.

The most fabulous success in this respect was, of course, the work of Talcott Parsons. The ultimate justification for the elaboration of his extraordinary system, so obscure to uninitiated outsiders, lay in the historical narrative set down in *The Structure of Social Action*. For generations, many social scientists identified that work as establishing Parsons's model of closure as the unique theoretical node through which all successful analytical routes must pass.

Evidence of the inaccuracy of that narrative, I have argued, was never far to seek. Nevertheless, what ultimately undercut the supremacy of Parsons's system was not critical attention to any fatal flaw in the historical pedigree he claimed. Rather, people simply stopped *caring* about the historical scenario he preached, and the concepts he derived from it. Other virtues, other forms of meaning came, after the 1970s, to matter more.

This is the common – one might almost say, the universal – fate of comprehensive theoretical visions, whether they base their claims on reconstructions of intellectual history or some other appeal to meaningful status. At some point, the distinctive accomplishments of the theory – or its "core concepts," "basic structures," or the like – simply no longer strike people as essential, or perhaps even as particularly noteworthy. If anything at all endures from such systems, it comes down to us in the form of discrete chunks – single concepts, empirical findings, analytical strategies, and so on – rather than as a comprehensive program of inquiry.

Was Parsons's "theoretical convergence" indeed the stunning advance in theoretical understanding that it was purported to be? One might ask the same question about ethnomethodology or any number of other once ascendant theoretical programs whose appeal now has largely or wholly subsided.

One could temporize, insisting simply that these innovations represented an advance "for their time," only to be superseded by subsequent "advances." But such a position begs the question that matters most here: Do the theoretical "accomplishments" touted for any theoretical system matter for analysts today? Do any of their distinctive insights represent promising tools for analytical ends likely to matter to thinkers from other generations or social contexts? Are the questions that they answer, and their ways of answering them, likely to engage the interests of those whose thinking is framed in quite different expressive contexts? Or is it more accurate simply to describe these now largely anachronistic theoretical enterprises as responses to what have proved to be transient expressive tastes – tastes that their proponents sought, for a time successfully, to foster as widely as possible?

SAFETY IN NUMBERS

One approach to such provocative questions, consistent with a broadly expressive view of theoretical success, might go as follows: These ideas were successful so long as they continued to give shape to the thoughts and actions of those who believed them. Theories succeed, in this view, insofar as they provide a vision of life that "works," and perhaps a basis for concerted action, as defined by those who embrace it. The action involved might be anything from the creation of a learned society, to defense of privileged social arrangements, to the creation of a social movement. Thus, ethnomethodology, rational-choice thinking, or Marxism would be considered successful – that is, progressive – insofar as the meaning-systems they generate continue to move people to action in directions implied by the theory. By the same token, one might hold, the sign that the ideas in question are no longer "moving ahead" might be the fact that people cease to be moved by them.

Such a view clearly points to a noteworthy feature shared by social science theories and other idea-systems – the fact that they may "work" as "self-fulfilling prophecies." A rhetorically compelling portrait of the personality of one's worst enemy, after all, may be so engaging as to convince both one's self and others of its truth, regardless of observable discrepancies between it and the actual conduct of the person concerned. Similarly, many theoretical ideas from social science offer their adherents a worldview so seductive and so comprehensive as to bear all sorts of implications for the conduct of social action – vide rational-choice thinking and certain versions of feminism. Insofar as the relevant theory is indeed shared among a wide constituency, it may "succeed" by providing its adherents with a set of principles to live by. In this view, one might say, theories enjoy "safety in numbers."

This form of theoretical success obviously represents an enormous force in human affairs. Yet it is essentially indistinguishable from the sort of success that might be attributed to *myth* – that is, to the power to justify and direct human action regardless of any other criterion of validity.

Most social scientists, I believe, expect something more of their analytical equipment than what myth provides. What we require is the ability to distinguish between ideas whose success is purely mythic or ideological and those for which reasoned justification can be offered. As Chapter 2 noted, witchcraft was a "theory" that enjoyed wide success in terms of the numbers embracing it in its heyday; even some of the victims of the theory seem to have shared its premises. But in light of current understandings of witchcraft, we cannot afford to be satisfied with a view of theories in which their currency represents the last word as to their truth value. Accordingly, we need forms of theoretical analysis capable of identifying ideas that may find safety in numbers, yet which must ultimately be judged misleading as bases for dealing with the world.

There can be no doubt that doctrines with affinities to the safety-in-numbers principle have come in recent decades to exercise considerable influence. In the sociology of science, as Chapter 2 noted, both followers of Merton and their sometime critics, the constructivists, have embraced what might be called behavioral criteria of theoretical success. For the constructivists, scientific "truth" consists simply of those ideas which particular scientists succeed in winning acceptance for. For the Mertonians, the success of scientific ideas is manifest in the frequency with which their expression is cited by other scientists or by other outward manifestations of collegial assent, like scientific awards.

Such views fit well enough with certain commonsense criteria for professional success. Typically, we identify the most successful figures, ideas, and themes in terms of their ability to "generate interest," to attract attention, or to spark communication. The ability to provoke such attention is apt to make the author "well-known" and the work widely read, or at least widely alluded to. These are of course key concomitants of academic success.

For similar reasons, it is no secret that aggressive organization of scholarly communication – the founding of new academic organizations, for example, or the editing of new journals, or the convening of conferences – is often tantamount to theoretical success. There is nothing obscure about such processes. The sponsorship of new scholarly activities – whether devoted to the study of social movements, the Holocaust, new techniques of statistical analysis, or any other subject – helps foster demand for theoretical representations of the same kind. Further, should the orchestration of such demand succeed, it will surely conduce to establishing of university courses, curricula, programs, and departments.

As long as sheer attention is seen as equivalent to theoretical success, we must acknowledge that *there is no bad publicity in scholarly communication.* Putting forward an argument, an interpretation, or a conceptual system that strikes many people as bizarre or outlandish need hardly be damaging – to the contrary – so long as the scholarly public can be made to pay attention to it. The fact that an idea is taken up and discussed is, after all, evidence in itself of the power to generate interest, provoke discussion, or focus analytical attention.

A story is told, in America's rural West, about the prospects for lawyers: A small town may be unable to support a single lawyer, it is noted; but it can always support *two* lawyers. Scholarly communication in social science has this same self-sustaining quality. The meanings and assertions generated by any one author, viewpoint, or tradition of inquiry in fact create opportunities for others, either in support of or opposition to them. Like the practice of law, social science tends to grow without limit, filling the institutional space accorded to it. And, as with law, the doing of social science often seems as though it was designed to foster demand for more of it.

Social scientists, like lawyers, are a status group. We assert our status by communicating – by generating the streams of books, articles, theses, monographs, and the like that publicize our views and generally remind the world that we are here. In a strictly expressive view of our work, such aggressive communication, and the activities associated with it, could be considered tantamount to success. But more lawyerly *activity* does not assure greater justice for the community as a whole. For similar reasons, we should be skeptical about the idea that the sheer extent of communication of theoretical ideas is indicative of greater enlightenment.

THE LIMITS OF THEORY AS EXPRESSION

I hope by now to have persuaded the reader on two points. First, that the dynamics of theory in social science show far-reaching parallels to those in the expressive visions governing art, drama, fiction, and other disciplines of pure imagination. Second, that any view of our work that draws no distinction at all between the aims of theoretical social science and those of art ought to give pause.

The increasing appeal of such expressive visions of theory in recent decades is unmistakable. That appeal surely derives in no small measure from skepticism concerning what I have called "neutral mapping" models of scientific progress. The idea that knowledge somehow unfolds simply as a process of documenting or recording features of the social world onto some universal conceptual grid simply does not capture the realities, or the possibilities, of social inquiry. The relative importance of facts, principles, relationships, and the like cannot be measured by any objective "grid," as on a map. For the mapping analogy to make sense for social science, we must think in terms of a great variety of maps of the "same" territory: one for tourists, for example, one for speleologists, one for mineral exploration, one for the adjudication of property rights, and so on. In short, the theoretical "maps" that we create need to correspond to the kinds of things that we need to know.

For an increasing number of thinkers, we have seen, such observations do not go nearly far enough. The unfolding of theory, in these views, is simply an expression of forces internal to the consciousness of theorists themselves. As Alvin Gouldner wrote, in an early expression of such views, "Questions of fact – that is, concern with what the facts are – seem to enter surprisingly little into much social theory" (1970, p. 483). The overall tenor of Gouldner's book suggests that he found this state of affairs quite acceptable.

Many have followed where Gouldner led. Consider the words of Jeffrey Alexander:

The omnipresence of discourse, and the conditions that give rise to it, make for the overdetermination of social science by theory and its underdetermination by what is taken to be fact. (Alexander 1988, p. 81)

In the last decade or so, such invocations of "the underdetermination of theory" by evidence have flowed freely from the lips and word processors of theorists; the phrase itself seems to be taken from terms of recent writings in epistemology.

Yet the sweeping position taken by Alexander in this statement hardly represents a majority view among epistemologists or philosophers of science. In an article in the *Journal of Philosophy* (1991), for example, Laudan and Leplin acknowledge that more than one theory can be propounded for the phenomenon for which any particular theory may be adduced. But this hardly means, they demonstrate, that such alternate theories are equally credible in the face of any or all empirical evidence that might be brought to bear. A number of successive tosses of "heads" may be equally compatible, they note, with theories that the coin in question is biased and with theories to the opposite effect. But,

the hypothesis of bias readily admits of evidential support from sources outside its consequence class that would not support purportedly equivalent hypotheses. An example is the information that the coin hypothesized to be biased was poured in a die cut by a chronically inebriated diemaker. (p. 464)

"It is illegitimate," they conclude, "to infer from the empirical equivalence of theories that they will fare equally in the face of any possible or conceivable evidence" (p. 466).

There is, to be sure, one element of value in the relativists' position. This is their appreciation that all analysis, indeed all perception of the social world, assumes some sort of conventions or (to invoke what has become a cliché) "paradigms." Where this line of reasoning goes wrong is in the assumption that the *same* set of intellectual ground rules that make it possible to formulate coherent questions about social life must *perforce* dictate the answers.

All analysis indeed requires some theory; but it hardly follows that "theory" in this sense is a seamless web, such that one either embraces or rejects the whole thing. We require some sort of "theory" even to judge which side of a coin is heads and which is tails. But it is quite reasonable to expect this theory to remain stable while investigators examine the numbers of heads and tails produced in a series of trials.

Peter Galison makes the point well in his celebrated historical study of particle physics (1987). He shows, throughout the book, how contending positions in a series of researches early this century stemmed from distinctive theoretical visions. But Galison also shows that they shared a common theoretical "ground" – though this ground was in turn highly distinctive in relation to the thinking of those outside this specific domain of scholarship. The common ground shared by participants in the debate sufficed for them to arrive at interpretations of experiments that distinguished between successful and unsuccessful solutions to the theoretical problems at hand:

> Obviously the establishment of experimental results requires theory. No one but the most obdurate positivist would deny that. But the truism that "experiment is inextricable from theory" or that "experiment and theory are symbiotic" is useless. . . . At issue should not be *whether* theory enters, but *where* it exerts its influence in the experimental process and *how* experimentalists use theory as part of their craft.
>
> Before either question can be answered, clarification is needed to avoid the implication that there is a single set of beliefs usefully referred to as "theory." Especially when philosophers pronounce data to be "theory-laden," they have a tendency to lump together all ideas, ranging from the home truths of electronic circuitry to the metaphysical assumptions about universal symmetries of whole *classes* of theories. (1987, p. 245)

Galison is right. We cannot get along without theory – that is, without "paradigms" to organize our analytical work. But neither can we afford to choose among theoretical visions strictly in terms of which ones best encapsulate our inner sensibilities. There is simply no end to the variety of models of closure that could, in principle, organize the work of social inquiry. If we reject the simplistic course of anointing the most widely entertained theories as ipso facto the "best," we need to consider other criteria for theoretical success. In doing so, we surely ought to consider seeking out those approaches that maximize our ability to cope with a world in which theories represent indispensable bases for action, and in which the results of action bear on broadly shared interests in coping with the social world.

8

Theory for coping

Strictly expressive criteria for the elaboration of social inquiry might suffice, were it not for the pervasive need to cope with the constraints of social life. The fact is, we do not form images of the social world only for our own satisfaction in the contemplation, but also as bases for dealing with social forces that impinge upon us, whether we recognize them or not.

Like expressive interests, interests in coping with social life take many forms. These range from individuals' needs to understand and anticipate the workings of their immediate social contexts to broadly shared interests in grasping and dealing with basic features of social life – for example, social stratification, political upheaval, or economic growth and stagnation.

What all these concerns have in common is their focus on forces that *constrain* experience. From individual needs to get along with associates at work or at home to broadly shared interests in responding to the changing social organization of technology or world economic change, people realize that life is subject to forces that bear on human interests, whether recognized as such or not. If we want to make the most of social life, we must develop theories offering guidance concerning such forces and constraints.

For consistent constructivists, of course, any notion that our analytical faculties might afford such guidance is simply a theoretically induced illusion. But it is difficult to imagine constructivists, or anyone else, making such a premise a basis for the conduct of everyday life. Instead, most people operate on the assumption that they have an interest in understanding the social processes that form the context of their lives as a basis for coping with such processes.

In fact, people approach social life assuming a modicum of coherence in such processes. One notes, at the very least, that actions which produce a certain result on Monday will often do much the same on Tuesday. Indeed, most people can and do master much subtler forms of coherence. They distinguish between dealings with public officials that proceed according to the overt and official rules, for example, and those which require special inducements or reciprocity. Or, one notes that certain actions will satisfy one's spouse when he or she is in one frame of mind, but elicit the opposite reaction under other circumstances.

In short, virtually everyone recognizes the possibility of identifying *contingencies* in social life – "contingencies" in the sense of events, states, or arrangements that are dependent on or connected to others. For the purposes of these discussions, aspects of social life are "contingent" not when they are indeterminate, but when their relations to one another are knowable and relatively stable. Contingent social elements "hang together," in other words, so that by knowing one thing about the world we operate in we can infer other things.

Without such knowledge, social life would be an impossible proposition. One readily learns that a particular bureaucrat will resist efforts to induce her to act when one portrays one's wishes as orders, yet readily comply when they are packaged as requests for expert assistance. Or, one notices that workers in a particular plant are slow to challenge management when business is slow, but that they grow more demanding when there is a backlog of unfilled orders. Such insights are essential bases for coping with the situations in question.

The formal study of social life, much like the everyday conduct of it, involves efforts to grasp and understand such contingencies. Of course, beyond this minimalist, bare-bones characterization, one finds the most various doctrines as to how to conceive of and study the coherence of social life. Part of the reason for this is undoubtedly the extreme variety of the forms taken by contingencies underlying our subject matter. These range from relations properly expressed in quantitative formulas – Markov models of mobility among offices in a complex bureaucracy, for example – to dependencies, no less theoretically significant, that take a much different logical form – for example, the notion that the first manifestations of capitalism were contingent on a certain conception of the religious significance of work. But whatever the form, any contingency we might posit invites empirical inquiry aimed at learning whether things that we think *ought* to go together really do so – and how widely, across time and changes in social context, the contingency may hold.

Theories are statements of contingency that hold across some variety of contexts. Someone once characterized theory as "a guide to the unknown"; and that it is, both in everyday life and in scholarship. We construct theories in the hope of gaining a grip on what would otherwise be randomness and indeterminacy in a world that impinges on us. Here I see no fundamental difference between social science and the "theories" underlying the conduct of everyday life. When theories work, when they succeed in identifying contingencies that matter to us, we are less at the mercy of social processes and in a better position to cope with them. And to this elementary extent, theoretical efforts to understand the social context of human action differ not a particle from those directed at the natural world.

HERMENEUTIC EXCEPTIONALISM

I have tried to cast this simple characterization of theory in the most generic, broadly applicable way possible. But for some, even this one-size-fits-all account is bound to seem too restrictive. Among those likely to object are proponents of interpretive or hermeneutic views. For them, any understanding of the study of social life that fails to note the radical distinctness of its logic from that of natural science is doomed to miss the essential point. Social relationships are invariably mediated by *meanings*, they would insist, and accordingly only analysis in terms of meaning-systems reveals the true mainsprings of social process. Such insistences, of course, have a very long pedigree in social thought, extending back at least as far as the distinction in German thought between the cultural and the natural sciences.

Thoroughgoing proponents of this view reject any account or explanation of human affairs not couched in terms of meanings shared by the parties concerned. As all social institutions, practices, and arrangements are predicated on shared meaning, only accounts in these terms can successfully illuminate social life. In the words of Charles Taylor:

> convergence of belief or attitude or its absence presupposes a common language in which these beliefs can be formulated, and in which these formulations may be opposed. Much of this common language in any society is rooted in its institutions and practices; it is constitutive of these institutions and practices. It is part of the intersubjective meanings. (1979 [1971], p. 49)

On first consideration, all this may sound uncontroversial. Who could doubt, after all, that the sense people make of their worlds plays a basic role in shaping both individual actions and the workings of large social aggregates? And who could doubt that we often go about understanding social processes by seeking to understand how the people involved understand their situation and the actions of parties to it?

But consider Taylor's insistence that *only* such accounts can legitimately serve to explain social phenomena. Can it really be that the sense people make of their own actions, or of the situations they confront, taps some *ultimate* level of social reality? If so, how do we deal with cases where different participants make different hermeneutic sense of situations with which both are closely familiar?

What if someone does not "see" the adequacy of our interpretation, does not accept our reading? . . . for him to follow us he must read the original language as we do. . . . If he does not, what can we do? The answer, it would seem, can only be more of the same. (p. 28)

Thus, an insistence on hermeneutic criteria for hermeneutic arguments. But we need to think harder about the standard entertained for "success" in such exercises. Does success lie strictly in the conviction of all parties to a particular account that it "fits" the meanings immanent in the situation? Is it possible that a given interpretation might be deeply satisfying in this way but *wrong*? If so, how could one ever know?

The alternative is to adopt a far less categorical and to this extent more reasonable position than Taylor's. That is, simply that meaning-systems represent one among many possible contingencies shaping human affairs – and that accounts based on hermeneutic analysis are neither inherently superior to those based on quite different sorts of contingencies nor immune to evidentiary requirements binding elsewhere.

Consider an analytical problem where hermeneutic explanations face serious competition from those based on quite different contingencies. Suppose that a rash of strikes has broken out in a particular industry after a long period of labor quiescence. A hermeneutically minded analyst, perhaps inspired by Elton Mayo, attributes these developments to "mis-understandings" between workers and management. After painstaking textual analysis of the actions and statements of the two sides, the social scientist in question identifies the sticking point. It is said to lie in certain differences between the two sides' ideas of their mutual rights and obliga-tions – an interpretation whose validity is affirmed, let us imagine, by the parties concerned.

But suppose that another analyst identifies a quite different sort of contingency. The outbreak of strikes, this investigator notes, corre-sponded to the point where demand for the product had sharply increased just as the companies involved were acquiring backlogs of unfilled orders. The second analyst accordingly concludes that the reason for the outbreak of strikes at the time in question was the calculation of strategic advantage on the part of workers.

These two accounts need not necessarily be in conflict. The strikes in question could plausibly be contingent both on shifts in strategic advan-tage and on the parties' understandings of right and wrong. But one can also imagine evidence showing that ideas of justice played little effective role in the formulation of action on either side – statements by the parties concerned notwithstanding – but that conscious or unconscious calcula-tion of the likelihood of winning was decisive. For example, if understandings of the principles at issue between the parties appeared relatively constant, and relations of strategic advantage were rapidly shifting, the latter explanation would appear for most purposes stronger as an account of the outbreak of strike activity.

The point is, hermeneutic connections deserve no privileged role among the array of contingencies to which analysts of social life must attend. And when hermeneutic explanations are pursued critically, rather than simply by taking the expressions of parties at face value, the methods are not essentially different from those required for the investigation of other contingencies. As the philosopher of science Dagfinn Follesdall points out, hermeneutic analysis of a text, like other forms of theory making and explanation, involves hypotheses as to how the text should unfold, given certain assumptions about the author's meaning (1979, p. 324). And often investigation must be extended over a wide range of material before such hypotheses can be confidently confirmed or rejected. So, Follesdall writes, citing the example of decipherment of the ancient Greek script known as Linear B:

Michael Ventris' now so famous decipherment of Linear B was not immediately accepted as a final solution. Only when more inscriptions were found that fit in with his decipherment, was it generally acknowledged as *the* correct solution. (pp. 332–333)

Let us agree, then, that many outcomes which engage our practical and theoretical interest in social life turn on one or another system of meanings. And let us agree that decipherment of these meaning-systems typically involves mastering special sets of contingencies. None of these assumptions should lead us to imagine that interpretations of such meanings are somehow beyond evidentiary considerations. Nor should we assume that these are the only kinds of contingencies that we need to attend to.

One wonders why the tendency to insist on radical distinctions between the "methods of the natural sciences" and those underlying the study of social life asserts itself so persistently. Part of the reason, one suspects, is an undervaluation of the true diversity of contingencies embodied in the work of natural scientists (see Knorr-Cetina 1993). The principles linking analytical elements of interest to molecular biologists – for example, in the communication of genetic inheritance via DNA – are worlds apart from those governing the contingencies of interest to seismologists or population geneticists. Are these principles any less different from each other than all three are from those governing human meaning-systems? I can see no reason to think so.

Yet it seems to be an occupational disease among social scientists to yearn for a world of "pure theory," where effects would always be defined in the same terms as their causes. This is indeed a utopian aspiration, in the least appealing sense of that term. The things that we need to under-stand in social life are apt to be governed by the widest variety of con-tingencies. Sometimes the dynamics of meaning-systems affect material life, as when new definitions of the meaning of work or consumption give rise to new forms of economic action. Sometimes, by contrast, changing material conditions may affect the elaboration of meaningful forms, as in the changes in architectural styles brought about by the demographic impact of the Black Death in Europe. This is the kind of disorderly but fascinating analytical environment that we inhabit. And if we wish to develop forms of understanding suited for coping with the social world as it is, we cannot afford to ignore any category of contingencies.

"SOFT CAUSALITY"

It would be hard to overestimate the effect upon the study of social life of a certain view of natural science. This view pictures, as the key achieve-ments in the study of the natural world, the discovery and codification of relationships among properties of nature that are *universal* in form and *nonlimited* in scope. This is to say, *law-like* relationships, ones applying without exception to open categories of phenomena.

The repercussions of this view on the study of social life have been extremely far-reaching – and quite opposite in tendency. Some have taken the quest for universal laws as the master model for all social inquiry. The result, of course, is to turn analytical attention away from all relationships that appear to lack the universality seen as essential to rigorous science.

For another constituency, the effect has been a turning-away from such "scientific" models altogether out of a conviction that they are irrelevant to the study of social life. Sometimes these views take the form adopted by Charles Taylor. In other cases, the objection has to do with what is seen as the uniquely historical character of the relationships encountered in social life. Students of social life must concern themselves not with invariant relationships, it may be held, but rather with the particularities of specific situations. Thus attention turns to efforts directed, not at large numbers of cases, but rather at in-depth understanding of complex, one-of-a-kind wholes.

In reacting to what I see as a skewed and overdrawn view of natural science, proponents of both these persuasions miss something essential. The obsession with relationships that are universal in form and non-limited in scope has distracted attention from the kinds of contingencies that are standard in our subject matter and highly informative – those in which *various elements of social reality are dependent on one another, yet in which that dependence itself is predicated on a welter of contextual conditions.*

Perhaps the trouble is that we conflate the "scientific" assumption of an orderly universe with the notion that order is known to us only in invariant relations. Recall John Stuart Mill's statement from *A System of Logic:*

what happens once, will, under a sufficient degree of similarity of circumstances, happen again, and not only again, but as often as the same circumstances recur. . . . The universe, so far as is known to us, is so constituted, that whatever is true in any one case, is true in all cases of a certain description; the only difficulty is, to find what description. (1893, p. 223)

Our typical situation in the study of social life is that we can document authentic contingencies in our subject matter but typically find it impossible fully "to find what description" – that is, to enumerate all the things that have to hold true of the context for the contingency to have force. The kinds of coherence that make our subject matter intelligible and that engage our interest, in other words, depend on contexts that are knowable in varying degrees and ways, but rarely totally.

Have social scientists identified *any* relationships among properties of the social world that even approach being both invariant and universal, in the sense of applying across all social contexts? Some, perhaps. The relationship between the size of social systems and their internal organization, as first formalized by Spencer, is one candidate. It would appear that the requirement of social units to grow more specialized as they grow larger holds across a vast range of settings and kinds of organization. Another candidate might be Engel's formulation that the higher the relative income of families, the lower the proportion devoted to subsistence.

But relationships of this kind are few and far between. To insist on concentrating on the pursuit of relationships cast in such noncontextual terms may lead to statements that are indeed universal and nonlimited but lacking in content. A good example is the Skinnerian "law of effect" – the assertion that actions are more likely to be repeated to the extent that they are reinforced. The trouble is, we have no way of assessing the reinforcing quality of any experience, apart from whether or not it is indeed repeated.

More important, the relationships that ought to hold most *interest* for us are rarely of this kind. We are much more likely to want to know about the future social organization of the world's most complex and prosperous social systems; or the changing nature of family relations in newly industrial countries; or the evolution of supra-state organizations in international affairs. And insofar as we address such utterly pertinent issues, we must perforce focus on contingencies that hold true of rather particular, historically specific ranges of cases. Thus we find ourselves seeking to understand and document specific contexts in terms of culture, institutional arrangements, technology, and historical circumstances. This is not to say that contingencies that prevail among social elements of interest in these systems are random or inaccessible to study. It is simply to say that the force of the contingencies in question presumes a complex variety of necessary conditions *many of which we cannot specify in advance.* One could call such context-bound connections "soft causality."

As I argued in *Theories of Civil Violence,* the most informative form of theoretical knowledge available to us is not simply that of associations but that of *causal systems.* By this I mean the broad sets of conditions in which particular kinds of contingencies prevail. And such conditions are typically historical. They are arrangements of social elements thrown together by adventitious or contextually unique processes, and subject to change with historical circumstance.

The emerging world economy of the late twentieth century is an apt example. We may legitimately claim to trace contingencies of much interest in causal systems like the apparent linkage between economic growth and certain forms of decentralization of economic power. But such connections are always a bit like those between pulling on a loose strand of a knitted garment and the unraveling that follows somewhere else: The two events are certainly contingent, but one can rarely specify *all* the interconnections that make the contingency work. Thus we should not persuade ourselves, in the example given here, that the institutions that foster rapid growth among the economies of the late twentieth century will necessarily display the same effects in other settings.

This view thus counsels skepticism regarding the acontextual search for "relations" among "variables." This quest has led some authors to imply that meaningful results will be forthcoming as a matter of course, if only we adopt sufficiently consistent and rigorous procedures, and continue looking long enough. But not all associations are equally interesting, and (for similar reasons) our interest in any one association has much to do with the contexts in which we expect it to prevail. The fact that turning a particular switch is highly correlated with the lighting of a room may hold no interest for us, if we look at the bulb and notice that the filament is broken. A tiny bit of theory is worth more than a infinitely strong record of association, if only it bears on the conditions under which the association holds.

Sometimes we know a good deal about the elements necessary to give a causal system its efficacy. Consider a system in American political behavior that endured steadily for some decades: the once predictable tendency of male, urban, blue-collar voters to identify themselves and vote as Democrats. From the 1930s to the late 1960s, one could predict, with high probability, the party identifications of citizens who fit this description. Then the contextual forces that had assured this predictability began to break down. Some origins of these changes are fairly well known: the identification of the Democratic party with social protest and counter cultural symbolism; the growing tax burden upon middle-income Americans and the conviction among them that government spending was wasteful; and, especially important, the decline of trade-union membership and power. Yet it would be rash to imagine that our understanding of the changes in this causal system is in any way exhaustive.

The realization that the causal system of interest here has substantially dissolved hardly threatens our sense of the orderliness of social process. It simply reminds us that most of the coherence, most of the determinacy, in social relations stems from complex conjunctures of elements that remain in place only temporarily. They are subject to change through alteration of one crucial element or a shift in the relationship of existing elements to one another.

Causal systems, as I have described them, come in all degrees of complexity and robustness. Sometimes we can be virtually sure that any unit that meets what we see as "a certain description," to use Mill's words, will sustain contingencies of a specific kind. For example, the physical laws relating volume, temperature, and pressure of gases appear to hold across an enormously wide variety of contexts, extending, as far as anyone can know, well beyond our part of the solar system. Thus if something is a gas, and is enclosed within a defined space, we can assume with some confidence that contingencies in its states will be as described in these laws.

Such confidence is far more rare in the study of human and social phenomena. True, some relatively durable, predictable causal systems appear to be all but "hard wired" into human psychology. Skinner's "law" stating that *intermittent* reinforcement produces learning more resistant to extinction than *consistent* reinforcement is a good example. It is logically possible to imagine a behaving organism that does not manifest this contingency. Perhaps some sophisticated neurosurgery could even produce a rat or pigeon whose behavioral organization did not embody it. But short of this, the elements of this causal system seem to be stamped into the organism itself.

By contrast, few if any of the causal systems made up of strictly social elements – families, international markets, constitutional systems, and so on – seem fixed to this extent. The elements involved are simply too multifarious; they are not stable in relation to one another but thrown together by changing circumstance. Psychological mechanisms governing learning in the face of sustained versus intermittent reinforcement appear fairly robust across changes in context. But the workings of government institutions, family roles, or religious institutions in relation to their contexts are vastly less predictable; the juxtapositions of elements making up the causal systems involved simply appear far more transitory.

We constantly grasp, and cope with, just such loose and transitory causal systems in everyday life. In university life, for example, one often finds that one sees another person predictably at more or less the same time and place every week. We are hardly surprised that we catch sight of, say, a specific colleague at a particular spot on campus every Tuesday. Rather, we are apt to posit that his or her movements, and our own, are governed by causal systems that have us each heading for class, or attending a meeting, near each other at the relevant moment in our weekly cycles of activities. Yet we also know that small alterations in the elements composing those causal systems – a change of venue for a class, the dissolution of a committee, or a child's illness – may undo the regularity overnight. Many contingencies in social life are no more enduring than this. Yet that does not make them unsuitable as bases for understanding the regularities that they produce or for mobilizing such regularities as bases for coping. And the dissolution of such contingencies, when some element of the conjuncture changes, hardly shakes our view of the orderliness of the social universe.

Much important theoretical work consists of identifying and documenting conjunctures of elements that give specific causal connections force in very specific ranges of settings. A celebrated example is Theda Skocpol's *States and Social Revolution* (1979). This work is best appreciated not as a "theory of revolutions" in general, though it has often been discussed in those terms. In fact, that category of events which we bracket as "revolutions" is enormously heterogeneous in its social characteristics. Accordingly, any generalizations about the causal systems giving rise to any and all revolutions – which would presumably range from the helots' revolt in Sparta to the popular overthrow of Bolivia's authoritarian regime in 1952 – is apt not to be very informative.

The theoretical virtues of Skocpol's analysis lie instead in her sensitivity and thoroughness in tracing the workings of a causal system involved in a handful of rather similar revolutions of very special historical import. What Skocpol does is show how a particular conjuncture of historical and social conditions bearing on certain regimes – including sagging internal revenues, fraying international commitments, and a decaying aristocratic class – came together to produce especially far-reaching institutional changes. Our interest in the causal system delineated by Skocpol does not have to do with the frequency of instances of such systems in history, for they appear to be rare. Instead, the study gains its import from the value-relevance of this particular handful of cases.

The variety of causal systems that legitimately command theoretical attention is vast. Some of these are massive, far-flung holistic systems like the one that governed the political economy of the former Soviet Union. Conceived of as a unique causal system, the Soviet state embodied contingencies that nevertheless had repeated instantiations. Thus one can observe, at various points in the history of that system, efforts toward "reform" made by central power holders, attempts by such figures as Khrushchev and Gorbachev to foster more initiative and accountability at the peripheries. The fact that these efforts repeatedly met with similar resistance and reaction from predictable parties, notably local and regional party officials, demonstrates the systemic quality of the analytical unit. The fact that the USSR might be considered a unique phenomenon, a single "thing," thus does not make the analysis of its workings any less theoretical.

Other causal systems are reproduced in the most diverse settings, a good example being the systems embodied in "asylums," as analyzed in Erving Goffman's famous work of that title (1961). As Robert Alford points out (personal communication), it was a measure of Goffman's theoretical imagination to note that institutions as diverse as "boarding schools, armies, mental hospitals, prisons, and concentration camps" shared certain systemic characteristics.

Many contingencies in social life reflect the workings of immense numbers of roughly similar causal systems aggregated over many cases. When we speak of theories of "the American family" or "the multinational firm," we are thinking of conjunctures of elements that occur repeatedly in many distinct units – units which remain similar enough that similar causes in all will produce a predictable aggregate effect. Thus it is reasonable to characterize "the American family" today as more likely to have more than one breadwinner and to experience lower "moral costs" of divorce than it did a generation ago – and to invoke these changed causal constraints in explaining particular changes in typical family circumstances such as higher divorce rates.

In cases like these, where single causal systems of the same form aggregate their effects across many separate instances, it is often clear that not all of what appear to be the "same" units indeed embody the essential system. The cost of divorce (in terms of its moral or symbolic unacceptability) is obviously not low in *all* American families. But the low costs that are so widely noted characterize enough American families to represent a legitimate element of any account of current divorce rates. The same kind of reasoning serves in epidemiological studies of phenomena like smoking and cancer or sexual activity and AIDS. We know that some individuals appear invulnerable to the diseases in question, even upon unlimited exposure, though we cannot now identify the element within the causal system in question that provides this immunity. Nevertheless, in analyzing and coping with populations as wholes, it makes sense to direct inquiry and intervention to the contingencies that appear most typical. Thus we are prepared to advise vaccination or other preventive measures to attack certain diseases, even though we are certain such measures are unnecessary for some members of the populations in question.

Between the extremes of large, unitary systems and aggregations of many small ones, our work obliges us to confront causal systems of the greatest variety. One of the things that makes social analysis so fascinating – and so problematic – is the fact that so many different *kinds* of contingencies may affect outcomes of interest. Therefore we can never afford to exclude the possibility that effects for which we wish to account respond to causes of qualitatively quite different sorts. Much of the change in sexual customs and mores of the last generation seems to have been contingent on innovations of birth-control technologies. Similarly, changes in European architecture in the century after the Black Death appear to have resulted from strictly demographic contingencies leading to scarcities of certain kinds of skilled labor. It simply will not do to assume that social systems arrange themselves so neatly that effects of particular kinds must always stem from causes of the same kinds.

Most causal systems confronted by social scientists are to a large degree historical. The contingencies involved depend on conjunctures of elements that occur at one stage but need not always do so, and that, in many cases, certainly will *not* always do so. And again, it is a complicating fact of life in our disciplines that we rarely know all the elements that must be "in place" for a given contingency to hold. Thus, at some point in the history of the Soviet bloc, mechanisms for economic management and political rule that had worked for decades simply lost their viability. What the crucial change was in that highly complex, sui generis causal system will surely preoccupy analysts for decades to come. The practical implication here is that, at some point, familiar contingencies will often cease to hold simply because what appears to be "the same" system has undergone a sea change – often in ways that we cannot specify.

It would be wrong to imagine that the circumstances in our disciplines are qualitatively different in these ways from those prevailing in the natural sciences – or, at least, in *all* of the natural sciences. There, too, analysts address causal systems of widely varying structures. Some natural scientists devote tremendous efforts, as in social science, to specifying complicated webs of contingencies implicated in single, sui generis systems – the population ecology of species inhabiting the Amazon Basin, for example, or the seismic system of the San Andreas Fault. Other natural scientists, again like social scientists, focus on the aggregation of many unitary causal systems – as when epidemiologists, ethologists, or agronomists generalize about the contingencies of the human body, the social behavior of animals, or the growth of plants.

And causal systems in the world of nature are often also historical. In many natural science disciplines, contingencies of much analytical interest depend on arrangements of elements that have not always existed and almost certainly will not always do so. The formulations inspired by plate tectonics in geology, for example, have this character: They apparently did not hold for periods in the earth's history before the formation of such plates; nor will they necessarily always hold in the future. A similar assumption has to be made in much research on disease, given the propensity of viruses and bacteria to evolutionary change. AIDS is a historical development; obviously everyone hopes that someday, like smallpox, it will no longer command the interest of anyone but medical antiquarians. As long as the virus continues to infect people, however, the causal system that gives rise to the disease itself is subject to change, so that both theoretical analysis and coping measures have to track what amounts to a moving target.

SOME THEORETICAL SUCCESSES

A common approach to writing about theory is to begin from first principles. That is, one starts with doctrines of how theories ought properly to be constructed and applied. From such beginnings, commentators typically go on to take stock of current practice in their disciplines – praising those uses of theory which meet the proclaimed standards and viewing with alarm those which do not.

I have tried to proceed a bit differently, seeking to stress that *any number of theoretical programs may "work,"* in the elementary sense of serving to organize and direct the efforts of those who embrace them. My question is, rather, which of these countless possibilities shows the best promise of meeting the most enduring of analytical *needs,* needs of the sort that most predictably draw people to reflect critically on social life in the first place? What sorts of things do thoughtful people most typically need to know about social relations, and what sorts of analytical forms appear most likely to generate such insight? Only in the context of answers to such questions, I maintain, can one reasonably assess the prospects for progress in theoretical understanding.

Such assessments turn on two questions. The first of these has to do with the nature of the contingencies that engage our analytical interests. Is the social world coherent enough that contingencies established at one point may reasonably be assumed still to prevail later on? Are the causal systems governing the things that interest us stable enough to make it worth our while to study them?

The second question has to do with the stability of our interests in those systems. Are the things that we need to know themselves sufficiently enduring that insights gained at one point have a chance of proving useful for future analysts? Or – to take the extreme alternative – are the interests that students of social life bring to their work so transitory and context-bound as to be doomed to irrelevance for analysts in other settings?

My answers to these two questions are affirmative – with considerable qualification. I have sought to show how certain issues in social relations, as reflected in first-order questions, bear on relatively enduring and predictable analytical interests. These interests are all but built into the social conditions in which thoughtful participants in complex social systems live their lives. Our interest in such questions obliges us to direct analytical attention to causal systems that bear on these interests. Although nearly all such systems are time-bound to some degree, some are stable enough so that insight derived at one point may prove invaluable for those who approach similar subject matters later on.

Consider a few promising examples of such insight from *Theories of Civil Violence*:

1. The fact that, contrary to one major theme in the literature, participants in militant events do *not* seem to be disproportionately drawn from the ranks of the deviant, the defective, or the socially isolated.

If anything, these categories seem underrepresented among the participants in such events, according to a variety of studies over the years (Rule 1988 p. 109). The first systematic expressions of what I called the scum-of-the-earth theory of participation seem to have come from a group of turn-of-the-century theorists inspired by the conservative historian of the French Revolution, Hippolyte-Adolph Taine. But I suspect that the inspiration is all but universal among those antagonistic to social agitation. It is simply comforting to imagine that those engaged in demonstrating, rioting, or otherwise militant acts do so in response to some form of social deficiency or pathology. Or, to put matters the other way round, it is disturbing to consider that those who rise up to take actions one regards as shocking are for other purposes "normal," "reasonable" people.

Thus, I imagine that those who are disdainful of militant mobilization will always be tempted to embrace some version of this theory – just as those categorically favorable to such actions will always be inclined to oppose it. But, in this case, empirical inquiry has given at least a partial answer to what looks like an enduring question. Though no one can assert that the deviant, the isolated, or the unsocialized may *never* predominate in militant phenomena, we can be certain that militant phenomena are not the work of such people as a rule. And this insight, I suspect, will *matter* to future students of militant action, regardless of their expressive or rhetorical dispositions toward the subject.

2. The fact that participants in militant events are *not* necessarily the most deprived or aggrieved, either by objective standards or in terms of their own self-perceptions.

The assumption that such an association exists also has had a deep intuitive appeal. It seems easy to think of social life as a kind of hydraulic system, such that those subject to the most pressure are bound eventually to explode. The notion appears to portray rebellious action as a manifestation of some sort of basic instinct of justice – rather, say, than simply an expression of greed or opportunism. This idea was systematically developed in theories of *relative deprivation,* positing that human action is governed by a kind of master sense of equity which, when too severely violated, results in militant action of one kind or another.

Whatever the appeal of this notion for rhetorical purposes, systematic inquiry has left it with virtually no support as a general account of militant action. As a variety of studies have shown, those who actually take part in militant action are not necessarily those who report themselves the most aggrieved. While recourse to militant action in some cases is associated with the strength of self-reported indignation about specific issues, there seems no reason to believe that protest behavior is governed by any master calculus of overall social well-being.

Both of these insights, circumscribed and qualified though they are, appear to me strong candidates to endure. The reasons have to do both with their apparent robustness and with their relevance to what seem to me predictable human concerns. Certainly, it would be rash to suggest that such judgments could never be reversed. Their empirical content might be upset by future inquiry – findings that studies to date have somehow been defective, and that the socially isolated or the relatively deprived really did predominate among militant actors, after all. Or – what is much more imponderable – these issues could somehow lose their relevance for future analysts of militant action.

But such developments appear unlikely. The empirical findings seem fairly strong. Moreover, the inherently disturbing quality of civil upheaval, it seems to me, predictably spurs reflective thinkers to wonder, "Who are the people who do these things? What has happened to move them to these extreme actions?" And predictable attitudes of disdain or sympathy for militant action make it appealing to answer these questions by characterizing participants either as socially defective (and hence unworthy of serious consideration) or unjustly deprived (and hence entitled to very serious consideration).

Readers of *Theories of Civil Violence* will recall that these candidates for enduring status are drawn from a quite restricted category of such ideas noted in that work. Most theoretical ideas come and go without exhibiting any such claims on enduring analytical attention – and without receiving anything like such systematic scrutiny in empirical inquiry. The same holds for the history of social thought more broadly. Yet a searching look at the history of our disciplines does yield many ideas that show good prospects of enduring analytical utility.

Consider a few more examples:

3. The notion, first formalized by Spencer, that the size of social systems – organizations, social movements, governments, and so on – constrains their inner organization. Thus, as in living systems, growth requires specialization.

This idea seems to me both accurate and useful for coping with the social world. No one who were to imagine that a large political party could operate with the same internal structures of a small sect or interest group, for example, could make much headway in coping with political realities. True, social theorists today hardly grow excited over this insight, but that should not blind us to its importance. Like many of the best and most enduring theoretical achievements, this one may have become less conspicuous by virtue of its very acceptance.

4. The idea, dating from Marx, Weber, and other classic authors, that every entrenched elite fosters and diffuses high-minded justifications for its claims to privilege.

No dominant group in any autonomous social system, in other words, is content with interpretations of its special position as having resulted from luck, historical accident, or brute force. Instead, established regimes typically portray themselves as destined to privilege by virtue of an array of special qualities, ranging from the favor of the gods and the excellence of their ancestors to their embodiment of proletarian interests to the fostering of economic productivity.

5. The defeat of the idea that what Sumner called "mores" – in the form, for example, of long-established justifications for hierarchies of race, ethnicity, or gender – cannot quickly be undone without threatening the very bases of social order.

This notion has had an enduring appeal for conservative thinkers, who suspect that any effort to change customs or arrangements to which people seem to have become inured would throw all other social arrangements into question.

Sumner's ideas on these points served in the 1930s in the United States as bases for resistance to racial desegregation. People can hardly be expected to alter their entire social mind-sets overnight, the argument went. Accordingly, any changes must be slow and incremental at most, to avoid unraveling the entire social fabric. Moreover, it was held, deliberate efforts to enforce change are likely to be counteracted by automatic self-equilibrating forces tending to restore the status quo ante.

Opposing this position were many social scientists, most notably Gunnar Myrdal, who insisted that social change might actually be self-reinforcing rather than self-dampening. In Myrdal's view, the demonstrative effect of seeing certain forms of social change as viable faits accomplis could accelerate the pace of change, by belying self-serving myths about the inevitability of the old ways.

Myrdal's view has ultimately prevailed on this point – at least to the extent of the rejection of Sumner's view as the only possible model for actual events. A key blow against the Sumner position was the rapidity with which many Jim Crow arrangements were dismantled in the Deep South of the United States, once the political battle to preserve them was lost in Washington and the state capitals. Obviously racial inequality in the United States remains marked. But the dramatizations of second-class citizenship in public accommodation, in schooling, in employment, and elsewhere through maintenance of formal "color bars" not only were dismantled relatively quickly; they also passed with little of the social disorientation predicted by conservatives.

Similar lessons seem clear from the opening up to women of occupational categories that were formerly exclusively male preserves – as in the field of printing (Roos 1990). To be sure, there was opposition to all these changes. But it seems difficult to defend Sumner's position in anything like its classic form, at least as applied to overturning established social hierarchies. This insight seems a good candidate to command attention from any conscientious future students of social change.

6. The idea that networks of personal acquaintance afford transmission of certain kinds of information, and for this reason sustain certain distinctive social processes not sustained by mass communication. The classic reference here is Granovetter's study of access to jobs (1974), which shows that chains of personal acquaintance can systematically provide access to "superior" jobs in relation to access afforded by official announcements and the like. This discovery suggests that the paths traveled by socially relevant information make an enormous difference to what options are available to whom – and that social position within these information flows has sweeping effects on all sorts of life chances.

These insights make it impossible to take at face value certain universalistic claims made for markets and certain other institutions. It suggests that access to services, competition for advantage, and a variety of other social processes in fact depend on complicated molecular formations of microrelations that are, so to speak, "invisible to the naked eye." In a social world made up of large organizations conducting their affairs through mass appeals – job announcements, policies, product warnings, and the like – the idea that "telling everybody" does not produce uniform effects is a revealing if sometimes disturbing innovation.

And surely such insights are of value for coping with the exigencies of social processes. Any social analyst who sought to deal with the allocation of jobs, or the dissemination of information about social benefits, or the diffusion of environmental policies, or anything else would stand to lose by ignoring these insights. For this reason, these ideas seem good candidates to endure.

7. The idea that people's perceptions of their own well-being are predicated on reference groups rather than on any absolute level of well- or ill-being.

This insight, of course, held great cachet in the 1940s and 1950s, in the wake of the dramatic findings of *The American Soldier* and subsequent survey studies done by Lazarsfeld and others. Today, I suspect, most social scientists would consider such ideas rather ordinary. Ordinary they may now be, but hardly less useful. Anyone seeking to understand and cope with the ways in which people react to illness, career experience, or economic success and failure, would be incompetent indeed not to start with some inquiry into the reference groups that they have in mind.

Again, I can offer no absolute guarantee that any or all of these insights will continue to prove useful for future analysts. My most important aim in proposing these examples is to clarify the underlying rationale for choosing them. I want to distinguish between those insights whose appeal lies strictly in their expressive payoffs, and those likely to appear useful and persuasive whether they bear any expressive rewards or not. Insofar as ideas like these above earn their keep as means for coping with social reality, we can regard them as constituting one element of progress in a largely transient flow of theoretical ideas.

Note that the logical form of these insights is mostly very simple. It seems to me that analytical ideas general enough to be widely applicable must also, perforce, be stated in simple terms. No doubt some applications of these and other durable insights could be expressed in more complicated form – in terms of mathematical functions, for example. But the effort to make such ideas more mathematical would tie them more closely, I believe, to specific ranges of data.

Nor do the most enduringly useful analytical insights necessarily come in the form of single contingencies among social states – even relationships as broadly put as those above. Some of the theoretical ideas most likely to prove their analytical utility in the very long run, it seems to me, are models of *alternate possibilities* for accounting for important outcomes. The models are useful not because they predict specific events or outcomes, but because they alert us to possible contingencies of much interest that might otherwise pass unnoticed. Thus they enter what Coser has termed a "toolbox" of analytical options, as elements the usefulness of which is demonstrated by the recurring need for recourse to them (Coser 1981).

A perfect example comes from studies of stratification. This is a domain of social life so salient in social experience, and so chronically contested, that it is unlikely to disappear from theoretical attention. Years of debate over the origins of stratification have produced two broad analytical accounts of its origins – functional and power models. In the former, as nearly every social scientist knows, systematic social inequality is understood as a mechanism serving the interests of all. Certain roles are more richly rewarded than others, in this model, because their fulfillment benefits everyone. Should special rewards not be provided for political leaders, physicians, professional athletes, and the like, the logic goes, everyone would be worse off, because the most talented and dedicated people would then not be recruited to these roles. Thus an empirically relevant, and in principle falsifiable, account of what are obviously highly charged social arrangements.

By contrast, power models treat stratification as the imposition of systematic inequality upon the less powerful by those who benefit most from those inequalities. In these views, the widest variety of doctrines and arrangements – from notions of the divine right of kings to the imposition of formal educational requirements for access to certain jobs – reflect efforts to defend ideas and practices that benefit those on top at the expense of those on the bottom. Functional doctrines of stratification may themselves be seen as part of these justifications of inequality.

Both of these broadly applicable models find significant application in empirical inquiry. Randall Collins's *The Credential Society* (1979), for example, convincingly mobilizes power models to account for the rise of wide-ranging institutional arrangements, including much of modern public education. Similarly, functional models of occupational stratification seem to fit certain of the historical material presented in Paul Starr's widely celebrated history of American medicine (1982). The fact that the status and income of American physicians has risen over the last hundred years, for example, appears consistent with evidence that the efficacy of modern medicine in preserving life and health has in fact increased, when measured from a rather low nineteenth-century baseline.

Note that invoking one of these models for certain ranges of phenomena is by no means inconsistent with embracing the other for other explanatory purposes. Some of the most stultifying chapters of social thought have been devoted to efforts to "prove" the superiority of one or the other of these models in some generic sense. In fact, the models have their greatest usefulness not in this way, but in an endless dialectical tension with one another. At their best, they identify in sharp analytic form possible accounts for contentious realities that would otherwise often remain only dimly perceived. Surely this is preferable to any foredoomed effort to secure definitive supremacy for either model.

Thus it should not be too much for those attracted to power models to acknowledge that salaries and other benefits among major league baseball players are differentially allocated to players with higher batting averages and to pitchers who win more games – a functional process, clearly. Similarly, even enthusiasts of the functional model of stratification ought to acknowledge that this model cannot tell us much about why the Daughters of the American Revolution enjoy higher status than, say, daughters of welfare recipients.

The point is, anyone concerned with understanding specific forms and instances of stratification has an interest in keeping both these analytical possibilities accessible. One could say the same for a variety of ideal-typical alternatives that have emerged from various theoretical traditions: models of deviance as arising from the personalities of deviant individuals versus those which see deviance as produced by social structures; or models of adherence to norms as a result of rational calculation versus internalized commitment; or models of militant collective action as a rational or a nonrational process. The list could be extended at length.

The very articulation of these possibilities, I hold, amounts to substantive progress. The models do not tell us what processes of stratification will prevail in a particular setting, or what forces will be responsible for specific deviant acts, or whether particular instances of civil violence will be governed by rational or nonrational patterns. But they do alert us to analytical possibilities that we might well otherwise miss. The durability of these controversies makes it a good bet that knowledge of these possibilities will continue to serve the requirements of future thinkers.

CONCLUSION: IN QUEST OF GENERALITY

One of the main targets of the arguments developed here, it should be clear, is a certain genre of programs for "general theory." The common characteristic of such projects is to posit one kind of analytical principle – a conceptual order, for example, or a single category of facts or properties, or a specific set of causal principles – that must be invoked if any theoretical analysis is to be considered successful. The attractions of such systems have reasserted themselves in the study of social life from its earliest days to the present – from Comte and Hegel down to present-day proponents of presuppositional generality or reductive methodological individualism. In every era, these grandiose idea-systems have arisen and then, just as predictably, dropped from currency. Like so many abandoned cathedrals, they dot the landscape of our intellectual past, subjects of passing curiosity but little practical interest.

Yet for a time, they convince. They convince us to the extent that we accept that the specific processes, facts, or concepts on which they focus provide indispensable *means* for all important analytic *ends*. "See the world in our terms, adopt our mode of analysis," proponents of such views imply, "and you will be empowered to answer any legitimate theoretical question you might wish to ask."

Such claims should hardly be rejected out of hand. We accept something like them, for example, in the study of languages – to the extent that we are willing to invest much effort in the study of irregular verbs or sentence construction in the hope of achieving a general means of expression or understanding in the new tongue. And perhaps such compelling means– ends logic can be claimed for single bodies of general principles in other domains of inquiry. Perhaps the causal systems prevailing in celestial mechanics or molecular biology are so insulated from exogenous considerations that a single genre of principles can, indeed, account for everything and anything that needs to be understood in those disciplines.

But surely it strains credulity to apply any such argument to the study of social life. The simplest evidence for this is the sheer diversity of causal connections and other forms of contingency that hold theoretical interest for students of social life – as illustrated, for example, in the examples given in the preceding section. Surely it would be very difficult to claim that such a diverse array of insights and principles reflects any one set of causal forces or any single conceptual order.

Yet we cannot do without *some sort* of generality. We cannot plausibly propose to go about our work, in other words, without some sense of priorities – some idea of what features of social life command most attention, what strategies of investigation promise most satisfactory results, what analytical procedures produce the most reliable conclusions. Without some such criteria, we have no rationale for determining what knowledge to transmit to newcomers to the study of social life – either to our students or to the broader public of nonspecialist consumers of our work.

In short, we have to proceed with some sense of what matters and what doesn't. But there is no reason to imagine that such a sense must be tied to any single conceptual order or causal principle. Instead, we can – and indeed, must – take our priorities from interests in the workings of the social world that arise from the human condition. The things that we need to know, and that those who come after us are likely to continue to want to know, are not given by any a priori formula. But they are not random or unaccountable either.

Thus there is every reason to believe that more theoretical attention deserves to be focused on the form and character of personal-acquaintance networks than on the form and character of bottlecap dispersion. Such judgments have to be regarded, to be sure, as provisional. They have to do with the extent and variety of human interests engaged by the contingencies associated with the two kinds of phenomena. Perhaps some ingenious future researcher will establish bottlecap patterns as an index to systemic properties of social relations of far-ranging import. Should such patterns reveal something about patterns of mental health in the neighborhoods concerned, or their potential for economic growth or stagnation, the theoretical standing of bottlecap research will need to be reconsidered.

We cannot avoid judgments of this kind. Neither the forms of data nor the formal qualities of their analysis establish theoretical import in their own rights. Instead, we must constantly ask what advantages knowledge drawn from the most diverse theoretical contexts offers for coping with conditions that matter to human interests. And we can never afford to assume that such contingencies will always come in the same form. Eclecticism is the only prudent strategy.

Thus we can, and must, seek to develop certain forms of general knowledge in the study of social life. But these insights are more like those underlying general medicine – or general automotive repair and maintenance – than, say, astrophysics. Both general medicine and general auto maintenance require recourse to principles from physics and chemistry, as well as from other theoretical sources. But no practicioner of general medicine or auto repair could possibly deal with any normal range of cases on the basis of any form of "pure theory" alone. What makes for excellence in these activities is more the ability to distinguish what particular *kind of contingency* is apt to govern the various phenomena most likely to be encountered in a typical "caseload."

Thus the training of physicians has to give some priority to the characteristics of the circulatory system – a causal system in the sense invoked here – simply because so many vital outcomes depend on it. Similarly, any auto mechanic needs to pay more attention to, and develop more detailed knowledge of, the electrical system of cars than, say, the color of their exterior paint. There may be some problems confronted by auto-repair specialists that are somehow contingent on the color of the car's finish. But it would be ridiculous for any mechanic to begin the effort to diagnose the failure of someone's car to start by taking an exact measurement of the car's color. Nor would we expect a training program for auto-repair specialists to devote the same attention to analyses of exterior paint that it did to generators, spark plugs, and batteries.

The situation is much the same in the study of social life. Both historical precedent and our own analytical judgment do suggest that certain issues will continue to represent "first-order questions" – that is, bases of recurrent and pressing demands for insight. The origins of stratification, the causes of deviance, or the conditions of civil violence – and a range of other basic matters – will in all likelihood continue to demand attention, despite shifts in social context. Such questions arise so directly from the predictable sturm und drang of social experience that they are unlikely to go away any time soon. And our best hope for making sense of such questions, and for responding with insights that endure, is to remain skeptical of notions that any single set of principles can resolve them.

9

Summary and conclusions

Workers in Arctic oil fields, it is said, make the following complaint about their gloves: You can't work with them, and you can't work without them.

Any independent thinker struggling to understand a particular slice of social life is apt to make the same complaint about theory. Theoretical advice is always cheap, as proponents of one approach or another offer to "theorize" our material, that is, to interpret it so as to reveal its latent, but authentic, ultimate significance. The question is, how is one to choose among the seemingly endless welter of such possibilities? Which approach ultimately serves the analytical purposes that matter most? Do the forms of understanding offered by available theories indeed address those purposes? Or do they ultimately reveal, as one often suspects, more about the obsolescent preoccupations of theorists past than about the subject matter at hand?

Yet we cannot work without theory either. Some form of theoretical reasoning is our only way of linking our own work with that of other analysts – past, present, and future. Few if any efforts at social analysis, after all, are absolutely sui generis. Instead, we almost always stand to learn something from the exertions of those who have gone before us – if only we can separate the useful insights from the rest. And we almost always strive to make our work address concerns of those who will come after us. To the extent that we adjust our analytical efforts thus to play a role in larger processes of unfolding enlightenment, we are pursuing theoretical aspirations.

The problem is to find forms of theory that we can work with, ones that fit the constraints both of our subject matter and of our shared interests in it. And this means committing ourselves to some understanding of the prospects – or lack thereof – for long-term cumulation and progress in social understanding.

Summary and conclusions

Let me briefly review some key elements of my argument.

I hold that the desire to "contribute" to *some* form of intellectual progress is all but universal among students of social life. Even the many who reject natural science as a model for their efforts share such concerns. Who would trouble to put words (or numbers) to paper, if not in the hope that the result might leave some overall fund of understanding improved?

The problem with such aspirations is the endemic uncertainty about what forms of understanding will hold interest for those who follow us. "Contributions" that appear utterly apposite at one time, that represent a dramatic "step ahead" from the standpoint of one historical moment or intellectual constituency, are liable to appear irrelevant or even embarrassing from other perspectives. Concomitantly, perceptions of the essential direction of growth in social understanding are notoriously volatile. And in light of such volatility, who among us can claim certainty that the vision of intellectual progress guiding his or her own work will outlast its current context?

Thus the need for a critical look at the models of closure adumbrated in our work. What sorts of long-term "accomplishments" do such visions aim at, and what reasons have we for believing that accomplishments of this kind will *matter* to future thinkers? Any response to such questions requires judgments upon the ultimate ends of inquiry. How can we characterize, in the longest view, the virtues of the sorts of enlightenment that we pursue? Whom do we identify as the ultimate "consumers" of our ideas, and what sorts of rewards should we expect these beneficiaries to reap from our efforts?

Much social science, I have argued, is oriented to the pursuit of essentially *expressive* rewards. The forms taken by such expressive satisfactions are many and various. Some theories appear to derive their appeals from their pure conceptual elegance or indeed from their baroque conceptual complexity – from intellectual "marvels" accessible to those sufficiently talented or properly indoctrinated to appreciate them. Other forms of expressive satisfaction are clearly earthier – as when theoretical visions gratify by upholding embattled values, status claims, material advantages, or the like.

In short, the expressive rewards afforded by social science theories are almost as varied as intellectual life itself, and there is no reason to suppose that the "same" ideas will offer the same consummatory rewards to different thinkers. As in art, music, or literature, what makes a particular form satisfying to a particular constituency at one period may have little to do with the bases of its appeal, or lack of appeal, at others.

The intellectual appeal of virtually all theoretical forms is closely linked to prevailing social, cultural, and political contexts. And to the degree that theory is context-bound in this way, its applicability to other settings, and any aspirations to long-term cumulation, are bound to be problematic.

Against strictly expressive forms of theoretical success, I have sought to uphold a vision of theory oriented to long-term, shared interests in coping with the social environment. Here the ultimate aims of understanding lie in widely experienced human needs to deal with social forces, processes, and arrangements that bear on human interests. Theory succeeds, in this view not by providing images that satisfy in the contemplation, but by affording guidance for responding effectively to a social world that impinges upon us regardless of the ideas we entertain of it.

To be sure, I have drawn this distinction between theory for expression and theory for coping in sharpened, ideal-typical terms. In practice, enthusiasts of any theoretical position are apt to claim both sorts of virtues for their favorite doctrines. Yet the underlying distinction is of great moment, simply because the two principles potentially have such divergent implications for the conduct of intellectual work.

Theory oriented to coping offers the possibility – though by no means the certainty – of cumulation or progress. If we posit a measure of continuity in the social conditions, forces, and arrangements that regularly bear on human interests, then it is reasonable to hope that one might come to understand such things more fully over time. Thus, extended study of social stratification, international conflict, deviance, or civil violence might, at least in principle, leave us in a better position to cope with these things.

I understand that some readers will find the vision of theory advocated here unattractive. But I hope that no one will miss the weightiness of the issues at stake. For the rewards of the two ways of knowing, and the steps necessary for their pursuit, are profoundly different.

If expression is taken as the sole end of theoretical work, for example, no one need worry about the accuracy of theoretical representations of the social world as bases for dealing with that world. Thus a vision of one's worst enemies as utterly mean-spirited and treacherous could be altogether superior to a more nuanced view, even if the people involved were to act expansively and honestly when one actually dealt with them. Or theories that picture civil protest as a contagious form of mental illness could be held superior to those interpreting the same phenomena as the result of political competition and calculation – provided only that the former theories were more pleasing for their immediate consumers to contemplate. All that would matter, in the extreme case, would be the satisfaction offered by theoretical representations as ends in themselves.

Furthermore, if the ends of theory are held to be solely expressive, one would have no grounds for criticizing any representation of the world inspired by them other than in terms given by the theory itself. One's favorite theory, for example, might depict all forms of slavery as a calculated response by the enslaved to an array of social alternatives, and hence as a reasonable or acceptable social arrangement. Such a depiction would be held satisfactory from a strictly expressive standpoint, so long as it met the canons of analysis of the theory giving rise to it. Or one might prefer a theory that depicts all enduring heterosexual relationships as ipso facto exploitative and unequal. No evidence derived from empirical study of those born into slavery, for example, or of apparently equal and harmonious heterosexual relationships would be relevant to the potential revision of such ideas, provided only that they fit the logic of the theory giving rise to them. One could not conceive, in other words, of a vision of the world that was satisfying and true to the logic of the theory but wrong as a source of guidance for action.

One can even envisage the overt elaboration of theoretical social science as a form of public consumption, without any pretension to other than expressive rewards. Thus we would expect public soirées featuring rational-choice accounts of slavery; or Sunday supplement articles on structural-functional theories of American government; or TV series presenting ethnomethodological accounts of everyday life. For those sincerely drawn to theoretical social science as an end in itself, such exercises would hold great appeal.

But the example is implausible, and its implausibility points to the severe limits in the expressive possibilities of our work. *The strictly consummatory satisfactions afforded by theoretical social science will never hold much appeal for anyone not indoctrinated to appreciate them.* The "marvels" of our theoretical worlds simply are not that accessible. For purely expressive rewards, standard modes of expression like drama, poetry, fiction, and art have everything to recommend them over the theories of social scientists. In comparison to these forms, the abstractions of social scientists, as objects of contemplation for their own sake, will always strike most people as dispensable.

What is not dispensable in this way is the sort of theoretical knowledge necessary for coping with social conditions. I maintain that we have no choice but to respond to issues in the conduct of social life involving social stratification – or political economy, or international conflict, or deviance, or any of a host of other far-reaching themes associated with what I have called first-order questions. Any effort to act in the face of such issues generates demand for understanding. How do crime and deviance (or international conflict, or economic growth, or social stratification) arise?

To what degree are they susceptible to change through enlightened action? What are the potential costs and benefits of various approaches to such action?

If social science turns its back on such issues – as, alas, it often has – they would need to be taken up by nonspecialists. But where the labors of social scientists succeed in shedding light on them, it is no exaggeration to claim that they leave all thoughtful participants in social life better off.

BETWEEN LITERATURE AND SCIENCE

Students of social life, I hold, are not in such desperate straits as arctic oil-rig workers. We do have forms of theoretical knowledge that we can work with, that fit the peculiarities both of our subject matters and of our interest in them. If we sometimes have trouble grasping these possibilities, the difficulty may stem from the distraction of attempts to conduct our work according to models drawn from other intellectual arenas. One might call these models the *infraliterary* and the *ultrascientific*. Instead of trying to force our work inappropriately into one of these extreme molds, we need to locate it intelligently in relation to both.

By infraliterary models, I mean views of theory as a strictly expressive enterprise. By the ultrascientific, I mean the notion of theory as a kind of "neutral mapping" of the subject matter – a matter of recording laws or other regularities whose importance is given in the "nature of things," independently of human interest. Whatever the applicability of this latter view to certain domains of natural science, it leaves unanswered some of the most pressing and ubiquitous questions faced by social scientists. These are questions of *which particular* patterns or regularities, of all the countless possibilities, most warrant analytical attention. Neither infraliterary nor ultrascientific models satisfactorily resolve the crucial question of how to set priorities in our intellectual agenda.

And yet, theories of the sort that we need – "workable-with" theories – show some elements of similarity both to models from the natural sciences and to literary and humanistic forms. With the latter we share the need to organize our inquiries with a sense of relevance to human concerns and values. Precisely because it makes no sense to expect the agenda of social science to be given impersonally, "in the nature of things," we need constant, critical attention to the value significance of what we study.

Thus the fact that any particular theme in social relations appears repeatedly in works of the imagination ought to suggest that it deserves some measure of attention from social scientists. The fact that so many novels, plays, or other fictional works have dealt with social mobility – or male–female relationships, or wealth and poverty – make it plain, if further clues were needed, that these are issues on which systematic theoretical inquiry by social scientists is apt to *matter*.

In these respects, theories developed by social scientists are not really very different from those pursued in such humanistic disciplines as history or archaeology. No one doubts that success in these fields depends on the analyst's sensitivity to the value-significance of his or her material – in distinguishing, for example, between highly significant historical questions or materials and trivial ones.

Yet it is also clear that, in contrast to works of pure imagination, historical or archaeological studies must do more than just create accounts that readers find highly meaningful. In 1993, New York television station WNET-TV carried a documentary showing the liberation in 1945 of Jewish concentration camp survivors by African-American units of the United States Army. The story evidently was profoundly meaningful to members of the two groups. According to the *New York Times* (8 September 1993, p. B1), "A special showing of the film at the Apollo Theatre in Harlem . . . moved an audience of 1,200 blacks and Jews to tears . . . ." Yet the work was unlikely to elicit much praise from historians, in that the events depicted apparently could never have occurred. This account was good theater but poor history. Mutatis mutandis, the same sorts of tradeoffs characterize much of theoretical social science.

The view of social science developed here also shares something crucial with virtually any view of natural science – that is, commitment to the possibility of theoretical revision through encounter with discordant evidence. Endless debate rages as to how much of such evidence, and what kind, ought to be necessary to warrant theoretical change. But any notion of theory that leaves no room for alteration at any point, in response to collisions with unexpected results of empirical inquiry, fails in a fundamental way. It fails because it leaves us in a less advantageous position to cope with the demands of our environment – either social or natural.

Theory is a good slave but a poor master. It masters *us* when it denies us the chance to alter our views in order to deal more effectively with a world ultimately indifferent to our wishful thinking about it. This is exactly what occurs when theoretical ideas are pursued strictly as ends in themselves.

The attractions of such pursuit should by now be abundantly clear. As in the dramatization of the liberation of Nazi death camps by African-American United States Army units, our theories offer the possibility of constructing a seamless web that reinforces our most treasured and meaningful conceptions of social life. But the pursuit of such satisfactions can come at the cost of isolating theoretical enthusiasts from proponents of other theories, as well as from those who approach the subject with no commitment to any established theory.

In the world of pure expression, such issues would pose no problem. There simply is no need to reconcile the cubist portrayal of the human face with that of the Pre-Raphaelites; so long as each "makes sense" as an object of contemplation to at least some viewers, it succeeds. In contrast, we have a right to expect representations generated by social scientists to be subject to reasoned adjudication – partly in the hope that narrowing differences in perception across theoretical lines may also reduce the breadth of dispute about social affairs.

We have the best chance at adjudicating such clashes of perception, not by endlessly spinning out the logic of theories as ends in themselves, but by challenging that logic as frequently as possible "from the outside." By this I mean, from the standpoint of those who approach the "same" subject matter from other theoretical worldviews or from no one theoretical position in particular. For outsiders to the theory, what does it reveal that anyone needs to know? What, in other words, is the "or-else" clause?

One of the best ways of pursuing such questions is by seeking out what one might call "contested terrain" – areas where two or more theories appear to offer quite different representations of "the same" subject. A good example might be the contrasting representations of certain dynamics of family life, considered from the standpoints of feminist thinking and rational-choice theory.

The latter have spawned a number of studies of topics such as mate selection, divorce, and parental inculcation of norms in their children (e.g., Coleman 1989, p. 297). Naturally, these studies aim at showing the role played by rational calculation of self-interest in such processes. In contrast, many feminist thinkers have seen in family life precisely the realm where calculative models break down, and where processes more exactly identified by feminist analysis prevail. Thus, Paula England faults rational-choice analyses for failure to grasp the ability of actors within families to make meaningful interpersonal comparisons of utility – something many rational-choice thinkers hold to be impossible in principle (1990, pp. 162–164).

This antinomy offers the opportunity for a potentially fruitful look at a provocative bit of contested theoretical terrain. Does feminist thinking indeed identify processes, forces, or relationships that rational-choice thinking leaves undisclosed? Can rational choice claim similar successes vis à vis feminist analysis? Are there situations or cases where the two approaches lead to distinctively different expectations? What light can empirical inquiry shed on these? Inquiries like these offer our best chance to build theoretical understandings offering guidance to something more than just our own inner sensibilities.

Summary and conclusions

To some, injunctions of this kind may seem to threaten to remove all passion from social inquiry. After all, who can be stirred by the prospect of directing attention to those aspects of social life most compelling to those with other theoretical instincts? In comparison, the satisfactions of upholding one's favored interests, values, or meaning-systems through theoretical expression are unmistakable.

But the motivating force of those satisfactions can be taken for granted. There will never be any lack of energy devoted to pressing the implications of gratifying theoretical worldviews as far as they can go. What takes discipline is the effort to make sure that they do not go too far – that they do not end up leaving us less suited to cope with the constraints of social life rather than more so. To that end, continuously exploiting the tension between the-world-as-it-makes-sense-to-us and the-world-as-it-makes-sense-to-them is our most promising strategy.

BETWEEN RELEVANCE AND SYSTEM

For some readers, the view proposed here may appear to deprive theory of its most enthralling, indeed most distinctly theoretical, qualities. Theory, they might hold, is precisely that domain furthest removed from practical considerations – the realm where ideas are pursued for their inherent elegance or profundity. Against this majestic vision, the idea of relevance to the conduct of human affairs as one key criterion of theoretical import is apt to disappoint. For some, it may seem to reduce the pursuit of ultimate truth to a banal form of social engineering.

But things are not quite this simple. My point is not to oppose abstraction, or the pursuit of ideas whose practical implications or value-relevance are not immediately clear, in any categorical way. What I do insist is that not all abstractions can possibly be equally worthy of attention. Accordingly, some criterion for choice among contending theoretical programs is indispensable. And the criteria most likely to yield insights that endure are those with some ultimate relevance to our shared needs to cope with long-standing issues in the conduct of human affairs.

Needless to say, such judgments of *ultimate* relevance are bound to be enormously subtle and interpretive. How are we to know which lines of inquiry are most apt, in the longest view, to produce insights that bear consequentially on human interests? Which conceptions of social relationships, intellectual strategy, causal dependency, or conceptual ordering will in time come to illuminate first-order questions? Surely anyone who professes certainty on these matters does not deserve to be believed.

Note that in poetry, art, or fiction such perplexities do not arise. The proper subject matters for such forms of pure expression arise from experience itself. Suffering, joy, conflict between duty and personal loyalty –

233

such themes require no further justification beyond their obvious poignancy and centrality in human experience.

But for theories in social science, different judgments are required. Relevance to human value is indeed essential in our theories, I have argued, but the relation between analytical strategy and value-relevance may be subtle and indirect. Forms of representation that convey immediate emotional impact may nevertheless not reveal much new understanding of the conditions in question. And theoretical departures that initially appear utterly irrelevant to critical values may look quite different when their implications are pursued.

Here our work has all sorts of parallels to study of the natural world. On close analysis, something as seemingly trivial as mosquito bites may hold the key to understanding – and coping with – a phenomenon of such profound value-relevance as malaria. By contrast, something as meaningful and evocative as the memoir of a malaria victim may be irrelevant to efforts to deal with the disease.

This is why we must be skeptical about models of closure that posit a sort of transparent and immediate "relevance" as the organizing principle for social inquiry. Recall the rejoinder of Lewis Coser to such insistences: that Freud's preoccupation with the obscure medical complaints of middle-class Viennese women would have seemed utterly "irrelevant" to most people at the time. Clearly, judgments of the potential relevance of theoretical departures for human interest are no open-and-shut case.

And yet, such judgments have to be made. It is simply not feasible to accord every model of closure, every project in theoretical abstraction, equal respect or attention. In the case of Freud's early research, it would seem, a positive judgment should not have been difficult to make, notwithstanding the apparently undramatic case material. The notion that conflicts of strictly psychological or interpersonal origin, conflicts beyond the conscious awareness of the sufferer, might result in strictly somatic symptoms should certainly not have struck any informed observer as trivial at the time. And part of the theoretical promise of these ideas, of course, would have been their potential usefulness in coping with a whole gamut of troubling symptoms and conditions.

Again, one recurrent theme of this book has been skepticism of a certain genre of "general theory." The perennial claims for discovery of ultimate "core concepts," I hold, ultimately pall. They may well tell us much about the expressive mood prevailing in the context of their origin; but whether they help in the analysis of any particular social situation or process is much more dubious. No one has come close to demonstrating, for any set of concepts or insights, that they offer indispensable means for all legitimate analytical ends. Instead, I have argued, social scientists need to accept that their purposes will always require openness to a wide variety of empirical contingencies and intellectual strategies.

Nevertheless, it would be absurd to assert that all theoretical ideas are equally relevant to the typical concerns of social analysts. We cannot get along without some conception of what analytic foci require most attention. Nor are such decisions at all beyond the realm of reasoned debate. We can readily justify allocating special attention – for example, in our teaching – to power versus functional models of social stratification, to Durkheimian ideas on the inputs of collective states on individual behavior, or to the logic of balance-of-power analysis in international affairs. It would be absurd to seek to force any of these ideas into the role of a general theory – that is, to insist that they serve as "core concepts" for any and all analysis. But they serve so widely, to such a variety of analytical interests, that they clearly warrant special attention.

Vastly complicating such judgments is the fact that every theoretical program generates its own enthusiasms – fixations on the specific concepts, relationships, or intellectual strategies that, in the minds of enthusiasts, represent the sine qua non of intellectual progress. Somehow it is inconceivable to enthusiasts of a particular theoretical persuasion that *any* subject matter or problem can be fully understood without due application of their most cherished concepts – whether these involve attention to the distinctive perspectives and interests of women, to the underlying patterns of network affiliation, to the class significance of the material in question, or to hidden power dimensions implicit in its prevailing "discourse." The formal progress registered within each special theoretical vision will always tend to appear to enthusiasts as progress in some ultimate assessment.

Claims to theoretical "advances" emanating from such "inside sources" should never be written off in advance. Ideas that initially appear as reflecting only rather special theoretical tastes may ultimately be shown to embody very broad analytical utility. Hard decisions are necessary to judge the potential of new ideas for such long-range payoffs. But it would be absurd to pretend that we have no grounds whatever for such judgments. History provides broad (though certainly imperfect) precedents for assessing the concerns and interests apt to animate the thoughts of future analysts. That leaves it to us to judge the extent to which the analytical principles enshrined in various theories promise to address such enduring concerns. This is inevitably a speculative business – as the middle chapters of this book have demonstrated. But we clearly have intellectual resources to exploit for such speculation.

Note that the judgments required are considerably more subtle than simply whether particular concepts or ideas are logically "general" in their applicability. Respiration, in some sense, is a general concomitant of all social processes; if people were not breathing, after all, all sorts of social events, arrangements, and processes would be impossible. But no one, quite properly, finds much interest in respirational accounts of social stratification, economic growth, demographic change, or civil upheaval.

One might make a similar observation about the claims to generality of many familiar social theories. One does not doubt certain key premises of ethnomethodology – for example, the notion that social life is predicated on countless complex, unstated, and taken-for-granted premises of face-to-face process. Harder to understand is why we need to attend to such processes in order to address the sorts of first-order questions considered in this book. If the claims to broad theoretical attention of, say, network analysis seem more compelling, the reason is not far to seek. It is that network thinkers have demonstrated a much wider range of situations where variation in network relations are contingent, in nonintuitive ways, on other social states of unquestionable value-relevance.

Network thinking in fact provides food for thought on many of these issues. It is a perfect example of a line of analysis which, in its early phases, presented to many the aspect of abstraction for the sake of abstraction. Yet as Chapter 5 showed, this form of abstraction shows many signs of illuminating issues of considerable moment for human values and interests. As with the once nonintuitive connection between mosquitos and malaria, network thinking promises to tell us things about labor markets, political alignments, and a variety of other areas that, from almost any perspective, we need to understand.

All of this offers a profound lesson. A basic (and desirable) condition of theoretical work in our disciplines is a constant tension – that between the allure of theoretical profundities as seen through the eyes of enthusiasts of the program in question and critical judgment of the prospective value-relevance of those ideas. We need to *exploit* this tension, for both sides of it reflect legitimate concerns. No one should ever be surprised to find that proponents of every model of closure perceive in their program the sine qua non of any "complete" analysis. But against such insistences, we must always pose an indispensable analytical counterweight: the willingness to ask, from the standpoint of theoretical outsiders, "What's in it for us?"

What *form*, then, should we expect good, workable-with theories to take? What logical structure, what intellectual "texture" should they exhibit?

My answer is, a vast diversity of forms and textures. Certainly we must reject the idea that theoretical success of the sort advocated here can be assured by following any single formal criterion. Remember the rigorous but vacuous exertions of the modeler who created the definitive theory of bottlecap distribution. That effort succeeded in every respect but that of identifying contingencies that *matter* for any enduring analytical interest. In the absence of a rationale for the value-relevance of the processes in question, the strictly formal success of the bottlecap modeling program has little claim on our attention.

But those contingencies that do bear such relevance take the most various forms. Some are knowable through life-tables and demographic models; some take the form of detailed historical exegeses; some require the spare, schematic models of game theorists; some require the classification of cognitive categories in the fashion of Lévi-Strauss and his followers – and on and on. The only reasonable assumption is that any of a vast array of logical forms may characterize contingencies linking elements that engage our legitimate analytical interests.

Consider certain insights that we inherit from Weber – and that appear to have especially good prospects to endure. I have in mind not so much the thesis that Calvinism was indispensable for the launching of capitalism. Much more important is the more general (and less disputable) notion that the way in which people approach work, wealth, and material well-being depends on the moral sense that they make of these things.

Utilizing this insight obviously involves a kind of hermeneutic analysis. It requires, in other words, that we put ourselves in the place of actors as they make their way in a meaningful world, as judged by the actions, speech, and other *texts* that they generate. Any social scientist who failed to consider these insights in analyzing, say, historical changes in prevailing forms of economic activity would surely be negligent.

But it would be vacuous to insist that these are somehow *more fundamental* than insights into quite different contingencies. Consider network analysis. In a way, the contingencies addressed by this theory represent a kind of conceptual opposite to those of hermeneutics. Network representations, after all, tell us virtually nothing in themselves about meanings entertained by flesh-and-blood human actors, whom they austerely depict as elementary locations in social space. Yet the sorts of contingencies that are identified in network thinking are no less crucial for all sorts of legitimate analytical purposes.

Certainly one could quote enthusiasts of both network thinking and hermeneutic analysis who are willing to insist that their favored theoretical mode uniquely grasps the ultimate level of social reality – or something to this effect. Indeed, a number of statements to this effect can be found in this book. From such viewpoints, contingencies identified by theories other than one's own are somehow epiphenomenal or illusory. The best approach to such overblown claims, I hold, is to ignore them – politely, if possible. At best, they represent distractions. At worst, they are invitations to abdicate the true breadth of our analytical responsibilities.

The best hope of social science lies in the development of a body of knowledge alerting us to the widest variety of contingencies. Such knowledge would not take the form of a hierarchically structured set of laws or concepts, as envisaged either in various schemes for "neutral mapping" or in projects for all-inclusive theoretical generality. Instead, it would amount to an array of rich and varied *literatures,* the elements of which embody quite different intellectual styles. Reading works generated by symbolic interactionists will always be a different experience from the encounter with the work of political economists, or rational-choice analysts, or demographic modelers. Yet it would be rash to rule out any of these theoretical lines as sources of inspiration. All have the potential to offer insight into contingencies that enhance prospects for coping with social life – if only their proponents do not insist on pursuing them as self-obsessed ends in themselves.

Social science will always be context-sensitive. The changing expressive resonance of theoretical ideas will always project some of them forward while casting others in the background. Indeed, similar effects are to be expected for the role of social science in coping with social conditions, as history brings different demands for personal and public action to the fore. Let us simply hope that these transitory processes do not altogether overwhelm our theoretical poise. If part of our responsibility lies in addressing current conditions, another part certainly requires a longer view. We need to do our best to build analytical sensibilities capable of dealing with the full range of contingencies apt to engage the interest of analysts – both present and future.

CAN SOCIAL SCIENCE SOLVE SOCIAL PROBLEMS?

The view of social science developed here is obviously pragmatic rather than consummatory. The most compelling ends served by theoretical social science, I maintain, are not those defined only by our theories themselves. Instead, they are ends that we social scientists hold in common with the broad and diffuse public of thoughtful participants in social life.

Any position of this sort raises a ticklish question. What *form* should the publicly accessible benefits of our work be understood to take? How are we to conceive of the public advantages afforded by our work, and what scenario can reasonably be entertained as to how such benefits should, in practice, accrue?

One influential and long-standing line of thinking offers an optimistic and uncomplicated response to such questions. This is the tradition, beginning with Saint-Simon and Comte and continuing down to the mid-century American functionalists, who see in theoretical inquiry the basis for "solutions" to "social problems." In this view, the abstract contributions of social scientists bear the same relation to social practice as those of the natural scientist do to the work of the engineer. As knowledge of social processes becomes more complete, the possibilities for making the environment – either physical or social – more suitable to human needs are enhanced. Thus the unconflicted optimism of Durkheim, noted in Chapter 1, as to the concomitance of theoretical progress and improvement of social conditions.

Unfortunately, this is one idea whose expressive appeal has all too often disarmed the critical response it deserves. Both social scientists and the broad public are subject to such appeals, which seem to run in cycles. A generation ago, especially in the United States, the conviction was abroad that public life was afflicted with grave "social problems" and that social scientists were the natural agents of their solution. In the words of a report issued in 1969 by a blue-ribbon committee of social science experts:

> Our society cannot delay dealing with its major social problems.
> The social sciences . . . are our best hope, in the long run, for understanding our problems in depth and for providing new means for lessening tensions and improving our common life. (National Academy of Sciences 1969, p. 17)

The moment passed some time ago when such pronouncements could receive much attention – and perhaps even when social scientists were willing to make them. Much of the evident public disenchantment with social science at the end of the twentieth century appears to stem from bitterness at the absence of expected "solutions" to "social problems."

Everyone concerned should have known better. As I have argued at length (1978), the very logic of social problem solving does not withstand close attention. The conditions most likely to be bracketed as "social problems" stem to a considerable degree from oppositions of value or interest. Poverty, racial tension, environmental disarray, unemployment – all are, strictly speaking, conflicts rather than problems in the sense of conditions equally deplored by all. Such conditions would not persist unless their continuation were gratifying to some parties or interests. And often those who benefit from those conditions are prepared to go to great lengths to perpetuate them. Thus, measures that constitute "solutions" from the standpoint of one group or interest may represent "problems" for others, and vice versa. For public consumption, for example, unemployment is generally stated to represent a problem. Yet for investors, managers, and government economic planners, certain levels of unemployment are a godsend – as a source of discipline to wage demands, for example, or as a dampening factor to inflation.

Such sober reflections have led some thinkers to despair of *any* positive role for social science in public affairs. If troublesome social conditions indeed amount to conflicts – where advantage to one side perforce means disadvantage to another – how can any insight, from social science or any other source, be said to benefit any sort of *general interest?*

But such a down-beat conclusion also reflects an oversimplification. True, in the extreme case, troublesome conditions may stem from pure, zero-sum oppositions of value or interest. One can imagine the clash of views between Muslim fundamentalists and Chicago-school libertarians on, say, public policy regarding families. Here, one imagines, the inevitable conflicts stem from diametrical differences of vision of "the good society." No new information or insight, from social science or anywhere else, would be apt to bring the parties to such disputes much closer to agreement.

But I hold that the debates over social practice that engage most of us, most of the time, do not approach this extreme. Rather, most such controversies involve efforts to weigh the actual consequences of pursuing different values or interests in situations where most parties share at least *some* such things in common. In the case of environmental controversies, for example, debates often turn on the reckoning of costs of environmental protection measures in terms of other values – for instance, jobs, economic growth, or public amenity. Similarly, in public controversies over crime, debate is apt to turn on questions of what changes in compliance can be expected to result from changes in enforcement and deterrence, or what the cost of those enforcement and deterrence practices will be to those targeted in them and to other members of the public. And in considerations like these, social science has a vast role to play.

Consider social inequality – a theme that suffuses public debate on matters ranging from taxation to education to welfare policy. Undoubtedly, much of the passion underlying this debate stems from pure differences of interest or value. That is, some people simply prefer more (or less) egalitarian social arrangements as ends in themselves. But other elements of these debates turn on questions eminently susceptible to social science analysis.

Thus, few people are willing to endorse the maximum (or minimum) possible stratification without regard for the implications for other values or interests. One wants to know, instead, how much would be lost by increasing inequality – for example, in terms of the welfare of children and other dependent members of the public. Or one wants to know what stands to be gained, economically and in other ways, by decreasing subsidies to those at the bottom of the social hierarchy – for example, in order to release resources for purposes like capital investment. Or one wants to know the potential gains to be expected from redistributive policies, in terms of the future productivity of the labor force or the quality of public life. All such questions are of course complex and certain to be hotly contested – as much by social scientists as by nonspecialists. But they are certainly ones in which theoretical analysis of the sort advocated in this book has a critical role to play.

The same holds, mutatis mutandis, for the array of other issues implicated in what I have called first-order questions. In coping with crime, for example, one must certainly take into account pure value differences in terms of such matters as the severity of sanctions warranted against criminals. But any reasoned attempt to cope with crime also requires judgment on crucial matters like the sorts of social conditions and processes that give rise to crime or the forces and practices that can be expected to countervail against it.

Rarely, if ever, can social scientific insight be expected to settle public controversy on any topic like these in a decisive or definitive way. Our understandings are too tentative and context-bound, and too many other factors play a role in such judgments. What our work most definitely can do is *reduce the range of reasonable disagreement on questions of social practice.* Even where this reduction is modest in relation to what we might wish – even where the best of received wisdom still leaves vast room for speculation and contention – such guidance still places us all in a better position to cope with the exigencies of social living.

In short, in coping with all sorts of complex and troublesome social situations, we are better off proceeding with even a bit of theoretical insight. In dealing with civil upheaval, for example, we know that calculation of costs and benefits, both individual and collective, plays a role in the formulation of militant action. Activists assert or restrain themselves, in other words, in response to perceptions of the gains and losses likely to ensue from acting. For these reasons, repression often (though by no means always) works. And clear signals as to likely responses to various forms of activism, from governments or other activists, do shape militant activity. Such insights may not necessarily make for reassurance or self-congratulation. But they do represent an improvement over views of activism as a kind of unreflective outpouring of emotional impulses that marked earlier stages of public discussion.

Or, think of what has been learned about charismatic movements, starting with Weber's original inspirations and continuing through more recent research. We know that such movements, both in their political and religious form, have distinctive power structures and potentials for action. The leadership of such groups, for example, is less likely to be responsible for promoting interests that adherents brought with them to their affiliation and more likely to define, for the entire group, what its effective interests are. This means, for one thing, that such groups are more prone to incur drastic costs – from confrontations with repressive forces to mass self-destruction – than other political and religious formations.

Or, consider what we know about the role of transnational organizations in moderating international conflict. It seems clear that states may find it attractive to renounce the pursuit of some of their most immediate short-term interests if supporting transnational organizations promise certain long-term benefits. Examples are organizations dedicated to organizing and broadening world trade or to coordinating environmental policy. To acknowledge the role of such organizations hardly means denying the force of self-interest among nations. But it does leave us better off than we would be with an ultra-Hobbesian model of the preponderance of short-term interest.

Similarly, we know that the simple fact of social affiliation – participation in relations of an associational, familial, or communal sort – has all sorts of sustaining effects on both mental and physical well-being. Such relationships appear to provide protection not only against suicide, as in Durkheim's classic argument, but also against a variety of other mental and physical stresses. This insight not only underlines the credibility of Durkheim's strictly theoretical ideas on the social constitution of human experience; it also offers all sorts of practical insights for the design and improvement of social arrangements.

Insights like these have a value that goes well beyond any expressive significance, or lack of it. Whether or not such understandings make for reassurance or other satisfaction in the contemplation, the fact remains that they are *things that we need to know about the social world* – with the "we" understood as inclusively as possible. They represent hard-won understandings of perplexing and challenging forces that have shaped social experience, and are likely to continue to do so for some time to come. They do not purport to offer "theories of everything" or definitive pronouncements on the *ultimate nature* of charismatic authority, international conflict, social well-being, or civil upheaval. What they *do* offer is far more important: an understanding suited for coping with forces and circumstances that cannot help but engage our vital interests.

To the extent that our inquiries generate such knowledge, it is not too much to say that we are collectively *better off* – better off, in that we are less subject to fantasy and self-delusion in efforts to make the best of social life. And as our fund of such insight grows, we can legitimately claim that our work achieves authentic intellectual progress.

References

Alexander, Jeffrey C. 1982a. *Positivism, Presuppositions and Current Controversies.* Berkeley: University of California Press.

Alexander, Jeffrey C. 1982b. *The Antinomies of Classical Thought: Marx and Durkheim.* Berkeley: University of California Press.

Alexander, Jeffrey C. 1983a. *The Classical Attempt at Theoretical Synthesis: Max Weber.* Berkeley: University of California Press.

Alexander, Jeffrey C. 1983b. *The Modern Reconstruction of Classical Thought: Talcott Parsons.* Berkeley: University of California Press.

Alexander, Jeffrey C. 1987. *Twenty Lectures: Sociological Theory since World War II.* New York: Columbia University Press.

Alexander, Jeffrey C. 1988. "The New Theoretical Movement." In Neil Smelser, ed., *Handbook of Sociology.* Newbury Park, CA: Sage.

Alexander, Jeffrey C. 1990. "Introduction." In Jeffrey C. Alexander and Piotr Sztompka, eds., *Rethinking Progress: Movements, Forces, and Ideas at the End of the 20th Century.* Boston: Unwin Hyman.

Attewell, Paul. 1974. "Ethnomethodology since Garfinkel." *Theory and Society* 1 (2): 179–210.

Attewell, Paul. 1984. *Radical Political Economy since the Sixties.* New Brunswick, NJ: Rutgers University Press.

Bales, Robert Freed. 1950. *Interaction Process Analysis; Method for the Study of Small Groups.* Cambridge: Addison-Wesley.

Barnes, John A. 1954. "Class and Committees in a Norwegian Island Parish." *Human Relations* 8:39–58.

Becker, Gary. 1968. "Crime and Punishment: An Economic Approach." *Journal of Political Economy* 76:128–47.

Becker, Gary. 1973. "The Theory of Marriage, Part 1." *Journal of Political Economy* 81 (4): 813–846.

Becker, Gary. 1974. "The Theory of Marriage, Part 2." *Journal of Political Economy* 82 (2): 511–526.

Belenky, Mary Field, Blythe McVicker Clinchy, Nancy Rule Goldberger, and Jill Mattuck Tarule. 1986. *Women's Ways of Knowing: The Development of Self, Voice, and Mind.* New York: Basic Books.

Bellah, Robert. 1957. *Tokugawa Religion.* Glencoe, IL: The Free Press.

Benhabib, Seyla. 1987. "The Generalized and the Concrete Other." In Seyla Benhabib and Drucilla Cornell, eds., *Feminism as Critique: On the Politics of Gender.* Minneapolis: University of Minnesota Press.

References

Blau, Peter. 1964. *Exchange and Power in Social Life*. New York: John Wiley.

Blau, Peter. 1978. "A Macrostructural Theory of Social Structure." *American Journal of Sociology* 83 (1).

Blau, Peter, Terry C. Blum, and Joseph E. Schwartz. 1982. "Heterogeneity and Intermarriage." *American Sociological Review* 47:45–61.

Blok, Anton. 1973. "Coalitions in Sicilian Peasant Society." In Jeremy Boissevain and J. Clyde Mitchell, *Network Analysis: Studies in Human Interaction*. The Hague: Mouton.

Boden, Deirdre. 1990. "The World as It Happens: Ethnomethodology and Conversation Analysis." In George Ritzer, ed., *Frontiers of Social Theory: The New Syntheses*. New York: Columbia University Press.

Bott, Elizabeth. 1964 [1957]. *Family and Social Network*. London: Tavistock Publications.

Braithwaite, R. B. 1953. *Scientific Explanation: A Study of the Function of Theory, Probability and Law in Science*. New York: Harper and Row.

Breiger, Ronald. 1981. "The Social Class Structure of Occupational Mobility." *American Journal of Sociology* 87:578–611.

Burt, Ronald. 1982. *Toward a Structural Theory of Action: Network Models of Social Structure, Perception and Action*. New York: Academic Press.

Burt, Ronald. 1987. "Social Contagion and Innovation." *American Journal of Sociology* 92 (6): 1287–1335.

Camic, Charles. 1979. "The Utilitarians Revisited." *The American Journal of Sociology* 85:516–550.

Cancian, Francesca. 1992. "Feminist Science: Methodologies That Challenge Inequality." *Gender and Society* 6:623–642.

Cantril, Hadley. 1940. *The Invasion from Mars: A Study in the Psychology of Panic*. Princeton, NJ: Princeton University Press.

Chodorow, Nancy. 1978. *The Reproduction of Mothering*. Berkeley: University of California Press.

Chong, Dennis. 1991. *Collective Action and the Civil Rights Movement*. Chicago: University of Chicago Press.

Cicourel, Aaron Victor. 1973. *Cognitive Sociology: Language and Meaning in Social Interaction*. Harmondsworth, Eng.: Penguin Education.

Cole, Jonathan R., and Stephen Cole. 1973. *Social Stratification in Science*. Chicago: University of Chicago Press.

Cole, Stephen. 1970. "Professional Standing and the Reception of Scientific Discoveries." *American Journal of Sociology* 76 (2): 286–306.

Cole, Stephen. 1992. *Making Science: Between Nature and Society*. Cambridge, MA: Harvard University Press.

Coleman, James S. 1989. "Editor's Introduction." *Rationality and Society* 1 (1): 5–9.

Coleman, James S. 1990. *Foundations of Social Theory*. Cambridge, MA: Harvard University Press.

Coleman, James, E. Katz, and H. Menzel. 1966. *Medical Innovation: A Diffusion Study*. Indianapolis, IN: Bobbs-Merrill.

Collins, Randall. 1979. *The Credential Society: An Historical Sociology of Education and Stratification*. New York: Academic Press.

Collins, Randall. 1985. "Jeffrey Alexander and the Search for Multi-Dimensional Theory." *Theory and Society* 14 (6): 877–892.

Cook, Judith A., and Mary M. Fonow. 1986. "Knowledge and Women's Interests:

References

Issues of Epistemology and Methodology in Feminist Sociological Research."
Sociological Inquiry 56:2–29.

Coser, Lewis. 1975. "Presidential Address: Two Methods in Search of a Substance." *American Sociological Review* 40:691–700.

Coser, Lewis. 1981. "The Uses of Classical Sociological Theory." In Buford Rhea, ed., *The Future of Sociological Classics*. Boston: George Allen and Unwin.

Costner, Herbert, and Hubert Blalock. 1972. "Scientific Fundamentalism and Scientific Utility: A Reply to Gibbs." *Social Science Quarterly* 52 (March): 826–833.

Denzin, Norman. 1990. "Reading Rational Choice Theory." *Rationality and Society* 2 (2).

Edge, David. 1979. "Quantitative Measures of Communication in Science: A Critical Review." *History of Science* 8:102–134.

Elster, Jon. 1989. *Nuts and Bolts for the Social Sciences*. Cambridge: Cambridge University Press.

England, Paula. 1990. "Feminist Critiques of the Separative Model of Self: Implications for Rational Choice Theory." *Rationality and Society* 2 (2): 156–171.

Epstein, Cynthia Fuchs. 1970. *Woman's Place: Options and Limits in Professional Careers*. Berkeley: University of California Press.

Epstein, Cynthia Fuchs. 1988. *Deceptive Distinctions: Sex, Gender and the Social Order*. New Haven and New York: Yale University Press and Russell Sage Foundation.

Feyerabend, Paul K. 1975. *Against Method*. Atlantic Highlands, NJ: Humanities Press.

Finkel, Steven E., and James B. Rule. 1986. "Relative Deprivation and Related Psychological Theories of Civil Violence: A Critical Review." In Louis Kriesberg, Kurt Lang, and Gladys Engel Lang, eds., *Research in Social Movements, Conflict and Change*. Greenwich, CT: JAI Press.

Firestone, Shulamith. 1970. *The Dialectic of Sex*. New York: Pocket Books.

Fischer, Claude S. 1982. *To Dwell among Friends: Personal Networks in Town and City*. Berkeley: University of California Press.

Fisher, Sue, and Kathy Davis. 1993. *Negotiating at the Margins: The Gendered Discourses of Power and Resistance*. New Brunswick, NJ: Rutgers University Press.

Fishman, Pamela. 1983. "Interaction: The Work Women Do." In Barrie Thorne, Chris Kramarae, and Nancy Henley, eds., *Language, Gender and Society*. Rowley, MA: Newbury House.

Follesdall, Dagfinn. 1979. "Hermeneutics and the Hypothetico-Deductive Method." *Dialectica* 33 (3): 319–336.

Fox, Robin. 1971. *The Imperial Animal*. New York: Dell.

Frank, Robert H. 1990. "Rethinking Rational Choice." In Roger Friedland and A. F. Robertson, eds., *Beyond the Marketplace*. New York: Aldine de Gruyter.

Frank, Robert, Thomas Gilovich, and Dennis Regan. 1993. "Does Studying Economics Inhibit Co-operation?" *Journal of Economic Perspectives* 7, no. 2.

Fraser, Nancy. 1989. *Unruly Practices*. Minneapolis: University of Minnesota Press.

Friedman, Debra, and Michael Hechter. 1988. "The Contribution of Rational Choice Theory to Macrosociological Research." *Sociological Theory* 6:201–218.

Friedman, Milton. 1953. "The Methodology of Positive Economics." In Milton

Friedman, *Essays in Positive Economics*. Chicago: University of Chicago Press.

Galaskiewicz, Joseph. 1985. *Social Organization of an Urban Grants Economy: A Study of Business Philanthropy and Nonprofit Organizations*. Orlando, FL: Academic Press.

Galaskiewicz, Joseph, and Ronald Burt. 1991. "Interorganizational Contagion in Corporate Philanthropy." *Administrative Science Quarterly* 36:88–105.

Galison, Peter. 1987. *How Experiments End*. Chicago: The University of Chicago Press.

Gamson, William, and James McEvoy. 1972. "Police Violence and Its Public Support." In James Short and Marvin Wolfgang, eds., *Collective Violence*. Chicago: Aldine Atherton.

Garfinkel, Harold. 1964. "Studies of the Routine Grounds of Everyday Activities." *Social Problems* 11 (3): 225–250.

Garfinkel, Harold. 1967. *Studies in Ethnomethodology*. Englewood Cliffs, NJ: Prentice-Hall.

Gibbs, Jack. 1972. "Causation and Theory Construction." *Social Science Quarterly* 52 (March): 815–826.

Gilligan, Carol. 1982. *In a Different Voice*. Cambridge, MA: Harvard University Press.

Gilligan, Carol. 1986. "On *In a Different Voice*: An Interdisciplinary Forum." *Signs* 11, no. 2.

Goffman, Erving. 1961. *Asylums: Essays on the Social Situation of Mental Patients and Other Inmates*. Garden City, NY: Doubleday.

Goldberg, Steven. 1974. *The Inevitability of Patriarchy*. New York: Morrow.

Gorelick, Sherry. 1991. "Contradictions of Feminist Methodology." *Gender and Society* 5:459–477.

Gouldner, Alvin. 1970. *The Coming Crisis of Western Sociology*. New York: Basic Books.

Granovetter, Mark. 1973. "The Strength of Weak Ties." *American Journal of Sociology* 78:1360–1380.

Granovetter, Mark. 1974. *Getting a Job: A Study of Contacts and Careers*. Cambridge, MA: Harvard University Press.

Granovetter, Mark. 1976. Review of *Education, Occupation and Earnings: Achievement in the Early Career*, by William Sewell and Robert Hauser. *Harvard Educational Review* 46 (1): 123–127.

Green, Donald P., and Ian Shapiro. 1994. *Pathologies of Rational Choice Theory: A Critique of Applications in Political Science*. New Haven, CT: Yale University Press.

Guttentag, M., and P. F. Secord. 1983. *Too Many Women? The Sex Ratio Question*. Beverly Hills, CA: Sage Publications.

Harding, Sandra. 1981. "What Is the Real Material Base of Patriarchy and Capital?" In L. Sargent, ed., *Women and Revolution*. Boston: South End Press.

Harding, Sandra. 1986. *The Science Question in Feminism*. Ithaca, NY: Cornell University Press.

Harding, Sandra. 1987. *Feminism and Methodology*. Bloomington: Indiana University Press.

Harding, Sandra. 1991. *Whose Science? Whose Knowledge?* Bloomington: Indiana University Press.

Hartmann, Heidi. 1976. "Capitalism, Patriarchy, and Job Segregation by Sex." *Signs* 1 (3, pt. 2): 137–169.

References

Hartmann, Heidi. 1981. "The Unhappy Marriage of Marxism and Feminism: Towards a More Progressive Union." In Nancy Hartsock, ed., *Money, Sex, and Power.* New York: Longman's.

Hartsock, Nancy C. M. 1987. "The Feminist Standpoint: Developing the Ground for a Specifically Feminist Historical Materialism." In Sandra Harding, ed., *Feminism and Methodology.* Bloomington: Indiana University Press.

Hechter, Michael. 1987. *Principles of Group Solidarity.* Berkeley: University of California Press.

Hempel, Carl. 1965. *Aspects of Scientific Explanation.* New York: The Free Press.

Herman, Edward. 1981. *Corporate Control, Corporate Power.* New York: Cambridge University Press.

Hernes, Gudmund. 1992. "We Are Smarter than We Think." *Rationality and Society* 4 (4).

Hess, Beth, and Myra Marx Feree. 1987. *Analyzing Gender: A Handbook of Social Science Research.* Beverly Hills, CA: Sage Publications.

Hobbes, Thomas. 1968 [1651]. *Leviathan.* London: Penguin Books.

Homans, George. 1961. *Social Behavior: Its Elementary Forms.* New York: Harcourt Brace Jovanovich.

Homans, George. 1964. "Contemporary Theory in Sociology." In Robert Faris, ed., *Handbook of Sociology.* Chicago: Rand-McNally.

Homans, George. 1967. *The Nature of Social Science.* New York: Harcourt, Brace and World.

Irigaray, Luce. 1977. *The Sex Which Is Not One.* Translated by Catherine Porter with Carolyn Burke. Paris: Editions de Minuit.

Isvan-Hayat, Nilufer. 1986. "Rural Household Production and the Sexual Division of Labor: A Research Framework." Paper presented at the Annual Meeting of the Middle East Studies Association of North America, Boston.

Jongmans, D. G. 1973. "Politics on the Village Level." In J. Boissevain and J. C. Mitchell, eds., *Network Analysis: Studies in Human Interaction.* The Hague: Mouton.

Kanter, Rosabeth Moss. 1977. *Men and Women of the Corporation.* New York: Basic Books.

Keller, Evelyn Fox. 1985. *Reflections on Gender and Science.* New Haven, CT: Yale University Press.

Kelly, Allison. 1978. "Feminism and Research." *Women's Studies Quarterly* 1:225–232.

Keohane, Robert. 1984. *After Hegemony: Cooperation and Discord in the World Political Economy.* Princeton, NJ: Princeton University Press.

Keohane, Robert. 1986. "Theory of World Politics: Structural Realism and Beyond." In Robert Keohane, ed., *Neorealism and Its Critics.* New York: Columbia University Press.

Kleiber, Nancy, and Linda Light. 1978. *Caring for Ourselves: An Alternative Structure for Health Care.* Vancouver: University of British Columbia, School for Nursing.

Knoke, David. 1990. *Political Networks: The Structural Perspective.* New York: Cambridge University Press.

Knorr-Cetina, Karin. 1981. *The Manufacture of Knowledge: An Essay on the Constructivist and Contextual Nature of Science.* New York: Pergamon Press.

Knorr-Cetina, Karin. 1993. "Liminal and Referent Epistemologies in Contemporary Science: An Ethnography of the Empirical in Two Sciences." Mimeo; University of Bielefeld.

Komarovsky, Mirra. 1953. *Women in the Modern World: Their Education and Their Dilemmas.* Boston: Little, Brown.

Latour, Bruno. 1988. *The Pasteurization of France.* Translated by Alan Sheridan and John Law. Cambridge, MA: Harvard University Press.

Latour, Bruno, and Steve Woolgar. 1986. *Laboratory Life: The Construction of Scientific Facts.* Princeton, NJ: Princeton University Press.

Laudan, Larry, and Jarrett Leplin. 1991. "Empirical Equivalence and Underdetermination." *The Journal of Philosophy* 88 (9).

Laumann, Edward O., and David Knoke. 1987. *The Organizational State: Social Choice in National Policy Domains.* Madison: University of Wisconsin Press.

Laumann, Edward O., and Peter Marsden. 1979. "The Analysis of Oppositional Structures in Political Elites: Identifying Collective Actors." *American Sociological Review* 44 (5): 713–732.

Laumann, Edward O., and F. Pappi. 1973. "New Directions in the Study of Elites." *American Sociological Review* 38:212–230.

Lazarsfeld, Paul F., Bernard Berelson, and Hazel Gaudet. 1968 [1944]. *The People's Choice: How the Voter Makes up His Mind in a Presidential Campaign.* 3d ed. New York: Columbia University Press.

Lee, Nancy Howell. 1969. *The Search for an Abortionist.* Chicago: University of Chicago Press.

Lieberson, Stanley. 1980. *A Piece of the Pie.* Berkeley: University of California Press.

Linton, Sally. 1971. "Woman the Gatherer: Male Bias in Anthropology." In Sue-Ellen Jacobs, ed., *Women in Cross-Cultural Perspective.* Champaign-Urbana: University of Illinois Press.

MacIntyre, Alasdair. 1971. *Against the Self-Image of the Age.* New York: Schocken Books.

MacIntyre, Alasdair. 1973. "Is a Science of Comparative Politics Possible?" In Alan Ryan, ed., *The Philosophy of Social Explanation.* Oxford: Oxford University Press.

MacKinnon, Catherine. 1989. *Towards a Feminist Theory of the State.* Cambridge, MA: Harvard University Press.

MacMillan, Malcolm. 1991. *Freud Evaluated: The Completed Arc.* Amsterdam: North-Holland.

Magnarella, Paul J. 1979. *The Peasant Venture: Tradition, Migration, and Change among Georgian Peasants in Turkey.* Cambridge, MA: Schenkman.

Marx, Karl, and Friedrich Engels. 1959. *Basic Writings on Politics and Philosophy.* Edited by Lewis S. Feuer. Garden City, NY: Anchor Books.

McAdam, Doug. 1986. "Recruitment to High-Risk Activism: The Case of Freedom Summer." *American Journal of Sociology* 92:64–90.

McCloskey, Donald N. 1985. *The Rhetoric of Economics.* Madison: University of Wisconsin Press.

McRobbie, Angela. 1978. "Working-Class Girls and the Culture of Femininity." In the Women's Studies Group, ed., *Women Take Issue.* London: Hutchinson.

McRobbie, Angela, and Trisha McCabe. 1981. *Feminism for Girls: An Adventure Story.* London: Routledge.

Merchant, Carolyn. 1980. *The Death of Nature.* New York: Harper and Row.

Merton, Robert K. 1970 [1938]. *Science, Technology and Society in Seventeenth-Century England.* New York: Howard Fertig.

References

METSU (Middle East Technical University). 1963. *Hayriye Koy Arastirma ve Planlama Calismasi* [Hayriye Village Research and Planning Project]. Ankara.

Mill, John Stuart. 1893. *A System of Logic: Ratiocinative and Deductive.* New York: Harper and Brothers.

Mills, C. Wright. 1959. *The Sociological Imagination.* New York: Oxford University Press.

Mintz, Beth, and Michael Schwartz. 1985. *The Power Structure of American Business.* Chicago: University of Chicago Press.

Mitchell, James Clyde. 1960. *Tribalism and Plural Society: An Inaugural Lecture.* London: Oxford University Press.

Mitchell, Juliet. 1971. *Psychoanalysis and Feminism.* New York: Pantheon.

Mizruchi, Mark. 1992. *The Structure of Corporate Political Action.* Cambridge, MA: Harvard University Press.

Moe, Terry M. 1980. *The Organization of Interests.* Chicago: University of Chicago Press.

Moore, Barrington, Jr. 1958. *Political Power and Social Theory.* Cambridge, MA: Harvard University Press.

Moreno, Jacob L. 1934. *Who Shall Survive? Foundations of Sociometry, Group Psychotherapy and Sociodrama.* Beacon, NY: Beacon House.

Morris, Aldon, and Cedric Herring. 1987. "Theory and Research in Social Movements: A Critical Review." In Samuel Long, ed., *Annual Review of Political Science II.*

Nagel, Ernest. 1961. *The Structure of Science.* New York: Harcourt, Brace and World.

National Academy of Sciences. 1969. *The Behavioral and Social Sciences: Outlook and Needs.* Englewood Cliffs, NJ: Prentice-Hall.

Nielsen, Joyce McCarl. 1990. "Introduction." In Joyce McCarl Nielsen, ed., *Feminist Research Methods.* Boulder, CO: Westview Press.

Oakley, Ann. 1981. "Interviewing Women: A Contradiction in Terms." In Helen Roberts, ed., *Doing Feminist Research.* London: Routledge and Kegan Paul.

Olson, Mancur. 1965. *The Logic of Collective Action.* Cambridge, MA: Harvard University Press.

Parsons, Talcott. 1937. *The Structure of Social Action.* New York: McGraw-Hill.

Parsons, Talcott. 1961. "An Outline of the Social System." In Talcott Parsons, Edward Shils, Kaspar Naegele, and Jesse Pitts, eds., *Theories of Society.* Vol. 1. Glencoe, IL: The Free Press.

Parsons, Talcott. 1963. "On the Concept of Political Power." *Proceedings of the American Philosophical Society* 107:232–262.

Parsons, Talcott, and Robert F. Bales. 1953. "The Dimensions of Action Space." In Talcott Parsons, Robert F. Bales, and Edward A. Shils, eds., *Working Papers in the Theory of Action.* Glencoe, IL: The Free Press.

Parsons, Talcott, and Neil Smelser. 1956. *Economy and Society: A Study in the Integration of Economic and Social Theory.* Glencoe, IL: The Free Press.

Press, Andrea L. 1991. *Women Watching Television: Gender, Class, and Generation in the American Television Experience.* Philadelphia: University of Pennsylvania Press.

Reinharz, Shulamit. 1992. *Feminist Methods in Social Research.* New York: Oxford University Press.

Reskin, Barbara. 1978. "Scientific Productivity, Sex and Location in the Institution of Science." *American Journal of Sociology* 83 (5): 1235–1243.

References

Reznick, David A., Heather Bryga, and John A. Endler. 1990. "Experimentally Induced Life-History Evolution in a Natural Population." *Nature* 346, 26 July, pp. 357–359.

Riker, William H. 1990. "Political Science and Rational Choice." In James Alt and Kenneth Shepsle, eds., *Perspectives on Positive Political Economy*. Cambridge: Cambridge University Press.

Roos, Patricia A. 1990. "Hot-Metal to Electronic Composition: Gender, Technology, and Social Change." In Barbara F. Reskin and Patricia A. Roos, eds., *Job Queues, Gender Queues: Explaining Women's Inroads into Male Occupations*. Philadelphia: Temple University Press.

Rosenthal, Naomi, Meryl Fingrudt, Michelle Ethier, Roberta Karant, and David McDonald. 1985. "Social Movements and Network Analysis: A Case Study of Nineteenth-Century Women's Reform in New York State." *American Journal of Sociology* 90:1022–1055.

Rossi, Alice S. 1964. "Equality between the Sexes: An Immodest Proposal." *Daedelus* 93 (2): 607–652.

Rubin, Gale. 1975. "The Traffic in Women." In Rayna Reiter, ed., *Toward an Anthropology of Women*. New York: Monthly Review Press.

Rule, James B. 1978. *Insight and Social Betterment*. New York: Oxford University Press.

Rule, James B. 1988. *Theories of Civil Violence*. Berkeley: University of California Press.

Scott, Joan Wallach. 1988. *Gender and the Politics of History*. New York: Columbia University Press.

Sennett, Richard, and Jonathan Cobb. 1973. *The Hidden Injuries of Class*. New York: Vintage Books.

Silverman, David. 1972. *The Theory of Organizations*. London: Heinemann Educational.

Skocpol, Theda. 1979. *States and Social Revolutions*. Cambridge: Cambridge University Press.

Skolnick, Arlene. 1979. "Public Images, Private Realities: The American Family in Popular Culture and Social Science." In Barbara Myerhoff and Virginia Tufte, eds., *Changing Images of the Family*. New Haven, CT: Yale University Press.

Slater, Philip E. 1955. "Role Differentiation in Small Groups." *American Sociological Review* 20 (3): 300–310.

Smelser, Neil. 1962. *Theory of Collective Behavior*. New York: The Free Press.

Smelser, Neil. 1992. "The Rational Choice Perspective: A Theoretical Assessment." *Rationality and Society* 4 (4): 381–410.

Smith, Adam. 1976 [1759]. *The Theory of Moral Sentiments*. Edited by D. D. Raphael and A. L. MacFie. Oxford: The Clarendon Press.

Smith, Dorothy. 1974. "Women's Perspective as a Radical Critique of Sociology." *Sociological Inquiry* 44:7–13.

Stacey, Judith, and Barrie Thorne. 1985. "The Missing Feminist Revolution in Sociology." *Social Problems* 32:301–316.

Stanley, Liz, and Sue Wise. 1983. *Breaking Out: Feminist Consciousness and Feminist Research*. London: Routledge and Kegan Paul.

Stanley, Liz, and Sue Wise. 1990. "Method, Methodology and Epistemology in Feminist Research Processes." In Liz Stanley, ed., *Feminist Praxis: Research, Theory and Epistemology in Feminist Theory*. New York: Routledge.

Stark, Rodney, and William Sims Bainbridge. 1980. "Networks of Faith: Interpersonal Bonds and Recruitment to Cults and Sects." *American Journal of Sociology* 85 (6): 1376–1395.

Starr, Paul. 1982. *The Social Transformation of American Medicine.* New York: Basic Books.

Stimpson, Catherine H. 1983. "Contemporary Women's Studies." Paper prepared for the Ford Foundation.

Stinchcombe, Arthur. 1968. *Constructing Social Theories.* New York: Harcourt, Brace and World.

Stouffer, Samuel, et al. 1949. *The American Soldier: Combat and Its Aftermath.* Vol. 2. Princeton, NJ: Princeton University Press.

Tannen, Deborah. 1990. *You Just Don't Understand: Women and Men in Conversation.* New York: Ballantine.

Taylor, Charles. 1979 [1971]. "Interpretation and the Sciences of Man." In Paul Rabinow and William M. Sullivan, eds., *Interpretive Social Science: A Reader.* Berkeley: University of California Press.

Thibaut, John W., and Harold H. Kelley. 1959. *The Social Psychology of Groups.* New York: John Wiley and Sons.

Tiger, Lionel. 1969. *Men in Groups.* New York: Vintage Books.

Tilly, Charles. 1991. "Review Essay on James Coleman's *Foundations of Social Theory.*" *American Journal of Sociology* 96 (4).

Tuana, Nancy. 1993. "With Many Voices: Feminism and Theoretical Pluralism." In Paula England, ed., *Theory on Gender/Feminism on Theory.* Hawthorn, NY: Aldine de Gruyter.

Tversky, Amos, and Daniel Kahneman. 1974. "Judgment under Uncertainty: Heuristics and Biases." *Science* 185:1124–1130.

Wagner, David G., and Joseph Berger. 1985. "Do Sociological Theories Grow?" *American Journal of Sociology* 90 (4): 697–728.

Wasserman, Stanley, and Katherine Faust. 1994. *Social Network Analysis: Methods and Applications.* Cambridge: Cambridge University Press.

Wedow, Susan Marie. 1974. "Perennial Wisdom on Display: The Use of a System of Knowledge in Interaction." Ph.D. diss., University of California, Santa Barbara.

Wellman, Barry. 1979. "East Yorkers and the Community Question." *American Journal of Sociology* 84:1201–1231.

White, Harrison C. 1970. *Chains of Opportunity.* Cambridge, MA: Harvard University Press.

White, Harrison C., Scott A. Boorman, and Ronald L. Breiger. 1976. "Social Structure from Multiple Networks. I. Blockmodels of Roles and Positions." *American Journal of Sociology* 81:730–780.

Wilson, Edward O. 1975. *Sociobology: The New Synthesis.* Cambridge, MA: Harvard University Press.

Wilson, Edward O. 1978. *On Human Nature.* Cambridge, MA: Harvard University Press.

Wittig, Monique. 1981. "One Is Not Born a Woman." *Feminist Issues* 1 (2): 53.

Wolfe, Alan. 1989. *Whose Keeper? Social Science and Moral Obligation.* Berkeley: University of California Press.

Wrong, Dennis Hume. 1995. *Power: Its Forms, Bases, and Uses.* New Brunswick, NJ: Transaction Publishers.

Yonay, Yuval. Forthcoming. *When Black Boxes Clash: The Struggle over the Soul of the Economy.*

Index

action, theory of, 105
advance, scientific (*see also* progress), 57
aesthetic criteria for theoretical success, 11–13, 174, 191
Alexander, Jeffrey, 98–99, 101–119, 187, 201
Alford, Robert, 213
American Sociological Review, 65
Aristotle, 9, 24
Attewell, Paul, 53, 66

Bacon, Francis, 157
Bainbridge, William, 128
Bales, Robert Freed, 60–63, 67, 72, 101, 115, 192
Balesian small group studies, 166–167
bank hegemony over corporations, 131–132
Barnes, John, 123–125
Becker, Gary, 80
behaviorism, 3, 79
Belenky et al., 159
Bell, Daniel, 98
Bellah, Robert, 101
Benhabib, Seyla, 159
Berger, Joseph, 31
Black Death, 208, 214
Blalock, Hubert, 108
Blau, Peter, 80, 110, 137
Blok, Anton, 123–125, 138
Blum, Terry C., 110
boards of corporate directors, 130–132, 134–145
Boden, Deirdre, 67, 137, 196
Boorman, Scott A., 137
Bott, Elizabeth, 124–125, 127, 138
bottlecap dispersion, analysis of, 32, 111, 176, 236–237
Braithwaite, R. B., 29
Breiger, Ronald, 126, 137

Burke, Edmund, 9
Burt, Ronald, 135

calculation, role of in social action, 36, 84
Camic, Charles, 100
Cancian, Francesca, 155
Cantril, Hadley, 122
capital, aggregation of, 24
causal systems, 210–211, 223
charismatic authority, 118, 241
Chicago School, 82
Chodorow, Nancy, 162, 168
Chong, Dennis, 90
Cicourel, Aaron Victor, 65
citations, enumeration of, 69, 71
civil rights movement, 35, 90
civil violence, 34, 44–45
closure in theoretical inquiry, 26–34, 40, 42–44, 48, 72, 76, 98, 101, 120, 155, 176, 202, 236
Cobb, Jonathan, 181–182
Cole, Jonathan, 58–59
Cole, Stephen, xiv, 57–59, 70
Coleman, James, 65, 85, 86, 92–95, 97, 125–126, 135, 232
collective behavior, theories of, 35–36, 176
Collins, Randall, 102, 221
communal knowledge, 71
construction, constructivism, 49, 52–57, 66, 68, 69, 71, 149, 156, 180, 182, 183, 199, 203
contextual analysis, 160
contingencies, 88, 204, 223, 224, 237, 288
Cook, Judith A., 150, 154, 156
coping, as a criterion for theoretical success, 11, 14, 118–119, 171–172, 184–185, 202, 203–225, 228–230, 231, 234, 241–242

Index

Coser, Lewis, 33, 43, 220, 234
Costner, Herbert, 108

"dead ends" in scientific inquiry, 68
de Beauvoir, Simone, 147
Denzin, Norman, 96–97
Derrida, Jacques, 192
deviance, causes of, 45
disaggregation, as an analytical strategy, 120, 141
discontinuity of militant action, 36
discourse, 115, 149
discoveries, in science, 50, 52, 57
discovery, in social science, 3
Durkheim, Emile, 7, 9, 29–30, 40–42, 44, 80, 82, 86, 113, 122, 140, 235, 239, 242

economic growth, conditions of, 45
economic theory, neoclassical, xii, 42, 80, 83, 129, 187, 188, 189
Edge, David, 59
Elster, Jon, 85
emotions, role of in militant action, 36
empirical inquiry, role of in theoretical change, 16, 36–37, 40
empowerment, of women, 156
Engel, Christian, 209
England, Paula, 232
epistemology, feminist, 149
Epstein, Cynthia Fuchs, 148, 152
ethic of care and response, 158–159
ethics, 46
ethnomethodology, 24, 52–53, 63–67, 72, 137, 166, 196–197, 236
explanation, deductive, 28–30
expressive appeals of theoretical ideas, 77, 82, 83, 96, 123, 161–162, 163, 165, 171, 172, 173–202
expressive criteria for theoretical ideas, 11, 15, 16, 48, 198, 220, 227–229, 232, 242

family organization, forces shaping, 45
Faust, Katherine, 121
feminism, 198
feminist analysis, 144–169, 198, 232
Feyerabend, Paul, 38, 39, 52, 70
Firestone, Shulamith, 147
first-order questions, 45–47, 75, 119, 224, 233, 241
Fischer, Claude, 127, 130, 133
Fishman, Pamela, 147
Follesdall, Dagfinn, 207–208
Fonow, Mary M., 150, 154, 156
formal models for theoretical formulation, 30

Foucault, Michel, 149, 193
Fox, Robin, 147
Frank, Robert H., 83, 188
Freud, Sigmund, 33, 191–195, 234
Friedan, Betty, 147
Friedman, Debra, 90
Friedman, Milton, 81
functionalism, 41, 118, 221, 238

Galaskiewicz, Joseph, 127, 136
Galileo, 38
Galison, Peter, 202
game theory, 3
Gamson, William, 35
Garfinkel, Harold, 64–66
genome mapping, 175
Gibbs, Jack, 108
Gilligan, Carol, 158–159
Gilovich, Thomas, 83, 188
Goffman, Erving, 213
Goldberg, Steven, 147
Gorelick, Sherry, 145
Gouldner, Alvin, 200–201
Gramsci, Antonio, 24
Granovetter, Mark, 126–131, 133, 138, 219
Green, Donald P., 87
Guttentag, M., 85

Habermas, Jurgen, 192
Harding, Sandra, 147–148, 152, 157, 161
Hartmann, Heidi, 147
Hartsock, Nancy, 159, 162–163
Harvard Business School, 184
Hechter, Michael, 86, 90, 92
Hempel, Carl, 29, 174
Herman, Edward, 131
hermeneutics, hermeneutic analysis, 3, 96, 105, 205–208, 237–238
Hernes, Gudmund, 86, 91
Herring, Cedric, 35
historical character of theoretical analysis, 46, 210–211, 214–215
Hitler, Adolf, explaining rise to power of, 7
Hobbes, Thomas, 24, 35, 79, 99–103
Homans, George, 26, 28–31, 80, 81, 108, 175–178

ideal types, 117–118
identification, as a basic social process, 93
idiographic inquiry, 7–8
Iliad, the, 28
indexicality, 64–66
information flow within social networks, 127, 131, 138
Institute for Advanced Study, Princeton, 173

instrumental character of human action, 80
Interaction Recorder, 60–61
internalization, of norms, 93
international conflict, causes of, 45
inventions as an index of scientific advance, 50
Irigaray, Luce, 147
Irrationalists, 35, 164
Isvan-Hayat, Nilufer, 146

Japan, economic success of, 106–107
jobs, access to, 126–127, 142
Jongmans, D. G., 123–125

Kahneman, Daniel, 84, 91
Kanter, Rosabeth Moss, 148
Katz, E., 125, 135
Keller, Evelyn Fox, 157–160
Kelley, Harold H., 80
Kelly, Allison, 150
Keohane, Robert, 117–178, 180
King, Dr. Martin Luther, Jr., 140
Kleiber, Nancy, 149
Klein, Melanie, 162
Knoke, David, 120, 127, 128, 132–133, 137
Knorr-Cetina, Karin, 52, 55, 66, 207
Komorovsky, Mirra, 148

Latour, Bruno, 52, 55, 56, 182
Laudan, Larry, 201
Laumann, Edward, 127, 132–133
laws, scientific, 175
Lazarsfeld, Paul, 125, 220
Lee, Nancy, 126
Leplin, Jarrett, 201
Levi-Strauss, Claude, 137, 237
libertarianism, 82
Lieberson, Stanley, 111
Light, Linda, 149
Linton, Sally, 148
luck, as subject for explanation, 129
lynchings, 35

Machiavelli, Niccolo, 9
MacIntyre, Alasdair, 117
MacMillan, Malcolm, 192
Magnarella, Paul J., 146
Marsden, Peter, 127
Marx, Karl, 9, 23–24, 35, 80, 113, 116, 218
Marxism (*see also* Marx, Karl), 3, 137, 144–150, 153–155, 188–189
mass action, theories of, 82, 122, 128, 139–140
maximalist version of feminist analysis, 151–154

Mayo, Elton, 184–185, 206
McAdam, Doug, 128
McCabe, Trisha, 149
McCarthyism, 35
McClintock, Barbara, 158–160
McCloskey, Donald, 42, 186, 194
McEvoy, James, 35
McRobie, Angela, 149
meaning, in social analysis, 30, 31
meaningful, perception of theories as, 18, 180–181
Mendel, Gregor, 69
Menzel, H., 125, 135
Merchant, Carolyn, 157
Merton, Robert K., 23, 50, 69
Mertonian approach to study of science, 49, 53–54, 57, 58, 68, 199
METSU (Middle East Technical University), 146
Mill, John Stuart, 105, 209, 211
Mills, C. Wright, 28, 33–34
minimalist version of feminist analysis, 152
Mintz, Beth, 132–134
mistakes, in recognition of scientific achievement, 70
Mitchell, James Clyde, 147
Mizruchi, Mark, 134–138
molecular view of social structure, 121
Montesquieu, Baron de, 100
Moore, Jr., Barrington, 28, 30, 33–34
Moreno, Jacob, 123
Morris, Aldon, 35
Moe, Terry M., 70
Myrdal, Gunnar, 12, 218–219
myth, as model for social science, 198

Nagel, Ernest, 29, 174
narrative, role of in theoretical persuasion, 196–197
National Academy of Sciences, Washington, D.C., 239
natural science, 214, 230
Nazism, 35
neoclassical economics (*see* economic theory, neoclassical)
neorealism, in theories of international relations, 177
network analysis, 3, 120–143, 236–237
Newtonian theories, 176
New York Times, 98
Nielsen, Joyce, 152
normality, of militant social action, 35
norms, explaining compliance with, 94

Oakley, Ann, 149
obsolescence, built-in, in social science theories, 171

Olson, Mancur, 80, 89, 90
order, as topic in social theory, 105
or-else clauses, 16–17, 48, 77, 83–86, 99,
    112, 128, 152, 157, 163, 165, 232
organismic models of society, 41
outsider, to theoretical schools, xiii, 6, 9,
    193, 236

Pappi, F., 127
Pareto, Vilfredo, 24, 37, 118, 188
Park, Robert, 24
Parsons, Talcott, 28–29, 30, 37, 61, 79,
    98–103, 137, 192, 197
Pasteur, Louis, 56
peace movement, 35
periodic table of elements, 101, 113
personality formation, 45
pluralist theories of U.S. politics, 24
pornography, 156
pragmatic criteria for analysis, 49, 57,
    171, 190, 199, 202, 238
Press, Andrea, 149
presuppositions, 105–106
progress, claimed for social science, 25,
    171, 173–174
progress, formal, 5, 32, 67
progress, substantive, 5, 25
progress, theoretical (*see also* advance, sci-
    entific), 4, 75–79, 171, 226–228
propaganda, role in theoretical social sci-
    ence of, 38
propaganda, in scientific communication,
    70
prophecy, self-fulfilling, 198
psychoanalysis, 61, 191–195
Puritan ideology, role in science of, 50

RAND Corporation, 61
rational calculation, 80, 141
rational-choice thinking, 18, 79–97, 105,
    118, 145, 188–189, 195, 198, 232
rationality of militant action, 35
reflexivity, 66
Regan, Dennis, 83, 188
Reinharz, Shulamit, 154
relatedness, as a principle of feminist anal-
    ysis, 158–160
relative deprivation, role of in civil vio-
    lence, 37–38, 217
relativism, 38–40, 52, 149, 151
relevance, 30
religious conversion, as a model for the-
    oretical change, 13
residual categories, 112–114
Reskin, Barbara, 148
revolution, explanation of (*see also* civil
    violence), 25

revolutions, theoretical, xiii, 3, 19, 23, 24
rewards for scientific achievement, 51
Riker, William, 79
risk, attitudes toward, 90
Roos, Patricia, 219
Rosenthal, Naomi et al., 128
Rossi, Alice, 148
Rubin, Gale, 147
Rule, James B., 82, 153

Sacks, Harvey, 66
saloons, 156
Schumpeter, Joseph, 9, 24
Schwartz, Joseph, 110
Schwartz, Michael, 132–134
Science Citation Index, 59
science, feminist analysis of, 157–159
Scott, Joan, 147–149
Scottish moralists, 100
second-order questions, 47, 77
Secord, P. F., 85
Sennett, Richard, 181–182
Shapiro, Ian, 87
Shils, Edward, 101
Silverman, David, 65
Skinner, B. F., 209, 211
Skocpol, Theda, 109, 212
Skolnick, Arlene, 148
Slater, Philip, 61
slavery, 94–95
Simmel, Georg, 123
Smelser, Neil, 29, 101, 193–194
Smith, Adam, 9, 114–115
Smith, Dorothy, 149
social exchange theory, 80
social problems, 33–34, 42, 238–240
social stratification, 40, 221–222
social structure, meanings ascribed to
    term, 136
sociometry, 123
solipsism, 16
Soviet Union, as causal system, 212
Spencer, Herbert, 209, 218
Stacey, Judith, 164, 166
Stalinism, 35
Stanley, Liz, 150–151, 155, 179–180, 182
Stark, Rodney, 128
Starr, Paul, 221
status attainment analysis, 129
Stimpson, Catherine, 151
Stinchcombe, Arthur, 198–199
Stouffer, Samuel et al., 141
strikes, explanation of, 7
structural equivalence, 135–136
structural functionalism, 3, 24, 28, 51,
    120, 123, 195
structuralism, 3

Index

Sumner, William Graham, 168, 218–219
Swanson, Guy, 65
symbolic interactionism, 3, 64

Tannen, Deborah, 147
taste, theoretical, 3, 16, 17, 72, 75, 95, 99, 116, 119, 197
Taylor, Charles, 205–206, 208
technical improvement in social science, 6–7, 36
text, role of in social analysis, 108
theoretical yearning, 7–8, 10
Theories of Civil Violence, xi–xiii, 11, 34, 36, 37, 39, 100, 106, 176, 177, 186, 188, 210, 216–218
theory, definition and use of term, 25–26
theory as end in itself, 42
theory as means, 15, 42
Thibaut, John W., 80
Thorne, Barrie, 144, 164–166
Tiger, Lionel, 147
Tilly, Charles, 35, 95
Toennies, Ferdinand, 130
Tuana, Nancy, 155
Tversky, Amos, 84, 91

unobservables, as elements in social theory, 108
utilitarians, utilitarianism, 79

values, role of in Parsons's thought, 99–101
Veblen, Thorstein, 145, 189

Wagner, David G., 31
Wallace, Anthony F. C., 65
Waltz, Kenneth, 177–178, 180
Wasserman, Stanley, 121
Weber, Max, 9, 80, 110–111, 218, 237, 241
Wellman, Barry, 127, 130, 133
White, Harrison, 126, 137
Whitehead, Alfred North, 33
Wilson, Edward O., 147
Wise, Sue, 150–151, 155, 179–189, 182
witchcraft, theories underlying, 71, 198
Wittig, Monique, 147
Wolfe, Alan, 82–83
Woolf, Virginia, 147
Woolgar, Steve, 53, 55, 182

Yonay, Yuval, xii, 80